S0-BFB-090

MUSEUM PEOPLE

for Phyllis, a people person,
dogs person, houses person
who lets people sign her
table — here is a signed
book (much worked over
in the Parter House)
with love from Peggy

December 1977

9

12

Pennsylvania Avenue

15 Street

14 Street

Constitution Avenue

2

Madison Dr

Washington

Adams Dri

Jefferson D

Washington Monument

17 Street

Independence Avenue

Map of Smithsonian Institution

 1. Smithsonian Institution Building

 2. National Museum of History and Technology

 3. National Museum of Natural History

 4. Air and Space Building

 5. Arts and Industries Building

 6. Joseph H. Hirshhorn Museum and Sculpture Garden

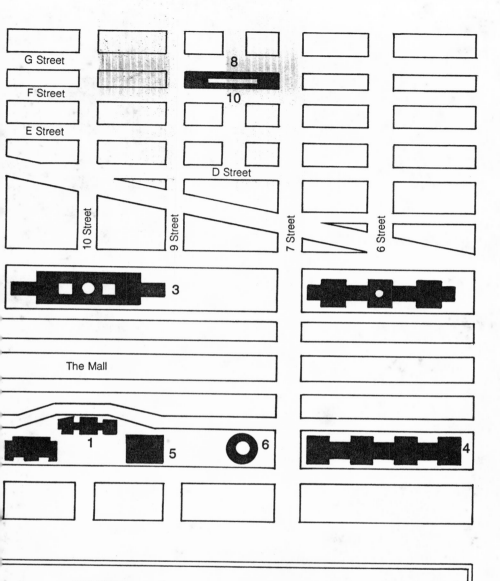

G Street

F Street

E Street

D Street

10 Street

9 Street

7 Street

6 Street

8

10

3

The Mall

1

5

6

4

  7. Freer Gallery of Art

  8. National Collection of Fine Arts

  9. Renwick Gallery

  10. National Portrait Gallery

  11. Folk Festival (The Mall)

  12. National Zoological Park

MUSEUM PEOPLE

Collectors and Keepers at the Smithsonian

by Peggy Thomson

illustrations by Joseph Low

Prentice-Hall, Inc.,
Englewood Cliffs, New Jersey

Copyright © 1977 by Peggy Thomson

Illustrations copyright © 1977 by Prentice-Hall, Inc.
All rights reserved. No part of this book may be
reproduced in any form or by any means, except for
the inclusion of brief quotations in a review,
without permission in writing from the publisher.

Printed in the United States of America   •J

Prentice-Hall International, Inc., London
Prentice-Hall of Australia, Pty. Ltd., North Sydney
Prentice-Hall of Canada, Ltd., Toronto
Prentice-Hall of India Private Ltd., New Delhi
Prentice-Hall of Japan, Inc., Tokyo
Prentice-Hall of Southeast Asia Pte. Ltd., Singapore

10 9 8 7 6 5 4 3 2 1

Library of Congress Cataloging in Publication Data
Thomson, Peggy.
        Museum people.

        SUMMARY: Uses interviews with curators, research
scientists, technicians, and zookeepers to present life
behind the scenes at the Smithsonian Institution.
        Bibliography: p.
        Includes index.
        1.   Smithsonian Institution — Juvenile literature.
[1.   Smithsonian Institution.   2.   Museums]   I.   Low,
Joseph, 1911-   II.   Title.
Q11.S8T47   069'.09753   77-3175
ISBN 0-13-606889-8

The symbols representing Smithsonian
Institution buildings are insignia of the
United States, registered with the U.S.
Patent and Trademark Office, and are
used with the express permission of the
Smithsonian Institution. The symbols may
not be reproduced in any form.

Contents

Preface

Almost the only employees you are apt to see on visits to the Smithsonian Institution in Washington, D.C., are the guards who point you in the right direction for the Kitty Hawk Flyer or the First Ladies' dresses or the dinosaurs or the pandas. This book is not about them. It's about the people you don't see. It's about the ones who work behind the scenes in the sprawling complex of museums, art galleries, and zoo which make up the Smithsonian Institution — the ones who work in cluttered offices and workshops and overstuffed storage rooms in the vast spaces beyond the exhibits.

It's a book about people, museum people, who tell about their jobs — what they do, how they came to be where they are, and how they like it. The book also goes into the museums' traditional tasks — of collecting, keeping track of things, conservation, and putting on exhibits — but always in terms of the people carrying out the tasks. It's always Smithsonian people talking, waving their hands excitedly in the air, pointing with paintbrush or shinbone as they describe their special interests.

Though this book describes exhibits-in-the-making, it isn't a guidebook for you to hold in hand while tramping from one exhibit hall to the next. It isn't a reference text telling how museums are organized. It takes you backstage but doesn't attempt to tell you everything that goes on there. It isn't a careers manual either, although — young or old — if you are still pondering what to be when you "grow up," you may be surprised by the variety of museum occupations you read about here. If you're a packrat of a collector, if you're curious about crickets or spacecraft, if you have a knack for working with your hands, for handling animals or machinery, or a flair for putting on shows, you may be a museum person yourself. Perhaps this book will suggest work that appeals to you, in museums like the Smithsonian. Since this is a people book, most of the material in it is based on interviews. Employees of the Smithsonian, working for national museums supported by the government, are used to interruptions — by telephone call and visit — from the public, from inquirers like me. It is part of their job.

Some of the people I talked to are curators — historians and art historians and scientists who collect neon signs and portraits and beetles, who study volcanoes, skins, skulls, twentieth-century folk art, or the behavior of golden marmosets.

Some are registrars, technicians, and collections managers, who keep track of the 100 million things in the collections, less than one percent of which are on display. They clock in the 800,000 new insect specimens that arrive in a single year. They make space for the second-best petrified logs and stuffed polar bears, which are not on display. And

because the Smithsonian, like most museums, sends objects and whole exhibits on tour, these people pack and ship antique saddles, a young giraffe, or the skeleton of a giant sloth for the public in other parts of the nation to see.

Other people working at the Smithsonian are conservators. They prolong the lives of old photographs and clothing and engines. They clean yellowed varnish from paintings and wash and wax outdoor statues. They perform delicate, finicky chores like removing corrosion crust from a bronze goddess or ink spots from a Teddy bear or insect cocoons from baskets or the dread and ubiquitous sticky tape from just about everything.

Still others at the Smithsonian are exhibits people, skilled in telling stories through three-dimensional objects. They are the artists and designers, the audiovisual wizards, the photographers, the riggers who hang airplanes from the rafters, the carpenters who take apart period rooms — like a kitchen or an Army barracks — and reassemble them inside the museum.

Searching for these people in the Smithsonian took me onto floors of the buildings reserved for the staff. It took me into the freeze-dry lab where frogs, robins, and bobcats are prepared for display, very much the way freeze-dried coffee or corn is prepared. Freeze-dry does away with the traditional but messy process of taxidermy. I went into greenhouses and storage hangars, into the rearing room where grasshoppers and potato bugs and dung beetles are raised for the insect zoo, into the various conservation labs for art work, for machinery, for Indian pots and Eskimo clothing, for ailing musical instruments. In the vertebrate paleo prep lab I watched through a cloud of dust a lineup of men grinding away at rocks in which fossil animals are embedded. My search took me into the fur vault and the alcohol room, a library of animals preserved in jars, and into the models shop where men and women in rubber aprons are modeling in clay and stirring mudpies in cottage cheese cartons. The results of their work, which looks a little like kindergarten play: fish and fish eggs, weeds, trees, lightweight fieldstones, and rodent-free fruit—all for exhibit. The day I was there the mannequin maker was sanding down an Indian head she held in her lap and she had a First Lady torso and arms on a sort of tea trolley beside her, awaiting her attention.

Exhibits-under-construction are exciting places to visit. Freight elevators clank open, spitting out an automobile or stacks of glass and lumber. Padded carts trundle by, carrying precious objects. Everywhere skilled craftspeople are at work—hammering, hanging, gilding, lettering. Designers and curators confer amid a jumble of paint pots, wires, ladders; how will they nudge a locomotive along a track with a bull-dozer, how will they pick (rigger talk for pick up) the gon-dola of the zeppelin *Hindenburg* (not the real one, which blew up in midair on its maiden voyage, but a full-size rep-lica). Walking into the "1876" exhibit area, I saw deliv-erymen skate-boarding out from it down the loading ramp on their empty dollies, past me, past the guards, past a sign that said TOUCH NOTHING BUMP NOTHING SCRATCH NOTH-ING GOUGE NOTHING. EXHIBIT UNDER CONSTRUCTION.

I liked the noisy excitement of all that, even just step-ping around the edges the way I did, when the totem poles and heavy machinery and cannon were set in place; and scaf-folding for the two girls rigging the 51-foot ship model *An-tietam* from mast peak to decks. But then I liked the quiet excitement, too, in other parts of the buildings—the absorp-tion and sense of purpose—where people were stitching sails or stirring rice paste or sketching pollen under a microscope, and where curators were writing in cubicles piled ceiling-high with books, maps, specimens, and stacks of print-outs from the computer.

Museum people are tinkerers, scholars, showmen. They're good at working with their hands. They have a sense of his-tory. They have a feeling for things—for wheels, tools, bones. You see that feeling in the concentrated way they bend over tiny rodents or blobs of pond algae or a clock or a shoe-crimping machine. You see it when a curator thwacks his hand on the lazyboard of a Conestoga wagon and says, "My great-great-grandfather Jacob drove one of these"; or when a photographer contorts his limbs in imitation of the moth he saw in his lens—a moth which was imitating a bent twig; or when a musical-instruments conservator ties a hog bristle or sharpens a goose quill for repairs to a harpsichord. That feeling is evident in the way an art conservator smooths a blockprint that looks like a crumpled shoe-box tissue. In some museum people the feeling shows as a deep respect. In others, a boisterous joy.

People in museums have a passion for authenticity. They use a replica of the real thing only when absolutely necessary and they label it plainly for what it is. In Air and Space exhibits, buttons which fall off World War I and World War II pilot uniforms are sewn on again with thread found in airmen's kits. When the wing of a 1930s airplane is being restored, care is taken not to use modern pinking shears to pink the edge of a tape because modern shears cut too-shallow notches.

The people I saw were totally engrossed in their work assignments. A bracket maker toured me all through his building and we saw only his own handiwork. A framer toured me through *his* building. We didn't look at a single picture, only at frames—the ones he admired and the ones he pined over because of their little flaws.

I've heard the Smithsonian called, as a place to work, a haven for the American eccentric. It's certainly a place that encourages people in their single-minded, passionate interests—in farm machinery or in mouse tails or the noses of dolphins. It's a place where no one has to explain how a lifetime can be well spent in getting to know a single living creature. The man who is in his fifty-fifth year of work on freshwater free-swimming flatworms (Turbellaria) says his latest publication on them can probably be fully understood by only six people in the entire world—one in Canada, one in Japan, and four in Europe—and that he still has a lot to learn about them himself.

xvi Museum People

The Smithsonian is full of people who picture themselves as living in the nineteenth century — who choose to work at rolltop desks with brown photographs on the walls and little iron, wood, and brass patent models of sadirons (solid flatirons) and side-saddle tricycles for decoration. The only uncluttered office I saw belongs to a collections manager for paleobiology. With 50 million specimens of fossil animals to keep track of, he feels that one misplaced fossil crab claw would set the other 49,999,999 a bad example.

The people in this book have come to museum work along different paths. Some held advanced degrees in sciences, communications, history, art history, conservation, and knew what they wanted to do and where. Some worked at and received degrees after they were already in their jobs. Many have no degree; and even though they continue to study and may lecture at universities and write for scholarly publications, they don't intend to get one.

Most of the people in this book said they never expected to find themselves working in a museum. They entered through a combination of interests, skills, hobbies. They were surprised that experience — working on a railroad, at sea, in a pickle factory — led to it. They were pleased that talents in electronics or gardening answered museums' needs.

Objects remain pretty much forever in the Smithsonian's collections, and Smithsonian people stay on pretty much forever, too. There are dozens of employees who come to work day in day out, some of them seven days a week, for ten and twenty years and more beyond the date of their retirement.

It would take a series of books to begin to tell about all of the Smithsonian people — people past and people present. I've left out whole categories of the ones working there today — not just the guards but the security alarms people, the accountants accustomed to figuring travel expenses in exotic-sounding currencies like rials and drachmas, the locksmiths (museum people all have bulky key rings jangling in their pockets), the lawyers who have to consider: Can the donor really give the statue to us or does it belong to his church, his tribe, his sister or his aunt?

Readers will see what began to happen as I researched this book. It soon became as cluttered as any of the museum cupboards. It's still that way. Like the Smithsonian itself, it has too many things in it and is overstuffed with ideas and faces, with kites, campaign buttons, and other treasures, with too many lists and quotes and conversation. I hope you can find your way.

The book may even have too many people in it. But one person led to another, and each said what a blunder it was to leave out his neighbor. I was forever having to see still more people to understand the work of ones I'd seen. I sympathized with the biologist who said he couldn't get on with his howler monkey research without first learning the fruiting characteristics (and just about everything else) of the hog plum tree on which the howlers feed.

The people I intended to skip—registrars and other keepers of records—turned out to be perhaps the most interesting of all. I asked about the difference between an accession number and a catalog number only to be polite, but it opened up a whole world to me of predicaments to be met in counting and storing and shipping. How would *you* file a microfossil you can't see? It's a problem. Here are more: How would *you* fly a live nene goose to San Francisco or an Akan drum from London or a Stamp Act box from Texas? The first traveled in a tomato crate, the second on a first-class seat, the third in a brown carton marked Tutti Frutti Twinkles.

Some of my encounters came about by chance, when I took a wrong turn at the end of a corridor. Smithsonian buildings are splendid places in which to get lost. Without question the Natural History Museum rates tops overall for behind-the-scenes spaces. It has the best attics, and behind a door in the basement marked Scientific Events Alert Network there's a young man counting everything from earthquakes to the worm diseases afflicting moose. The National Collection of Fine Arts has the best cellars, with warrens of shops (for framing, for silk-screening, gold-leafing), their doorways almost hidden by crates stacked in the halls. The Freer is as hushed and elegant belowstairs as it is in the exhibit galleries above. My shoes ruined the effect, clattering along its marble floors, but I felt hushed, too, with awe, as I peered into drawers of porcelain, jade, lacquer, rooms of scrolls, rooms of double six-panel screens, a whole pull-out wall of Whistlers in glistering frames of gold. Through a doorway there I watched a Japanese screen restorer kneeling by a low table, cutting strips of gold-flecked brocades in the speeded-up tempo of silent film, and marveled at his skill.

The Smithsonian's Zoo provides the best opportunities for eavesdropping and snooping. I overheard the vet intern say on the telephone, "Oh, Jimmy's coming along fine," as he described the Bactrian camel, bored with his alfalfa and molasses, now perking up with a change of diet. A note on the vet's desk reminded him of the green snake with gout and the spiny rat requiring dental pictures. I thought I'd never seen anywhere such green greens and appealing fruit, done up in tissue wrappers, and such rosy mice and frosty-white fish as in the commissary's walk-in refrigerators.

Gathering people and information was the best part of working on this book. When museum people complain about restricting what they collect for a single exhibit (it's hard to narrow down to 40 neon signs, say, from the 700 they photograph and consider), they should know how hard it is in writing a book about museum people to keep from collecting more of them than will ever fit into it.

I'm grateful to all of them — the ones named in the book and the ones unnamed. They unlocked their storage cupboards for me and let me peer over their shoulders as they worked. They moved piles of papers, books, cages, to offer me a place to sit, even rummaging among skulls in the dish drainer to provide an extra cup for tea. They gave time to talk about the pleasures of their work.

PART ONE
The Places

1. Places Where People Work

The people who work for the Smithsonian Institution are a mixed lot of scholars, artists, art handlers, conservators, animal keepers, carpenters, and mechanics. They work together in teams that are amicable or sparring. Or they work alone, walled off behind piles of books and specimen cases. Many of them are away from time to time on errands connected with their jobs. They are away on digs or they are scrutinizing foreign fruit bats or filming or collecting or cutting up whale carcasses on distant beaches. One geologist intends to make a field trip to the moon as the logical next step to mapping moon craters at his desk and assigning names to them.

Some of these people haven't spoken to each other in years. Their paths don't cross or even if they do, they haven't noticed. Some have never met, which is understandable since their places of work are scattered through a number of buildings.

Smithsonian people work in the cluster of eight museums and art galleries which face each other across the grassy Mall sweeping from the Capitol to the Washington Monument. They work in other galleries some blocks beyond the Mall and in the Zoo in Rock Creek Park and in installations still further afield — within the United States and across the seas. Some of them have offices, labs, and workshops in buildings which are dazzlingly new; some, in old buildings which are period pieces, as much on show as the things they exhibit.

All are based in Washington, D.C. In common they

have, as headquarters, the Smithsonian's famous "Castle" on the Mall.

The Castle , they share is a red sandstone fortress with arched windows, crenelated battlements, and a roof line spiked by eight towers—skinny towers and squat ones, pointy-roofed towers and flat. The first home of the Smithsonian, it was built a century and a quarter ago by architect James Renwick, Jr. The building was an oddity in its day, and is still. In a city where ordinary-looking government offices abound, its quirky dark shape stands out against sunny skies, against gray skies, against inky night skies, and has become a Washington landmark. The Castle with its flags flying has come to be a symbol of the Smithsonian, an invitation to adventure.

New buildings have been added over the years, giving shape to different aspects of the Smithsonian adventure and extra space to the growing collections. It takes a map with arrows pointing beyond its margins to show the places where today's employees work.

Starting at the Mall, there's the Castle as centerpiece, with its massive carriage porch and its founding father statue out front — and the other eight buildings lined up left, right, and opposite. Beside the Castle is the Arts and Industries Building 🏛 , a squatter structure, also red — but of brick — and resembling a carousel. It was first used in 1881 for President James Garfield's inaugural ball, an occasion which is remembered for the accidental death — from cold — of canaries intended to provide music and decoration. Recently the building was restored to its century-ago look and its entire exhibition space — consisting of a rotunda and four broad naves — was given over to the totem poles, the antlers and cannon, stuffed polar bears and steam-driven machinery of a single "1876" exhibition.

Opposite the Castle, across the grass, is the Natural History Museum 🐘 , huge, gray, classical, with a dome and widespread wings. The complicated floor plan and odd-shaped, wide-ranging spaces inside cover more than 20 acres. Natural History is best known for the giant 8-ton African bush elephant in the center of the rotunda. Thirteen feet two inches from shoulders to floor, it is shown in full-trumpet position, its trunk pointing up toward the balconies. It is believed to be the largest elephant ever. Radiating off from the elephant's fore- and hindquarters are the exhibit halls, which contain the great Diplodocus skeleton (80 feet long), the Hope Diamond (44.5 carats), all the artifacts of American Indian and Eskimo life, and the fiberglass model of a blue whale measuring 92 feet from snout to fluke. Out of sight, attic to basement, are the people laboring in the name of natural science — dissecting, cataloging, tending collections. In a dusty loft, volunteers reassemble earthenware pots from multitudes of shards.

Next door to Natural History stands the Museum of History and Technology 🏛 , a great white box of a building. Its ramps give it a modern Aztec look. When it opened in 1964 it provided space to display the huge original Star-Spangled Banner, 30 feet by 42 feet, stitched by Baltimore widow Mary Pickersgill, the equally oversized statue of George Washington looking uncomfortable in a Roman toga, and the

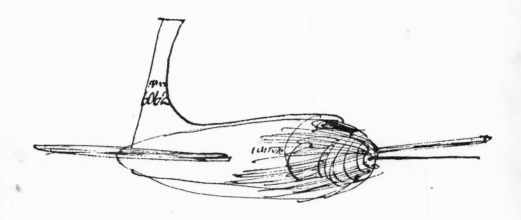

Foucault Pendulum, which swings to and fro from the fourth-floor ceiling and demonstrates the earth's rotation on its axis. History and Technology houses the First Ladies' gowns, Presidential memorabilia, starting with Washington's ivory-and-gold false teeth, stamps, fire engines, coins, and an atom-splitting cyclotron. This building was large enough to accommodate the Bicentennial exhibits *We the People,* on the political process, and *A Nation of Nations,* the story of immigration in America. Its basements contain conservation labs for musical instruments and for machinery and the central conservation lab for the entire Smithsonian.

The very new glass-and-marble-and-steel National Air and Space Museum   , which opened on July 1, 1976, has become the greatest magnet for crowds on the Mall, with two million people visiting it in its first seven weeks alone. Now guards close the doors when more than 10,000 are inside at a time. Though the building was expected to be something of an eyesore—a hangar, after all, and three blocks long—it was built by architect Gyo Obata along such open and airy lines and its airplanes were hung so inventively in midair in great glass bays that, in spite of the crush, people come out saying they feel they've been flying. Visitors see historic flying machines (the Wright *Flyer,* the *Spirit of St. Louis*), spacecraft (the Apollo 11 command module, the Skylab-Orbital Workshop), rockets and missiles. A space-age planetarium, called a Spacearium, helps visitors to picture space flight, as do many audiovisual shows and mechanical demonstrations, run and monitored from a single small control room in the basement.

There are three art galleries on the Mall. The Freer Gallery of Art   🔲   is a low-slung, elegant Renaissance palace, granite, built around a courtyard. It was a gift, in 1906 together with its works of art, from Detroit industrialist Charles Lang Freer. Freer quit school in the seventh grade to work and made a fortune in railroads while he was still young. With his money he bought works of art with such a fine eye and generous purse that his collection from the Orient, India, and the Near East is one of the best in the Western world. Also world-famous at the Freer is the work done in its basement — on research and conservation.

The Hirshhorn Museum and Sculpture Garden   🔲   , which opened in 1974, is a boldly modern circular building which its architect referred to as "a drum suspended on piers over a plaza," but which most people describe as a doughnut or a bagel or "Joe's Place." Along with 6,000 of its pieces of modern art, the building was a gift from financier Joseph Hirshhorn. Hirshhorn, who fell in love with calendar pictures at age 12, was the twelfth in a family of 13 children whose immigrant mother stitched pocketbooks for a living. A short man, he reached the microphone for making his speech on the museum's opening day by standing on a case of champagne. He spoke of the paintings and sculptures which he gave as his "children" — among them sculptures by Rodin (*The Burghers of Calais*) and by Moore (*King and Queen*).

The National Gallery of Art, completed in 1941, is a great classical building of marble which looks white under sunny skies and pink in the rain. It was the gift, along with a collection of Old Master paintings and sculptures, of financier Andrew Mellon, who asked that it not be named for him. It now has a two-part annex built alongside it, to the east, on the Mall's last patch of building space. The design for the annex by architect I. M. Pei was intentionally modern, lest it look as though the National Gallery had "whelped a pup." But the same man who went into the Tennessee quarries to select the rose-and-white marble for the original building also picked out the matching marble to be used on its neighbor 35 years later.

("People" from the National Gallery were not interviewed for this book. Nor were people from the John F. Kennedy Center for the Performing Arts, the three-theater structure on the bank of the Potomac River. The National Gallery and the Kennedy Center both come under the Smithsonian umbrella, but they are run quite independently of it.)

Off the Mall by a few blocks are still other Smithsonian museums. Two share a building. The National Collection of Fine Arts 🎨 (showing work by American artists such as Winslow Homer, Albert Pinkham Ryder, and George Catlin, famous for his paintings of Indians) and the National Portrait Gallery 🖼 (likenesses of famous Americans — Presidents, Pocahontas, Einstein, Joe Louis) share what once was the old Patent Office Building, which President Eisenhower saved from being torn down for a parking lot. The small Renwick Gallery 🏛 across the street from the White House was Washington's first art gallery, designed by Renwick, the architect for the Castle. Today it is a museum of American crafts and design.

Further afield but still in the city are the Anacostia Neighborhood Museum (across the Anacostia River from downtown Washington), a storefront museum run by the neighborhood which it serves and celebrates; and, in Rock Creek Park, the National Zoo 🐾 . The Zoo in recent years has had such remodeling and reshaping of terraces and pens and ponds that Zoo people say the antics of bulldozers and giant yellow cranes have been as much on show as the white tigers, the Chinese pandas, and the pygmy hippos.

Still further afield are the Zoo's breeding park for endangered species and Smithsonian research installations such as the radiation laboratory in Maryland, the astrophysical observatory in Massachusetts, the oceanographic sorting center in Tunisia, and a tropical research institute in Panama.

The whole Smithsonian adventure and the proliferation of buildings and programs began with a totally unexpected gift from a mysterious figure about whom almost nothing is known — an Englishman named James Smithson. Born in 1765, the illegitimate child of a nobleman, Smithson became a chemist and mineralogist. He identified a new mineral, later called Smithsonite. He died in 1829, a wealthy man, and he left his fortune to the United States, a country he had never seen, but clearly admired. He asked that his money, which amounted to 105 bags of gold — worth then more than half a million dollars — be used to establish in his name a scientific institution for the "increase & diffusion of knowledge among men" (his phrase is a quotation from George Washington's Farewell Address).

Honoring the memory of Smithson, members of the staff named the pair of barn owls who nested in the spring of 1977 in the northwest tower of the Castle, Increase and Diffusion. Earlier, in 1904, Alexander Graham Bell brought Smithson's bones from Italy, where he was buried, and President Teddy Roosevelt sent the USS *Dolphin* and the Marine band to welcome them on arrival. Natural History's physical anthropologists practiced a bit of forensic osteology — detective work on bones — in 1973 at the time Smithson's crypt in the Castle was being refurbished. They reported after examining

the skeleton: Smithson stood five feet nine, his forehead was shorter than it shows in his portraits; he fenced, smoked a pipe, and died of natural causes.

One museum curator — from Air and Space — has a fantasy regarding Smithson. He'd like to pilot him about the Mall in a helicopter, introducing him to the buildings, to Increase and Diffusion as they swoop in and out of the Castle, to the fact that 4,700 people owe their museum jobs to him, and 20 million visitors a year owe him a debt of pleasure. This loyal employee — 57 years at the Smithsonian — pictures himself breaking the news to Smithson that the original bags of gold have multiplied 10,000 times. The Smithsonian Institution today is valued at between five and six billion dollars. Its budget for 1976 ran to $100 million from Congress, a further $11 million from private sources, and more from grants. "I think Smithson would be pleased and astonished."

At the start, a doubting Congress was slow to take up Smithson's gift. It mulled over the matter for eight years before authorizing the first building — the Castle — and appointing the first Secretary, Joseph Henry. Henry was a physicist, distinguished for his work on the electromagnet (a "henry" is an electrical unit named for him). He would have preferred more functional work space to a Castle, but he made the best of the elaborate building. He not only moved in with his family, but also offered living quarters to bachelor scientists, explorers, and illustrators, so that they could be close to their labs, library, and specimens. One paleontologist occupied a tower room with its floor-to-ceiling rose window for eighteen years.

Henry's family played croquet on the Mall, then known as the Smithsonian Reservation. His daughters gave concerts. President Lincoln is said to have come as a relief from war cares to talk with Henry about the stars. It was Henry who in 1861 arranged for a balloon ascension from the Smithsonian grounds to demonstrate to the President the usefulness of ballooning for military reconnaissance. The public came to the Castle for lectures on subjects ranging from politics to snakes. Visitors looked at the objects on display in glass cases on the ground floor of the Great Hall and could see the scientists and taxidermists at work on the iron balconies above their heads.

It didn't suit Henry when Congress transferred to him all the objects from the National Cabinet of Curiosities in the Patent Office building. He thought a scientific institution should be separate from a museum. He thought research and exploration, on which the greatness of the Smithsonian depended, would be hobbled if money and time and space went to keeping house for curiosities and playing host to curiosity-seekers.

But for all his complaints about museum chores, Henry collected widely — books, art, Indian artifacts, examples of human ingenuity. He pioneered in collecting weather reports from around the country by telegraph. He collected, he said, not to swell the Smithsonian holdings but to save things from destruction and to make them accessible. In saying that, he sounded like a museum person in spite of himself, though to his mind collections always meant collections for scientific study — not for public education, and certainly not for public entertainment.

At the close of the Philadelphia Centennial Exposition of 1876, the contents of many of its exhibitions came down to Washington in forty-two boxcar-loads — kites, cookstoves, totem poles, machinery — to be housed in a new museum, next to the Castle, now called Arts and Industries. From that time, the Smithsonian was in the exhibits business on a large scale. It never let go and it never stopped. How to interpret "increase & diffusion," how to strike a balance between research and exploration on the one hand and exhibition for the public on the other, has been a puzzle for every Smithsonian Secretary from Henry's time until today.

The present Secretary, S. Dillon Ripley, who began his term as the eighth Secretary of the Institution in 1964, says, "It's a funny thing about museums; you have to do two things. You have to play two tunes on the harmonica at the same time. You have to be concerned with the role of research, which is a very scholarly, esoteric, erudite kind of business. And you have to speak to the citizens, reach out to people, show them the collections which are really theirs, excite them, interest them, serve them.

"I wasn't the first in this," says Ripley, citing the kinship he feels with the third Secretary, Samuel Pierpont Langley, that "prissy, fussy old bachelor," who built steam-driven aircraft models with 13-foot wingspreads. While Langley was studying astrophysics and building his flying machines (which he called aerodromes) he let grass grow knee-high around his laboratory shed beside the Castle to discourage visitors. But it was Langley (Secretary from 1877 to 1906), Ripley points out, who established a Children's Room in the Castle, with special exhibits to beguile the eye—live fish in aquariums and glass cases of dead but realistic birds—and with chatty labels to excite curiosity. Langley's labels put ROBIN REDBREAST first, followed by bits of information and verse, and the Latin name and scientific data last.

It was Langley, too, who put live animals on display by establishing the National Zoo. The animals had been accumulating in pens behind the Castle, brought there originally for the taxidermists to observe their expressions. In 1890, Langley moved them—94 mammals, including six of the endangered American bison, plus 60 birds, five snakes, three tortoises, 17 alligators, and one bullfrog, in a borrowed wagon, to their present location in Rock Creek Park.

Ripley is an exuberant birdman who has presided over the Smithsonian during the years of its greatest growth and extraordinary flowering. A research person like his predecessors, he writes in the odd hours when he can slip away to his laboratory. He has co-authored a ten-volume work on the birds of India and Pakistan, and written other books on waterfowl and rails. He has traveled by yak to study high-altitude birds of the Himalayas. He delights in scholarship and has attracted numbers of leading scholars in their fields to the Smithsonian and has found the money to support their work.

we supply a memory bank, let our successors know that we even knew we had them and, as well, what we thought about them."

Central to everything a museum does is conservation — the proper caring for precious or unique objects. One aspect of conservation is the breeding program which is being carried on at the National Zoo for reproducing endangered species, a program which Ripley calls a last hope of showing numbers of wild animals to zoo-goers in the future.

"An honorable task," Ripley says of museum work, "and an onerous one, not easy. There is no school in which to learn it except experience."

There is no school in which to learn how to be Secretary, either. Ripley's predecessors learned on the job as he has done. Research people all, they seemed to be blessed with energy and long lives, working on at their special interests well past the dates of retirement. Charles Greeley Abbot, who served as fifth Secretary until he was 72, stayed on in one of the tower rooms in the Castle, recording sunspot activity into his hundredth year. Abbot was one of the first living people to have a crater on the moon named for him. And he was the

oldest person, at age 100, to be granted a patent, for his device to harness solar energy. As a youngster he'd mended his family's pots and pans, built a forge on which to mend farm machinery, made himself a bicycle out of wood, with iron tires. As an old gentleman correlating sunspot activity with weather on 18-foot lengths of paper rolled around oatmeal boxes, he was happy to prophesy wedding-day weather for brides. Smithsonian people remember his singing sea chanties at his desk and baking brownies on his solar cooker.

Alexander Wetmore, the sixth Secretary, *another* birdman, recorded a pelican as the first entry in his field notebook when he was eight. When he retired from the Smithsonian's top post, he returned to his four-volume work on the birds of Panama. He was on the job, in his khakis, in the Natural History Museum all through his eighties.

When Ripley sums up the responsibilities of running the whole Smithsonian museum complex, he says the job is "like the old Hungarian horse act where the man comes out jumping up and down on the rumps of eight or nine Percheron horses. You just have to keep jumping from rump to rump." Ripley has also said that being Secretary of the Smithsonian is "the most fascinating of jobs." Not all Smithsonian people agree with him. Among the many who find their own work completely to their taste, at least one, a carpenter at History and Technology, believes his job is better than the Secretary's and he wouldn't care to swap.

PART TWO
The People

In History

In Science

In the Arts

2.People in History

 MARGARET KLAPTHOR
Political Historian

The collection of dresses worn by the nation's First Ladies attracts more visitors from all over the world than any other exhibition in the Museum of History and Technology. The carpet in front of Jacqueline Kennedy, supposed to be indestructible, was threadbare within four years. But it is their history, not the dresses themselves, that most interests Margaret Klapthor, their curator. "I'm a historian pure and simple," says this outspoken, direct museum person who dresses in no-nonsense clothes and holds her short dark hair away from her face with a barrette. "It's seeing the common thread running through costume and politics and furnishings that's exciting — the common thread distinguishing one period from another."

Klapthor thinks she was assigned the dresses when she first came to the museum in 1943, fresh out of college with a degree in history, because curators in political history were men not much interested in women's wear. The dresses at that time didn't look like much. They stood in a row in bare glass cases. Klapthor changed all that and moved the *First Ladies* show into period White House settings, surrounded by furniture they'd used, their musical instruments, the portraits and silver and rugs of their years in the White House. She found everything in other glass cases, where they had been arranged President by President. When the White House was renovated during the

Truman administration, the exhibition acquired important castoffs like mantelpieces and panelings and moldings. It also acquired, found under layers of plaster, a scrap of old wallpaper, which was copied for papering one of the parlors.

Today the First Ladies appear in glass-fronted rooms which reflect changing styles of decoration in the White House — for example, Martha Washington beside her tea table in a room representing the second-floor parlor in the Executive Mansion in Philadelphia; Louisa Adams beside her harp and music stand in a White House Empire-style reception room, along with Dolley Madison and Elizabeth Monroe. The more recent First Ladies, starting with Florence Harding, stand in a row from one side to the other side of the formal East Room; this is shown as it looked from 1902 to the time of Truman, with dark marble mantels, gold mirror frames, a gold concert grand piano.

Wives of recent Presidents know exactly what is expected of them. They send around their gowns without fail, to keep the collection up to date and complete. Even so, it takes six months from the time a gown travels from the White House to the Smithsonian for it to appear on exhibit. It takes that long for the mannequin to be made to the new First Lady's size and the paperwork to be done — and the photographs and the labels.

Mamie Eisenhower sent her gown promptly, as soon as the Smithsonian's formal request reached her. She included in the gift the accessories she wore with it on the occasion of the first Eisenhower inaugural ball — pocketbook, gloves, beads, shoes, stockings, and petticoats — though she once sent a White House chauffeur to the Smithsonian to borrow back for an afternoon her comfortable pink shoes.

Lady Bird Johnson sent her yellow satin dress and matching coat, with its cuffs of sable, after a slight delay. She explained that her husband especially liked the ensemble, and she wanted to wear it some more first. Pat Nixon was prompt with *her* yellow dress and beaded jacket. Though Betty Ford never had an inaugural ball, she sent Klapthor a lime-green sequinned chiffon crepe dress which she wore on a state occasion (1976) in the White House. Rosalynn Carter's Wedgewood-blue ball dress received considerable notice in the press at the time of her husband's inaugural in 1977. It made history by *not* reflecting current high fashion. First Lady Carter broke with the tradition of her immediate predecessors when she chose to wear an old dress, dating from her husband's inaugural six years earlier as Governor of Georgia. She maintained the stronger First Lady tradition, however, and gave her dress to the Smithsonian.

Some of the early First Lady clothing was hard for the Smithsonian to come by. The grandson of Abigail Adams said huffily that his ancestors "were not in the habit of keeping their old clothes." Descendants of Jefferson explained his daughters' dresses had been "cut up and worn to rags" during the Civil War. Lucretia Garfield said she thought her own dress was too ugly to send to the Smithsonian; she changed her mind only on her deathbed. Grace Coolidge wrote Klapthor to say she had second thoughts about having sent her red chiffon flapper dress with its short skirt and rhinestone hip-hugger belt. It was "so ugly," her friends thought. But Klapthor persuaded Mrs. Coolidge to leave it in the collection. "I wrote her it was a perfect example of high fashion of its period."

Klapthor has worked directly with every First Lady from Eleanor Roosevelt on — and with several of the earlier ones. The second Mrs. Woodrow Wilson was the only one who asked to have her dress shown from the back. Though Klapthor agreed the back was elegant, she thought it unfriendly — to turn the figure with its back to the viewer. It looked as if the second Mrs. Wilson were not speaking with the first Mrs. Wilson, even though, dressed in her favorite color, black, she seemed to be in mourning for her white-clad predecessor. Today's new showcases, which are glass on three sides, have resolved the problem.

From time to time, on occasions like the visit of the wives of astronauts and cosmonauts, Klapthor leads a tour of her hall, giving them at a steady, brisk pace an account of two centuries of Presidential life. She covers fashion from berthas (lace collars) to Empire waistlines, through hoops and hobble skirts to flapper hemlines, from leg-o-mutton sleeves to spaghetti straps. She describes the furnishings and accessories—the wing chair in which Washington sat to "catch his breath" the day he died, John Quincy Adams's bedpost watch-holder (a gentleman's watch was thought to benefit from being kept in a vertical position), Dolley Madison's turban, Louisa Adams's yard-square handkerchief with the number 17 woven into a corner, the silver chicken-legs coffee set that belonged to Mary Todd Lincoln, her fan, parasol, and wrist watch along with various examples of combs, tiaras, lockets, and mourning pins.

Klapthor calls attention to the bold and lavish decoration in the Blue Room during the Grant administration, which was matched by the heavy embroidery, the fringe and beadwork on the bustle dresses of the period. Julia Grant's stiff brocade gown could stand independently, without a mannequin in it. Klapthor wants no one to miss the patriotism on show by the womenfolk of Benjamin Harrison, whose slogan was "Buy America". Designs of burr oak leaves and acorns are woven into the fabric of Caroline Harrison's dress; daughter Mary Harrison's has goldenrod. The fabric of both is American. So is the design. So is the maker, although most fashion of the turn of the century was French. Klapthor points out the royal purple in the china as well as the dress of Mrs. Lincoln, whose lavish, spendthrift ways were a campaign issue.

White House china became such an area of expertise for Klapthor that at one time Mrs. Eisenhower asked her to help in identifying pieces in the White House collection and to correct the White House labels. At the same time Mrs. Eisenhower gave duplicate pieces of china to the Smithsonian. A set that always attracts attention is the one ordered by Rutherford Hayes to celebrate native American flora, fauna, fish, game, and fruit. Klapthor likes to show its platters painted with a very realistic wild turkey and with a shad caught and bleeding in its net. The same set has plates with big-horn sheep, cranes, buffaloes held at bay by wolves, soup plates shaped like laurel blossoms, fruit plates like apple leaves, ice-cream plates like snowshoes—a whole feast of Americana from persimmons to prairie hens to maple sugar-in-the-making. Klapthor has written a fat book on White House china, as well as books on the First Ladies.

Because she doesn't know how long the First Ladies' dresses will last—400 years is a guess—she is collecting a second string. She now has additional dresses (also the Ladies' own) for two-thirds of her ladies. She has three inaugural dresses of Eleanor Roosevelt's—from FDR's first, third, and fourth inaugurals. And she has numerous dresses from the fashion-plate First Lady, Mrs. Kennedy.

She is two-thirds of the way through the exhaustive project of documenting each dress on display. For this Sara Taft, a fashion designer from New York, comes several days a month to record every detail of each dress, the material, how it is put together, and its decoration. For each dress Taft makes a paper pattern and a mock-up stitched in muslin, and she compiles a workbook complete with swatches, threads, watercolors, with rubbings of the lace and embroidery. In case seamstresses in future generations will have forgotten how to do double French piping she includes step-by-step directions.

All the dresses are genuine. Klapthor is fierce about that. She will never put a copy of a dress on display. She thinks even one replica would cast suspicion over all the collection. She authorizes the muslin copies because she wants future students to have all the information, to know that Angelica Van Buren's skirt is eight yards around at the hem and that Sarah Polk's measures eighteen inches at the waist. The Polk dress was altered once, it seems, to fit a larger relative, but the later stitching—of three-ply thread—could be distinguished from the earlier stitching—which was two-ply. And Klapthor had the dress restored to its original size.

Klapthor crosses the hall from her office in History and

Technology to visit Sara Taft as she works in the storage room on the dresses. She watches her flip a tape measure from seam to seam across a bodice which lies in special buffered (acid-free) tissue paper, then remove her right white glove to write the measurements in a notebook. Klapthor sympathizes over Mrs. Harrison's dress, one which Taft had been dreading because it is one of the most elaborate structures in the batch. But Taft tells her she is moving along with it. "I tell myself, if I could do Florence Harding with that under-bodice, bodice, over-drape and beads, I can do anything."

Neither she nor Klapthor speaks in terms of favorites. Taft does say, "I get a clear picture of which were First Ladies of fashion and which were Girl Scouts. Lou Hoover was a Girl Scout." If that sounds like criticism, the fair-minded Klapthor adds, "Lou Hoover was also the first woman geologist graduate of Stanford."

Klapthor is in and out of the storage room on days Susan Wallace is there painting a First Lady mannequin. All the First Ladies are being given new bodies. When a First Lady is removed from the showcase — and a card left in her place saying "Object Removed For Study" — the old plaster of Paris bust with its wooden frame is replaced by a lightweight plastic body with hips, knees, and ankles, which make for better hanging of the dresses, and with nicely proportioned arms. Wallace strikes a caveman pose as she describes the old plaster casts with the all-purpose, one-size-fits-all arms which, on the smallest ladies, left them with hands dangling at their knees. As a mannequins expert, she works in the "magic shop" of the Smithsonian's central exhibits facility and is available for producing not only First Ladies but South American market-scene figures and World War I aviators. The aviator uniforms she finds fit better on standard female mannequin legs than on male ones, which are too big in the calf.

First Ladies have always been given the same face, copied from a museum bust of King Lear's daughter Cordelia.

It's the same face for Rosalynn Carter as for Bess Truman, the Smithsonian having decided to give the First Ladies a similarity not theirs in life. Originally the faces were left a plastery white. But now the individuality is brought out in skin coloring and in hairdos, over which Wallace takes great care. On the basis of a portrait, she recently altered Caroline Harrison's hair from solid gray to a livelier mixture of colors. A White House press secretary was her authority for how to streak Betty Ford's hair.

Protecting the collection is more of a problem for Klapthor than acquiring it. Light in the First Ladies Hall is kept dim and specially filtered. Visitors complain it's so dim they can't see, but it has to be that way to safeguard the dresses. Humidity is rigidly controlled. So is temperature, because cloth fibers expand and contract with changes from hot to cold, causing dust, if it is present, to saw through the fibers with the motion. Dust itself is attacked, though it's always a problem how best to do it.

Klapthor confers with Barbara Coffee over plans for the yearly cleaning of the hall. It takes conservator Coffee and two helpers several days to do each room, a week at least for the elaborate East Room alone. They wear white hospital coats for the work, with white cotton gloves and white booties. And they move cautiously.

The upper reaches of the room they get to with bamboo extension feather dusters that notch together like fishing poles. Around the necklines of the dresses they use sable paintbrushes, and across the smooth expanses of skirt they use low-pressure vacuum cleaners with fiberglass screens held in

front of them to keep from sucking in the material. Skirts are rehung into new folds. Satin shoes have dust blown off them with what Coffee calls "poofers." The discouraging part, Coffee says, is that "no matter what you do to clothing, you're damaging it. Brushes grind some dust in; poofers release it into the air. You just always try for the gentlest procedure to do the job." Bugle beads found on the floor and bits of rhinestone and pearl go into boxes to be sewed back on one day.

In the summer of 1975, Coffee traveled to England, Holland, and Sweden for advice on how to preserve Julia Tyler's net dress, which is crumbling, and Ida McKinley's silk dress, which is splitting. She felt she brought home very little news that was good. "Most experts were horrified that our gowns are on permanent display. Almost all other costume collections on exhibition elsewhere in the world are rotated and allowed to rest in storage. Some are changed every six months or even every two weeks." Coffee and Klapthor feel helpless about that. "We can't close down the hall," says Klapthor. As it is, they try to schedule their cleaning for raw winter days, in hopes they won't disappoint too many visitors. "Someone called this collection a national icon," says Klapthor, who is amused but doesn't altogether disagree.

To date Martha Washington's is the only gown to be absent for any long spell. It was retired because its salmon-color silk, painted all over with wildflowers and insects, showed signs of deteriorating. Technician Lois Vann spent a year, working four hours every other day, to stabilize the dress. She sandwiched the skirt in an almost invisible brown silk net called crêpeline (which is why the skirt looks a shade darker than the top). To do the job she used a needle several sizes finer than any that is commercially available. She used single strands of silk thread, straight from the cocoon. And she stitched only between the fibers.

Klapthor thought possibly Mrs. Washington should be made to stand in the future, to ease the strain on her dress. She was always shown seated, in the First Ladies Hall, because that was how she chose to greet her guests in the White House. The Smithsonian's chief conservator advised Klapthor against a change. He said: build a special chair seat and let the first First Lady have her way.

 ## HERBERT R. COLLINS
Political Historian

In the line of duty as political history curator, Herbert Collins attended both national political conventions in election year 1976, and he had a good time collecting. He collected badges, buttons, hats, bunting, horns, banners, and lots of posters — Jimmy Carter posters of smiling peanuts from the Democratic Convention in New York, and posters of elephants eating peanuts from the Republican Convention in Kansas City.

Some souvenirs he bought. Most he asked for as gifts to the Smithsonian. "I talked a Montana Delegate button off Indian Chief Big Spring, to go with the picture I have of him, wearing it, from the Kansas City *Times*," Collins reports shamelessly. "I asked Representative John Rhodes to donate his vest once he was through with it — the blue satin vest worn by the Arizona delegates. I told Senator Hiram Fong, 'Say, we'd like to have that Hawaiian shirt of yours. It's the most colorful thing in the convention hall.' And I talked a big paper sunflower off a Kansas lady delegate. I already had two — they were made in Italy — two new ones, which I'm keeping as backups for the collection. But I wanted the very one she waved when *Newsweek* took her picture."

Some items Collins traded for, using his duplicates, as any stamp collector would do. He tried to trade a spare Ronald Reagan horn for a Reagan Frisbee, but he was turned down. "I could barely pry any Reagan stuff out of his delegates," he recalls. "It was like asking for pieces of the True Cross. But once their candidate lost, they just threw the stuff away and I happily picked it up off the floor. One woman got in a great hassle with me, though, because I was taking a Reagan poster off a stick. She thought I was desecrating it. I tried to tell her I was just making it easier to carry but she made such a scene I had to drop it altogether."

Collins made a point of picking up a sign, THIS IS REAGAN COUNTRY, that was identical with the one Vice President Nelson Rockefeller tore up on the convention floor. He also got a hand-lettered sign someone carried the next day, which said, ROCKY, DON'T STEAL MY SIGN. "That's history," Collins says.

To a newsboy who asked him if he wanted the *Times*, Collins answered, "No, I want your hat." It was a white plastic helmet with Kansas City *Times* on it. The boy said he'd sell it for $2. Collins said that was too much. The newsboy next to him offered *his* hat for $1. "I bought it for 50 cents," says Collins, who is not called History and Technology's "great acquisitor" for nothing.

The Kansas City convention yielded the better crop of hats, he recalls, ones with more variety. The New York convention had the better posters, because the Democrats had more of the one-of-a-kind homemade items which he favors. He had to go through official channels to get a 12-foot WELCOME banner and a traffic sign that said: NO STANDING—DEMOCRATIC NATIONAL CONVENTION—POLICE DEPARTMENT.

"It was hard work," says Collins. "I loved it. I'd be up at seven, and one night in New York I didn't get to bed until four. That night after the crowds left I combed the convention hall for two hours. I went through the Carter staff trailer and the news trailers. I had my shopping bags so filled with stuff—Peanut Power T-shirts, used red, white and blue coffee cups, Carter face masks with their toothy smiles—I could scarcely fight my way to a taxi.

"You've really got to be aggressive for this. It's current events you're collecting, right on the spot, things that otherwise wouldn't be saved. More sophisticated objects, made of glass or ceramics, are always going to be available. But paper objects—who saves them? They decorate children's rooms for a while, fade, get dusty, and when the children grow up

they're thrown out." Even so he had to be realistic about space and be selective. In 1968 he let himself take big stuff—billboards from all the candidates. By arriving just at the critical moment, when Rockefeller lost his bid for the nomination, he was allowed to dismantle Rockefeller's Washington headquarters, climbing out of the windows himself to take down the street decorations and carry them off in his Chevrolet. He can't operate that way every year.

Back at the museum Collins stowed away his convention loot in the big shallow drawers of the cabinets in his storage room across the hall from his office, and set about his cataloging. He made notes that hats with green bands were worn by Carter people, that blue hatbands signified uncommitted delegates. "It will be my fault if people in 2076 don't have a complete record of the 1976 conventions. However, I can't answer for 1876. I wasn't here then."

Collins's political history cupboards are never bare. But they get a regular thinning as batches of items are put out on exhibit. A show like *We the People* has the Franklin Roosevelt microphone from his Fireside Chats, the Lewis and Clark expedition compass, Supreme Court Justice robes, a Ku Klux Klan hood, the cabin of the *Caroline* (John Kennedy's airplane), and hundreds of campaign buttons and banners. Even so there are still ten times more political mementos than are ever on show at one time—ten times more Presidential spectacles and hats, more ballot boxes, more historic gavels and chairs. And a high proportion of the items Collins has collected himself.

A strong sense of history underlies his genius for collecting. He has it in his bones, he says, from having been born in 1932 (the year Roosevelt defeated Hoover, as he puts it) in the oldest frame house in Caroline County, Virginia, and rocked in his grandfather's cradle. As a boy he collected arrowheads and clay pipes, hopping down from the tractor while working in the family fields, to pick them up. He saved as a child — and still has, all except for six — the Presidential portraits that came in cereal boxes. He has the Smithsonian postcards he got on a trip to Washington with the high school teacher who required her pupils to memorize the Presidents and Vice Presidents in order. He has the balls of tinfoil he wadded up during World War II. "No one ever told us what to do with them." And he looks back on the stint he spent in a pickle-sorting station, grading cucumbers by size, as a useful introduction to orderly curating.

Collins, whose degrees are in history, is a man of light build, who dresses conservatively, keeps his hair short, almost brush-cut, and wears the expression of an earnest schoolboy. His speech has the precision of a classroom combined with the cadences of the South. His manner is open, courteous, even courtly. The key to successful collecting, he says, is friends. He has a network of them all around the country — other museum people, private collectors, antique dealers, and the staffs and relatives and descendants of political figures. He keeps up with them regularly by letters and by long, news-filled, warmly personal telephone calls.

Clout has something to do with Collins's successful collecting, too, the clout that comes of representing a national museum. When he wants something, he's direct. "I'm just the opposite of an antique dealer who downgrades everything he sees. I let my enthusiasm show. I let the owners know that they have something so important they should protect it from fire and theft and family squabbles. They should preserve it, I even say 'enshrine it,' where the most numbers of people will see it."

He holds off from asking for an object till he sees a

place for it in an imminent show. Then he asks for it as a loan. "That initial separation of the person from the object is the main thing," he says. "If you do that and the person can get adjusted to living without it and can think it's better off in a national museum and can see how good it looks there, then nine times out of ten you'll wind up with it. You may even get," as he did with President Grant's horsedrawn carriage, "the extra money you need to restore it."

Of course you may not acquire it at all, Collins adds. Recent Presidents have hoarded things for their Presidential libraries. A lot of individuals with money have taken up collecting political memorabilia. And some things just get destroyed. When Collins read that an eagle named "Old Abe," a veteran of Union Army service in the Civil War, had been very much in evidence at the 1876 Centennial, squawking raucously at the Wisconsin pavilion, he wanted to get Abe for the Smithsonian's "1876" show. "I was dead certain someone must have stuffed that old bird and sure enough someone had, but years later the bird was lost in a fire." It was only when he was convinced the bird was not to be had that he settled for Old Abe paperweights, sheet music, and a portrait of the bird.

The best political history items, according to Collins, reflect an individual and his times. Collins will agree there probably isn't anything more precious in the American heritage than the original document of the Declaration of Independence, now at the U.S. Archives, but he thinks the Smithsonian's lap desk on which Jefferson drafted the document comes mighty close. It belonged to Jefferson and Jefferson designed it. Collins is also partial to Jefferson's linen sleeping bag, now in a political history drawer. It was used as protection from the dingy bedding in colonial taverns.

George Washington's crabapple walking stick has special luster for having been willed to him by Ben Franklin and then willed again by Washington to a nephew who willed it to the Smithsonian. A chair in the political history collection, which is worth $100 as an antique, is worth 50 times that much for having been used in the House of Representatives, Collins points out. He was elated in 1977 to obtain the chairs used by Kennedy and Nixon during the 1960 campaign debates. A bloodied cuff in the collection is valuable for its associations with the actress who cradled the dying Lincoln's head as she gave him a drink. Though a Presidential vest would always be welcome, the vest in the collection representing President Andrew Johnson is all the more so for having been stitched by Johnson while he was a tailor. It was a vest he made for a client's wedding suit. In the same way, Eisenhower's five-star pajamas are a reminder both of his wartime command and of the heart attack he suffered while he was President.

Collins frequently collects around a theme — like Presidents' hobbies. He went for Cleveland's trout flies, Lincoln's handball, Hoover's fishing reel, Kennedy's life preserver from the *Honey Fitz*. When he wanted Chester A. Arthur's fishing reel, he encouraged a Republican friend to form an association called the Friends of Chester A. Arthur to buy it for the Smithsonian. The association also bought Arthur's otter-skin laprobe. "We had to vacuum the dog hairs off it," Collins recalls. "Arthur's descendants were using the laprobe as a rug for their German shepherd." Collins did not save the hairs. "A predecessor of mine, a good many years before I came here," Collins adds, "used to save envelopes labeled 'dust from Washington relics,' and 'dust from Jefferson relics.' We don't go that far these days. Nor do we refrain from polishing away historic fingerprints even if they may be the prints of our founding fathers."

Collins likes pairs. Having the drum that beat a muffled cadence at Lincoln's funeral, he asked for — and got — a drum from Kennedy's funeral. He has black-rimmed menus that were used on the Eisenhower funeral train on the way out to Abilene, Texas, and the plain menus used on the trip back. He has the bullet-riddled speech Teddy Roosevelt was reading when he was shot in Milwaukee. He couldn't find a matching speech from George Wallace when the attempt was made on the Governor's life. He tried. But he learned that when this assassination attempt was made, the Governor was speaking extemporaneously.

Collins is pleased to have the packet of Everett Dirksen marigold seeds, named for the Senator who campaigned to substitute the marigold for the rose as America's national flower. He'd give just about anything for the pair to that — which would be a sketch of the wild turkey Ben Franklin had in mind as the national bird instead of the eagle — considered by Franklin to be a dirty bird, quarrelsome, and of bad moral character.

Much in fact of Collins's instinct for collecting comes from the regret he feels over things no one saved in the past. Why, he asks, did no one save the big log cabins on wheels that were pulled through the streets like floats in the 1840 campaign for the "log cabin" candidate? Or the huge ball that was rolled between Baltimore and Washington with the 1840 campaign issues written on it — the origin of the saying "Keep the ball rolling!" Why did no one save Benjamin Harrison's beaver hat? Collins has the Harrison coat. The hat he lacks is featured in a campaign jingle he likes to recite: Grandfather's hat fits Ben/ He wears it with dignified grace/ So rally around, we'll put Uncle Ben/ Right back in his grandfather's place.

In any case the Smithsonian does have the original 1903 Teddy Bear honoring Teddy Roosevelt. And Collins found, to go

with it, the original Hound Dog which was the symbol identified with Champ Clark's unsuccessful bid for the Presidency in 1912, as well as the sheet music for the campaign song "You Gotta Quit Kickin' My Hound Dawg Aroun'." He has batches of bridle rosettes which put candidates' pictures on horse bridles. Collins calls them the pre-automobile bumper stickers. And of course his cupboards contain batches of all kinds of bumper stickers, too. And drawers of campaign chewing gum and balloons and such things as Barry Goldwater and Lyndon Johnson soft drinks. Collins drank them. "They both tasted the same to me," he says. But he saved the cans.

Some things may not become as valuable as he thinks. He's saving the spittoon from the office of Speaker of the House John McCormack because he thinks McCormack may turn out to be one of the last public figures to use one. Some of the things in storage may not be exhibited for a hundred years. They may never be exhibited. Collins is opposed, for example, to putting on view the shackles which were used on members of the Lincoln assassination plot. "Sometimes we take things to get them out of circulation, if we think they are being used to misrepresent history or personalities" (Collins won't give an example). "Or if we think they need more research to authenticate them. We collect and leave the exhibiting to the people who come after us." Though not an activist, Collins went on the Pentagon anti-Vietnam War march to pick up posters, and he got himself teargassed in the process. But he picked up posters he prizes especially for the marks they show of having been trampled underfoot.

One day a week Collins saves for research, the basis for his own writing. His publications include two books on Presidents. One is on Presidential wheels — cars and carriages — the other on Presidential wills (Calvin Coolidge had the shortest). The theme of Collins's latest book, *The Threads of History*, is that if all the textbooks were thrown away the events of American history could still be documented through cloth things like bandannas and coverlets and banners. There would still be a record of battles and bridge openings and elections and inventions and Lindbergh's flight and the astronauts' landing on the moon.

"If we could only find out the truth about things," says historian Collins. "I thought about that when I was carrying General Washington's military camp stool from the auction in New York." Collins on that occasion spent $12,500 for what he wanted—no begging, no trading, no "talking it off" someone. "Here was that camp stool, which had been on Revolutionary battlefields, riding in a taxicab with me and on a train by my knees and being delivered at midnight to a museum guard. We take objects great distances from the locale in which they figured. And yet their history stays with them. It's like a soul to them," he says.

 ## JOHN WINK
Bracket Maker

John Wink braces himself for a tight show—the kind of exhibition so crowded with objects that a person standing in one spot for an hour can scarcely take everything in. Mounting this kind of show is a hard job for Wink, and a challenge to him. As chief bracket maker for the Museum of History and Technology, and working out of a shop full of rods of all kinds, he mounts objects for exhibit. He fixes them neatly and precisely in place with hoops or bands or claws of brass, steel, aluminum, sometimes plexiglass. He fashions fine brackets for elegant, fragile things like Dolley Madison's dancing slippers or Eleanor Roosevelt's pince-nez (her dainty eyeglasses). He fashions sturdy brackets for axes, cannon balls, buffalo heads, or the massive parts of an oil rig.

"You can make or break a show with your brackets," says Wink. "The lazy way is to line everything up on shelves or to fasten everything to a back panel where it will look like so many dead flounders. Good work calls for floating the objects, floating them out from the wall and spaced so they cast interesting shadows. You put some forward, some back, some

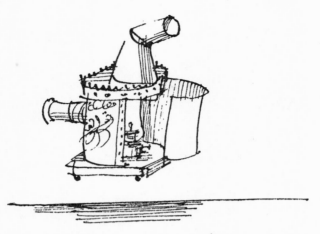

high, some low, and your most important ones you put pretty much at eye level. It gives your objects more life," he says.

The Bicentennial political history exhibit, *We the People,* was a tricky one for Wink. There was a multitude of objects in it, many of them superimposed and overlapping. In the plexiglass case on patents he had to float the original models of inventions in and out amongst each other and amongst the patent documents — plow, school desk, spinning wheel, stovepipe drum, oyster dish, animal trap, two sewing machines. The contraptions were odd shapes. Some were bulky, and the farther forward he had to carry them the harder it was to support them. Patent-model clothespins were easy, though. He strung them across the case, clipped to a clothesline.

For Herbert Collins's large display on campaign paraphernalia, Wink had to be inventive 400 times over, devising just the right claw to clasp a kewpie doll or a tiny bottle or a victory cigar, just the right arm to float a medal in front of a photograph or a campaign ribbon across a letter without putting a hole through the paper or even touching it.

Freestanding objects in the show — without cases around them — like a red, white, and blue umbrella and tavern signs and the eagle-decorated toilet (in the section on patriotic symbols) were a security problem for Wink. He solved it by keeping them high and back beyond reach and bolting them to a pipe or base. Small items — miniature Uncle Sams and eagles — he enclosed in plexiglass boxes secured by odd-size screws impossible to unscrew with an ordinary screwdriver. The boxes he fastened to pedestals anchored both to the floor and a subfloor. Breakable items—bottles, crockery jugs—even when they sat on shelves in cases and beyond public reach, he fitted with brackets, too, to prevent their shifting or toppling as the building vibrated.

Wink winces at the suggestion of a ready-made, standard-size bracket. It could never be satisfactory for the pleated paper fan which he had to display standing open and upright. Or for the pair of 125-pound ivory tusks, for which he made brass cups at the bases and brass bracelets to circle the tips. Ready-mades would come out wrong—too complicated or awkward or heavy—"like a dress without a fit," he says. The comparison comes to his mind because Wink used to run a dress shop. Before that he did window display. Before that, scenery painting.

Wink's first assignment when he came to the Smithsonian was mounting a guns display. "I went to see how other museums did it. What I saw was very crude—guns just wired to a panel. I figured: to hang them properly and to conceal the hanging I'd have to make a base fitted to the gun butt—I did that from metal lined with doeskin—and then hold the base out from the wall by a shaft. Up top I'd come out from the wall with a smaller shaft and fastener. I did pretty much the same thing with the swords."

Wink's procedure applied to most objects he found. He improved on it and refined it, so that it worked with china and glass and clothing. Occasionally he hangs things from the ceiling with fine wires in smoky, neutral, practically invisible shades. Where he needs transparent brackets he uses plexiglass. He used twine and ribbon to mount dried grasses for the State of Kansas plaque in the "1876" show.

No assignment has yet stumped Wink. He did find it surprising, though, when he was asked to make 1,500 coat-hangers for the clothing show called *Suiting Everyone*. First he made the hangers, then welded them together in a random pattern as a big 16-by-16-foot room divider. "I counted 10,000 welds," he says.

Wink's co-workers consider him a genius, the best brackets man in the country, fast at sizing up a job, fast and accurate in carrying it out. They also consider him super-critical of sloppy, homemade-looking work. "Well, if it's wrong it's wrong and I say so," Wink admits.

It pleases Wink that everything he needs for his work is contained in one closet-sized shop and that his tool box is no bigger than a fishing-tackle kit. From time to time, when he tours people through the museum to look at his solutions to brackets problems, it pleases him to learn they had not even noticed the brackets. Suddenly they realized the neatness and elegance of his work. "It's a good bracket," he tells them, "if you didn't see it."

 ## MELVIN JACKSON
Marine Historian

When Melvin Jackson came to the Smithsonian in 1961, it already had one of the finest collections of ship models in the world. But Jackson wanted to add more of the flavor of seagoing ships and of the men who sailed them. "I wanted to portray the life at sea," he says, "to portray it accurately and never mind the damn nostalgia. I've sailed square-riggers. There's no romance about them. They're mankillers. It's terrible, brutalizing work. Jack Tar was the lowest form of labor, the outcast, victimized, the dregs. He was a malcontent to begin with, driven to sea. The whole world was there surrounding him, yet he was confined to miserable quarters. He slept in a filthy fo'c'sle and he ate salted beef he called 'salt horse.' On shore he rarely ventured a block beyond the waterfront."

"It's a terrible story," Jackson says, his face rosy against a puff of silver hair. "And a hard one to research. I'm reading it pretty much backwards, learning about conditions by reading the bills proposed to do something about these conditions — to better the seaman's lot." Jackson is finding it next to impossible to collect artifacts to represent Jack Tar. "Who would save Jack's rags? They'd be burned. Or the handbills from boarding houses on the waterfront? They're gone. I traveled all over Europe looking for a tattoo shop to buy. I never found one. Gave up. And then, out of the blue, unasked, a tattooist's tool kit came to the museum, complete. It had all the tools for the 'professor's' trade — sample books, celluloid templates for inking in the outlines, powdered colors in jars, an early electric needle, calling cards, and pictures of his best work." Jackson has since gone on a search through Baltimore for the perfect oldtime waterfront bar. "Fruitless," he says. "I wanted to get the bar and the back bar (the one with the mirror and bottles). I'd have taken all the fixtures. But those things have already been bought up and put in people's recreation rooms. What's left is astronomical in price."

Jackson, who keeps plugs of chewing tobacco on his desk ("I'm a chewer but not a spitter"), is the son of a seaman and a seaman himself. When he was a high schooler he spent summers at sea as a cadet. He went to sea again in the merchant service in 1935 when he dropped out of Yale, "which I couldn't stand." In World War II he served in the U.S. Coast Guard, "in the Atlantic and the Pacific, everywhere *but* along the coast. I was always in trouble," he adds, "from hating discipline."

Jackson was in his late thirties when he got his college degree and a PhD in oceanic history from Harvard, writing his thesis on privateering in the Caribbean Sea during the Napoleonic wars. "It was a damned exciting time for me,

studying with all sorts of characters for fellow students." He has been to sea off and on since, and looks a real salt with his high color and exploding white eyebrows. He takes it as a compliment that his colleagues call him Captain Bligh. "A superb navigator, Bligh." He goes about his curatorial work with spirit and a great deal of grumbling.

The first thing Jackson wanted to do in setting up a new hall of maritime history was to inject a racket into it, real noise plus the mingled smells of oil and steam. "The designers kept telling me they needed big objects for the hall, more big objects. Well, I can't drag in the SS *United States*." But he did bring in, "live," the whole two-story engine room from the *Oak*, a U.S. Coast Guard buoy tender, knocking a great hole in the History and Technology floor to do so. It took months to take the engine room apart, months to reassemble it—to get the brightwork gleaming, the gray paint fresh, the piping covered in white, the 30-ton 750-horsepower triple-expansion steam engine in running, singing order again.

Because steam would have spread grease and oil throughout the museum, he had to power the engine by a hidden electro-hydraulic system. He also had to fake the superstructure of the deckhouse a bit, or too big a load would have been put on the floors. He substituted lightweight materials for the steel, and re-created such details as blisters of rust and chipped paint around the portholes.

Jackson wanted people to experience close up the rumble and quiver of the engine, the hissings of steam, the thrust of pistons. He made it possible for them to stand on the iron-grating floor of the deckhouse and to descend the spiral iron staircase to the engine room itself. He got a genuine radio rig for the radio shack. Then he put out word he needed an engineer, a real ship's engineer but retired, who would grease the engine, oil it, keep the cups filled, wipe it down, polish the brass. He wanted someone who could answer the public's questions and with them trace the piping so they could see where the steam goes—on a circuit from the boiler through the engines and back to the boiler.

After that he acquired a pilothouse, complete, from a modern inland-waterways towing boat. "Fully instrumented," he brags. "The visitor stands in the pilothouse with river scenes crawling past on long strips of film. I thought the museum should do credit to the tremendous traffic and unique flavor of our inland waterways. And I wanted to include also those incredible steam packets of the late 1870s, which were known for their speed and the elegance of their appointments." He added to the hall of American maritime enterprise a model of the *J. M. White,* the embodiment of the style of "steamboat Gothic," with its Victorian fretwork and furnishings.

Jackson also had made for the hall a 13-foot model under full sail of the tobacco ship *Brilliant.* It's an enormously complex model, substantial, made of pine and oak, one tenth actual size, with one mile of rope in twenty different girths to show for the ten miles of rope on the original. "I was looking for a ship some merchant had looked at and said, 'Now that one will make money for me.' Not a sleek-line privateer but this typical carrier, with its bluff, big, apple bow, its steep, abrupt lines in the stern, its short, squat rig. Oh, this one must have been a terrible sailor, a real dog of a sailor," says Jackson, "but an attractive piece of merchandise."

The original *Brilliant* was built in 1744 in Virginia to carry hogsheads of tobacco to Liverpool. "An all-purpose merchant ship, she could have been a sugar dragger," Jackson speculates. "We know she was bought by the Royal Navy in 1776 and served as a transport and convoy escort during the Revolution. She beat off the Continental frigate *Raleigh,* captured the Continental brig *Cabot,* was sold out of the Navy and became a whaler off Greenland till she sank near Spitzbergen.

"The *Brilliant* is a slice of maritime history. I can't divest it of romance — how I hate that word — but I use it to show something of the early part of our maritime history on the eve of the Revolution. We were turning out this kind of vessel, and it was pretty sophisticated."

It is because the Royal Navy had made — and kept — exhaustive inventories and descriptions of its ships that Jackson's model was so faithful to the original. When he talks about its making, an immense pride shows. Then he reverts to his grumbling. Just as he said of his period of merchant marine service, "You make some mistakes in life," he won't admit to pleasure in being a curator, either. "Museums are women's work," he snaps. "They're not a man's work at all."

 ## DON BERKEBILE
Transportation Historian

When he shows visitors around his exhibition of cars, carriages, and gas pumps in History and Technology, Don Berkebile starts them at the Conestoga wagon — the huge, six-horse, covered freight wagon of which he's particularly fond. He thwacks a hand affectionately against it, saying, "My great-great-grandfather Jacob drove one of these. He probably spent much of his time sitting here on the lazyboard, which pulls out from under the body like a breadboard from under a counter. From it he could reach brake chain or jerk line easily. Other times he'd ride the wheel horse, especially on a rough road. Going uphill he probably walked." The massive wagon Berkebile now leans against is an especially fine one, he believes, "close to 100 percent original, in very sound condition with unusually large wheels, and attractively designed. You see how its end bows and end gates slope outward at quite an angle? Its bed has a curvature — the sag in the middle — that's characteristic. It's what makes a Conestoga wagon so graceful-looking. I should think this particular one was used by a professional wagoner, on the road all the time, whole days, some nights, too, probably."

Berkebile is almost as fond of a farm wagon in the exhibition — a covered, two-horse workaday wagon, light compared to the Conestoga, and with simple straight lines. He found it on a farm in Bedford County, Pennsylvania, where the family had used it continuously for 85 years.

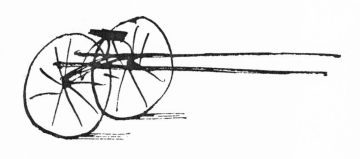

"When I came to the museum," Berkebile says, "it specialized in elegant, unusual vehicles, such as fine, handcrafted broughams and victorias, rockaways and coupes. It lacked the everyday, commonplace things. It didn't have a single wagon. For a country that was predominantly agricultural during a large part of its history, there doesn't seem anything more important. Nor did it have any commercial vehicles," he adds. "Most museums don't, partly because such vehicles just don't have a good survival rate. Once they're no longer earning their keep, nobody cares what happens to them. People save grandfather's carriage but not his laundry - or garbage- or water-wagon."

Berkebile set about filling in the gaps. He managed to find a laundry wagon, with handsome lettering and cherubs painted on its side. He found the Pennsylvania farm wagon, a weathered blue with its running gear painted in red lead. He found a buckboard, which he wanted, and several buggies. He's still on the lookout for a good road cart ("a lightweight two-wheel cart with little advantage over riding horseback") and a spring wagon ("the shallow box on springs which was good for carrying people, potatoes, or manure").

Berkebile, who can make almost everything except a wheel, which he intends to try someday, has an intense look about him. With a fuzz of fair hair, wide-open pale eyes, muscled arms and hands that hark back to his farmer ancestors, he has the look of a determined collector who acquires what he wants, however long it takes. The Knox tractor is an example. He made a search for it which took 11 years, and he considers it his most important find. He tells about driving

43

this 1912 vehicle all around the Smithsonian grounds the day it arrived. "Very maneuverable, with its three wheels," he says. "It was used to haul horse wagons. You could do wonderful things with it in a very tight space. The Knox was the first of the tractor-trailers, and very useful."

Berkebile enjoys showing the Simplex, and describes road-testing it. "It's a beast to steer," he says. He points out the chain-driven 1930 Mack "bulldog" truck (a pet of his). He shows, too, the cycles—the one hobby horse, the bone-shakers, the highwheelers (or ordinaries or penny farthings), and the safeties that started in the mid-1880s. Over by the gas pumps he tells about his good fortune in obtaining the very air-stand he had long admired at the gas station of a little old lady down the road from his own Pennsylvania home. He considers that 1920s stand vastly superior to today's.

When he comes to talk about the paving materials in the exhibit, though, Berkebile keeps his talk factual, playing down his habit of roaming about Washington in search of torn-up streets so he can make off with specimens. He has some Belgian blocks obtained that way, square paving stones with different dimensions from the standard ones, and he has standard ones, too. Sometimes he finds brick, cobblestones, or rubble stones (which are broken quarry stones, not round and smooth like the cobble). He looks a bit sheepish if he has to explain. "The rubble stones were not actually being torn up. I found a couple loose and lifted them."

Berkebile is, naturally, not against acquiring elegant vehicles as well, like the 1912 Pierce Arrow and the 1929 Cunningham. "I'll never turn down a Duesenberg, if I'm offered one though I have to be careful about overfilling my parking space. People today are collecting from years as recent as the 1950s. I may be cussed out for not doing it, but I feel I have to save my space for the rarer, earlier specimens. I'm not collecting recent cars at all, except to cover innovations like the first automatic transmission or the first power steering."

Nevertheless, Berkebile's store is large enough to permit quite generous lending. He lent History and Technology's *A Nation of Nations* exhibit one hack passenger wagon, one

farm wagon, one oxcart, a Model T, a VW, and a Columbia Electric car with battery charger. To the "1876" show across the Mall in the Arts and Industries building, he sent along a coach, a landau, a sleigh, and a drop-front phaeton.

Like most fanatic collectors, Berkebile thinks his exhibit's space is "shockingly deficient." He'd like to have a whole building instead of part of a transportation hall. "Our specimens are big, and we have a big story to tell." He envisions a life-size diorama of the Conestoga wagon crossing a bridge. Another of a line-up of early cars out on the road, with old-time gas stations and the cabins that were forerunners of motels, with room for the Burma Shave roadside signs strung out in a line: Within This Vale/ Of Toil/ And Sin/ Your Head Grows Bald/ But Not Your Chin/ Use Burma Shave. He'd put up repair shops from different periods, starting with the blacksmith shop. He'd like the space to treat such subjects as the automobile's influence on the economy and on suburban life-styles.

Instead he is collecting with prudence. And he is careful about restoration of what he has — trying to fix, for example, the squirrel-cage monocycle, with its interior swing-seat from which the rider was supposed to steer by twitching his body. "I'd be surprised if it ever worked," Berkebile says. He often attends antique automotive-parts flea markets to pick up old car-repair tools. And he is building up an archive of catalogs, manuals, photographs, tapes of his conversations with old-timers in automobile history, and correspondence he's had with people like a woman who raced in Stanley Steamer competitions and was a factory-trained Stanley Steamer mechanic. He subscribes to dozens of journals, including *The Draft Horse Journal*, *The Steam Automobile*, *The Flying Lady* (Rolls-Royce), and *The Wheelman*, for cyclists.

Though Berkebile does considerable writing about his vehicles, he says he had little schooling. "I didn't care for it. I was a kindergarten dropout. But I went back and stayed through high school. I collected, though, even as a boy, mostly guns. My father saw no use in buying anything you couldn't eat or wear, so I mostly collected guns in very poor condition, and had to repair them." He worked as a laborer in a steel mill, "pushing a wheelbarrow," and as a clerk. When in 1955 work ran out for him in Pennsylvania, he came to Washington, with a gun he had made that was a reproduction of an antique, and he was hired right away by the Smithsonian as a model maker.

"I got sick of models, though. Models didn't appeal to me much. A model is just a toy. Actual specimens were what interested me. Working on the real thing, you feel you have history trickling through your fingers." For six years Berkebile did restoration work—on "real" textile machinery, weapons, vehicles, engines—until the chance came for him to specialize. He became a curator in transportation.

Curator Berkebile recently went back to restoration work for the 1976 Bicentennial shows. He took apart a steam pumper fire engine for a replating job and put it together again. He made steam hammer and elevator parts. He reassembled the body and running gear of a peddler's wagon. "There was evidence it was a third marriage for both of them."

It was all welcome work for a fellow who rebuilds a stagecoach in his free time. He doesn't really like working on cars, though. "I've done it, I've torn down and built up antique cars. I use manuals and I'm rather mechanically inclined, so I just start and see where it leads me. But I don't like doing it. You have to handle each car as it needs to be handled," he adds. "Many need total restoration. Furniture can be rubbed up. But a car has been kept in an outbuilding. Mice and rats have lived in it, and moths. It's rusted. There may be nothing for it but total restoration. If possible, though, you try to save or bring back the original finish, and this takes ingenuity and skill and a lot more work. Many people can do a total job, but can't do that."

Berkebile says he is still living in Washington out of a suitcase, after 20 years. He goes to Pennsylvania on weekends to work on his family history, his buildings, his blacksmith shop, his collections of uniforms, weapons, vehicles. There he keeps the bike he got for Christmas in 1936 ("heavy as a motorcycle without an engine; I thought it was great") and the two-speed device he got for it in 1937 ("which I thought was the ultimate"). All that he lacks, and he's on the lookout for it, by serial number, is the 1940 Chrysler in which he learned to drive, that belonged to his father.

 ## PAUL GARBER
Aircraft Historian

"I wish I were an airplane," says 78-year-old Paul Garber, historian emeritus for the National Air and Space Museum, whose knees creak when he gets up from his desk. "I'd put some oil in my landing gear." As it is, in spite of the stiff knees, he taxis well. His compact figure gathers speed as he travels the corridors of the three-block-long NASM (pronounced "nassum") building, past the rockets, past the flying machines, many of which he collected, cared for, cleaned, patched, and protected, past the scale models, many of which were made by him. Without braking for corners, he's off to distant parts of the building on errands that have to do with interpreting the Air and Space collection to the public. Or he's out from the building entirely and away—to storage hangars or further still, to Bull Run battlefield, 35 miles from the museum, where he test-flies the copies he builds of historic kites.

Now that several hundred other people are doing the air and space work which he once handled alone, and now that he is retired and not required to do anything, he comes in to his office five days a week — full days that start at 7:30 in the morning — to do work he couldn't get to before. A big list-maker, he portions out his time on a daily list of things to be done and starts each new day by slipping yesterday's list in the trash with all its items crossed off. He keeps master lists, too, of "Got to Do," "Ought to Do," "Want to Do," to keep himself on course (his kite work, he says, appears on all three).

Garber, who answers the public's mail and telephone queries, is a one-man information service on the history of manned flight. Given a question, he spills out statistics on speed and distance records, personalities and events. He takes his correspondence seriously, in the Smithsonian tradition. "I think of the letter the museum received in 1899 from a bi-cycle maker, who wrote that he believed man could fly and asking what had already been done about it. An intelligent reply was sent to him, enclosing pamphlets, and suggesting other publications. That inquirer was Wilbur Wright. And in 1916, there was a letter from a college professor saying he thought he could send meteorological instruments higher than they have ever gone before, even with balloons, but he needed help. That writer was Robert Goddard, the father of modern rocketry."

Garber also shows the collection and gives lectures. An employee for 57 years, he tells people he works for James Smithson. "I *could* say I work for the director of Air and Space or for the Secretary of the Smithsonian or for the Board of Regents headed by the Vice President and the Chief Justice. But I always think of myself as working for Smith-son, that poor, lonely man. I wish I'd known him. I think we would have hit it off." Garber's duties include running the Smithsonian's annual kite-flying contest. Only homemade

kites flown by their makers are eligible to compete. The 1977 contest attracted — along with hundreds of box kites, bird kites, and tandem kites — a flying doghouse kite and a kite which dropped an inflated pink rabbit by parachute.

Garber's newest project is to produce films on the history of flight. He's starting, he explains, with "natural flight, myth and fantasy, witches on broomsticks, Icarus and man's primordial yearning to fly." Garber knows the yearning well. He was five when he flew a kite made for him by an uncle. "I was pulled splashing into the surf on an Atlantic City beach, clutching that string and headed for Europe when my uncle hauled me back." Later he made his own kites, one of which a Washington neighbor, Alexander Graham Bell, told him was not bridled properly. "I held it while he adjusted the string. Then it flew better, and he patted me on the head."

In 1909, aged nine, Garber rode the streetcar from Washington out to Fort Myer to see Orville Wright demonstrate an airplane for the Army. "I could hear the plane as I got off the streetcar. I'd never heard one before. And I'd never seen such a magnificent, enormous, wonderful 'kite' in the air as I then saw coming toward me with two men in it, the propellers whirling, the engine sputtering away. I stood there transfixed. Back home I was still so excited I couldn't put what I'd seen into words. I pointed to the picture in the newspaper and I said, 'That's where I was!' "

At 15 he was airborne himself, suspended by his armpits from a 20-foot glider which he made with his mother's help. The wing ribs were constructed with barrel staves. The wing covering was red chintz. His friends towed him by a clothesline for takeoff; then he soared off a bluff and over trees and a street to land in a field — safely and in one piece. Garber took flight training in World War I and served later in the airmail service. "Sometimes the train mail beat us between Washington and New York because we had to refuel in Philadelphia." In World War II Garber taught Navy gunnery officers on his ship to build target kites that would loop, dive, and climb.

From 1920 on, he served the Smithsonian and received a citation after the first fifty years for exceptional service as flyer, historian, collector, conservator, educator. Until 1958 when a director was appointed for the new museum, he was the chief person concerned with aeronautics. For much of the time he was the only person.

"I'm thankful I was interested in a forward-looking field," says Garber now. "Suppose I'd been interested in insects instead of flying, I'd still be pinning dead bugs on cardboard. As it is, aviation progressed and I went ahead with it. I've been on the crest of a marvelous wave. When anything happened toward the advance of aviation, I tried to acquire the related object for the museum.

"Someone once asked me," Garber says, "why I selected the aircraft I did. I thought to myself, 'Because it seemed a good idea at the time.' But I realized that wasn't the answer. The difference between a junkman and a curator is having criteria for collecting, having some yardsticks to apply to an object you're considering. You need those. You'd have, as one yardstick, technical importance. What does this plane embody of aerodynamic or structural significance? You'd have historical importance. With what notable historical event was it associated? And use. Does it represent some advantage to

the first such request to reach Lindbergh. At that point it was not this guy Garber who got it, because he thought of asking for it. It was the magnetism of the Smithsonian that persuaded him to place it here. That's true in all of our collecting. It's the prestige and fame and capability of the Institution."

A curator, Garber says, is responsible for understanding his subject, for knowing what to look for, where to find it, how to bring it in, record it, display it, preserve it. Lindbergh delivered the *Spirit* into Garber's custody at Bolling Field on April 30, 1928. "Lindbergh said to me, 'Here it is.' I said, 'Thank you. We'll take good care of it.' And we always have, as Lindbergh himself has said."

The plane was dismantled according to Lindbergh's directions. "We peeled the cuffs off the tops of the wing struts, removed the wings and tail, lifted the tail skid into the truck and towed the fuselage to the museum on its own wheels." These were so wide it was necessary to remove them, as well as the struts, and lower the fuselage onto a dolly to get it in the door of Arts and Industries and past the old locomotive, John Bull. When the *Spirit* was reassembled, Garber climbed onto the building's overhead trusses by way of the roof and a high window. He crossed the rafters in order to attach the cables which would suspend it ten feet in the air, safe from the crowds, safe from souvenir hunters and scribblers.

As curator Garber had his own methods for labeling acquisitions. He listed for himself 14 steps. "Number one is to say thanks. For labeling, my list is the old Who, What, When, Where, Why, and How. I put the name and date at the top. Then a brief statement on why the specimen is important, really brief, so that 'he who runs' can read it. Then a paragraph on history, a paragraph on technology, a paragraph on associated persons. And finally the source. Acknowledging a gift is so darned important. So it reads: *Gift of Charles A. Lindbergh and the Spirit of St. Louis Association,* and I listed the names, as Lindbergh asked me to do, of the nine men who helped him with financing his costs. When I write a label, I have the whole dining room table at home covered with references — and I end up with a few sentences. Well, you have to learn a lot in order to know a little."

If Garber gives the credit for his success in collecting to the magnetism of the Institution, he doesn't mind boasting a bit about his own handiwork. One of this listmaker's 22-item lists is for "Why I Exist." Tops on it: *originating and making things that add something worthwhile to the world;* on the bottom: *waiting for people who are late.* In between is: *repairing things.* "Repairing is good," he says, "because if you don't, things cease to exist."

A model of his own launched Garber on his Smithsonian career. He had just come, in 1920, to the end of a temporary three-month job at the museum. His boss was away. Garber stayed on without permission to build a goodbye present to the museum: a four-foot model of Leonardo da Vinci's *Ornithopter* — the human-bird flying machine. "The day I hung it, I was standing on a ladder looking up at my model, rereading my own name on its label, when an elderly gentleman came along and asked me about it. I gave him a lecture on Leonardo's wonderful concept of flight and said if anyone could have flapped aloft in such a thing, Leonardo could. He was strong." The old gentleman was Charles Doolittle Walcott, then Secretary (the fourth). He decided on the spot to rehire Garber.

Garber's job as preparator was to repair things. "And a heck of a lot around here was broken." He worked on locomotives, ship models, telegraph instruments, bicycles. And he interpreted his duties to include test-riding each one of the bicycles — cycling being to his mind something nicely akin to gliding and flight. If he didn't have an object to demonstrate an important step in development, he made a model of it. He was later promoted to aide. "Thank goodness I can use my hands. I never earned a college degree, but I got over the educational hump from subprofessional to professional status by studying at night and taking correspondence courses. Finally the front office agreed that I had the equivalent."

Even as curator Garber continued to clean and repair the collection. It was no small chore. To reach suspended planes he rigged up extra-long vacuum cleaner pipes and brushes, and he threw lines over the rafters to keep the weight of the equipment off the aircraft. "Cleaning was a constant thing," he remembers. "It was like painting the Brooklyn Bridge. I'd finish the 20 planes on display and it would be time to start over. I worked at night. Sometimes an airplane would require a turnbuckle job to level droopy wings. Or the erasing of vandals' names. Or putting another patch on the German Fokker D-7 — one of the last to be made — in 1918, when the Germans were short on materials. The fabric was deteriorating. In the old sheet-metal building heat was turned off at night. The frame and fabric would shrink and pop off like a gun, and I'd know I had another patch to apply. After a while I was patching the patches."

Today in the new NASM building, thanks to air-conditioning and the use of a giant crane and a forklift, such problems are easier to solve. Garber now applies his mornings to desk work. Perhaps he types a detailed reply to a schoolboy's inquiry: No, he writes, the *Spirit* was never "refinished." It has just been cleaned and patches re-doped where the fabric came loose. Yes, the engine is original, and though it has a replacement ignition harness, the one that was on the Atlantic flight is in our preservation facility.

Garber likes to remember the time he helped Lindbergh, who on one visit asked for a climbing line so he could go up into the cockpit of his old plane. Lindbergh wanted to check the marks he'd penciled on the dashboard during flight to help him keep his five gas tanks in balance. "I cranked up a ladder for him. And then I thought he'd want to be alone, so I sat on a nearby bench, leaving him up there — it must have been for half an hour. When he leaned out of the cockpit window to call me, even though I knew he was there, I had a feeling of awe at seeing him."

Garber remembers, too, the visits of Orville Wright to the Smithsonian, but he has one regret. "I wish I'd asked him more about control. Wings we have had from the first time a bug wiggled out of the mud 250 million years ago, gasoline engines for a century. A fuselage is just a body. But adequate control of an airplane did not exist until the Wright brothers developed it. It's the most important thing in aviation. I wish I'd asked Orville: how did you control your gliders of 1900 and 1901? I have a close idea but I'm not positive."

Garber was able to serve Orville Wright as recently as 1976 by giving the mannequin of that flight pioneer a new old-fashioned high white collar. In 1948, Garber placed the Orville Wright mannequin prone on the lower wing of the Flyer, so that visitors would see which way the airplane flew. He clothed the figure in a blue serge suit of his own that he thought Wright would have liked. He sacrificed a white shirt as well, bought shoes, and after a long search found a proper stiff high-standing collar in a Washington haberdashery that supplied such collars to Herbert Hoover. Over the years the mannequin's collar turned yellow. Garber wanted a new collar—"to look nice and clean"—for the opening of the new building. That's why with his wife's help he cut and stitched it of linen and buckram. It was a congenial task for a master kite maker—and an act of friendship.

 **PETER MARZIO**
Art Historian

It was the idea of Peter Marzio, curator for graphic arts, to use neon signs in the big Bicentennial *Nation of Nations* exhibition, which presented the history of immigrants in America. Two months before the opening of the exhibit, Marzio, a hefty young Italian-American, was hovering over the work in progress like a hen over its chicks, watching closely as each of his signs was hung. The neon signs he had chosen were from the windows of small ethnic restaurants and groceries, and showed the many nationalities in American neighborhoods — Greek, Chinese, Mexican, Italian, Spanish — still celebrating their origins. He had done most of the collecting himself. It is understandable that he was anxious as he watched workmen hanging the signs, all fifty of them, crowded together in a sort of stage setting that was one great black hole strung with wires — black ceiling, black felt walls, black carpeting.

"The signs with their glass-tube writing are extremely fragile and easily cracked. Neon is brittle stuff to handle, precarious to connect up. It requires enormously high voltage. Till all of the signs were up and safely wired to their transformers, with the juice on and the colors blazing, it was a pretty nervous time." When it was done — the hanging took several weeks — he was relieved, pleased, and vastly excited. Now he could throw back his head with the mop of dark hair and laugh at previous anxieties. The effect of the wall of signs was as he wished — both "wow" and "nice," a jumble of illuminated scribbling (pink, blue, orange, red, green) which sorted itself out to individual messages like KUAN SING DUMPLING HOUSE and IRISH-ROSE BAR GRILL and a hotdog -shaped WARSAW FOOT LONG.

Marzio had searched out the signs on walks through city neighborhoods in Cleveland, Washington, D.C., Brooklyn, Harlem, and Spanish Harlem. He photographed some 700 of the best candidates, narrowed the field down to 50 representing 19 nationalities. Then he contacted the owners to say the Smithsonian would like to take their signs for display in History and Technology and give them copies in return.

Most of the owners were foreign-born. Some didn't speak English. Many of those who did were still not sure they understood. "They'd screw up their eyes and squint at me. I wasn't asking for a pizza or a hotdog or a dumpling. I

was asking for the sign in their window. And it looked as though I were going to crazy lengths to get it when I could just copy it for myself. I told them, 'It's *your* sign we want. By touching it, you blessed it. We want your sign for the Smithsonian.' "

Most of the owners agreed to Marzio's switch. Some were even "sweet" about it. "You have to be a bit bold to collect, a bit worldly," says Marzio. Even so, several people turned him down flat. They were sure any collector from Washington was an income tax collector. Some had never heard of the Smithsonian. And one owner of an underground shop in New York, at a subway stop, thought if his sign were good enough to hang in a museum, then he should get $2,000 for it. "I said, 'For three little words—FRENCH ICE CREAM? You've got to be kidding.' From the argument we had you'd think we were negotiating the sale of his whole shop. I have days," Marzio adds, "when I can't collect anything. That day I couldn't have collected the dust off his floor."

The signs Marzio took had to fit in his space. That ruled out great jumbo neon signs like the ones on the Las Vegas "strip". And it ruled out a 30-foot fire-breathing dragon which he saw in New York's Chinatown. Signs he did take, which he especially liked, included THE GYPSY TEA KETTLE (Tea Leaves Read Gratis), featuring a gypsy woman in a yellow headscarf pouring into a cup from a kettle; JOE'S SICILIAN PIZZA, with a chef twirling a pizza crust; SOLA-MONE'S FRESH & SMOKED FISH, its lettering enclosed in a fishy outline. His all-time favorite was LA VIÑA, from a Spanish-American restaurant, featuring a green palm tree, blue pig, red chicken, pink crab, blue fish, red lobster, plus one yellow-eyed pink bull and a cup of coffee sending up a plume of steam.

He was also partial to his melting-pot mixtures: the signs for GOLDBERG'S PIZZERIA and the ITALIAN-FRENCH-SPANISH BAKERY. He'd like to have had the Chinese Rathskeller sign, too, but it was too large to include.

Marzio had the copies made, to send to owners of the originals, in a neon shop in New York. He describes his visits to the shop as a venture into the world of alchemy. "There were great piles of tubing everywhere and burners with blue flames shooting up a foot long. And rituals of arm-swinging and blowing to bend the glass in the fire, and vac-uum-pumping to get out impurities, and filling the glass with gas and bombarding it with electricity. When they zap the tube with the really high voltage—30,000 volts—it looks like lightning in there. It smells like lightning, too. And smoke goes up from the black paint that's used to block out spaces between the letters."

His sign collection is a bit of history, Marzio figures. "Neon is pretty much a dying art, with very few companies left making it. In the 1930s and 1940s Times Square was one big neon splotch. Sign shops meant neon. There was one in every neighborhood. Now New York has maybe only four or five good ones. Pretty soon you're not going to be able to prove the industry existed. Old neon breaks and gets thrown away. I got sick of hearing, 'Oh, if you'd only come in a year ago. Or last month. Or last week.' "

Marzio learned how to date his specimens — by the thickness of the glass, the way the tubing was bent, the type of writing. "Eighty percent of neon is writing plus simple symbols. When people asked if we dimmed any of the colors or changed them to make pleasing combinations for the show, I said, 'No. We don't tamper with them. They're museum specimens. They're as much museum specimens as a Van Gogh.' " It makes him laugh, though, to think that he *made* them so. "Neon is just such a curious street art. And it's such a curious act, for a museum to reach out in the streets this way, take the neon 'live,' bring it in, and in the process create an entirely new museum category. A new collectible. It's a little like candid photography. We're snapping a bit of life, freezing it, putting it where people can look at it."

From the start he felt sure visitors would like it. "There's just something about the colors and proportions that's nice. Like the MIDDLE EAST GROCERY sign. Not anything special. Just the total sign. Nice colors. Thick chunky letters. People come in expecting neon to be vulgar, and they're surprised to see how captivating and non-carnival it is. There's just an incredible quality to it."

Marzio says he was not showing the signs as art, though. If he were, he wouldn't have hung them in a big jumble. He was using them to make a point of the ethnic neighborhoods. They were also evidence of the small shop owner. "It's easy to go back in history and research the big companies. But what do later generations know about smaller enterprises? For these people a neon sign represented pride in their identity; it was as good as seeing their own name in lights. Each sign — custom-made, unique — was a way for immigrants to put their name and language on American streets."

Around the corner from the wall of neon, which Marzio called his "ethnic put-in" wall, he mounted an out-put wall.

Again he used signs to tell the story, but no longer old-fashioned neon. Here he shifted to classy modern plastics and fluorescents — to represent the superficial, style-of-living exports America is known for, like fast foods, blue jeans, motels, or comic books. He counted on the shock of recognizable American trademarks combined with foreign writing: the pack of *Wrigley's* chewing gum and words in Dutch, "Dubbel Goed"; *Kentucky Fried Chicken* and *McDonald's* in Japanese; *Holiday Inn* in Arabic; *Pepsi* lettered in Russian on the familiar bottle; and an Italian sign showing Michelangelo's statue of David wearing *Levi's*.

The end portion of *A Nation of Nations*, representing twentieth-century technology, moves on from the neon signs into film shows, television, an operating ham radio station. "It's garbage if you use a lot of audiovisual devices just to create an atmosphere," says Marzio, who had charge of that portion of the exhibit, "just to call attention to objects. But here the signs and sound and pictures *are* the objects representing the twentieth century. They're also a good change of pace from the pretty heavy material that came earlier in the show. They're a balance of the dipsydoodle with the solid. When you exhibit you want to be sure you transfer information, but you have to joke a bit, you have to be a bit playful."

His own penchant for playfulness paid off earlier with a highly successful show on cartoonist Rube Goldberg and his zany, deadpan drawings. *Doing It the Hard Way*, that show was called, and it featured the complex mechanical contraptions Goldberg drew to simplify such chores as slamming a screen door or swatting a fly. Marzio likes his memory of Goldberg, sick and old, walking through that exhibit with him. Goldberg was amazed at how good his funny-paper cartoons looked when they were blown up on the walls, bigger-than-life. "Why," he said, "it looks like my obituary written large and bright." That was 13 days before he died.

Getting people to look, with a little shock of pleasure, at city neon and newspaper cartoons and other such graphic arts is what Marzio prizes about his job. "I have the chance to change tastes, to interest people in popular images as well as fine art images." In recent years he put on several exhibits of chromolithographs, early mass-produced, cheap color reproductions of paintings. "Collectors and art historians have scorned them as garbage. What we're doing here in the museum would be like saving old TV shows today, not the rare ones, but shows like *I Love Lucy* and *Laugh In*. We're saying: these pictures are valuable because they indicate the taste of the second half of the nineteenth century and because they show how that taste was made."

One exhibit of the color lithographs he called *Perfect Likenesses*. There was irony in the title. The likenesses were far from perfect. On show were color pictures of Indians printed on lithograph stones. The prints were based on copies of a series of oil paintings which in turn were based on drawings of Indians from life. Drawings, paintings, the copied paintings, and prints were all shown in a row. People examining them could see the changes along the way as copyists altered colors of warpaint and feathers, refined Indian noses, and idealized the faces till the Indians looked more and more like businessmen in fancy dress.

"I was trying to get people to play detective," says Marzio, "to learn to distinguish one art form from another and to learn about the demands which democracy puts on fine art. These color prints were an exciting step. If you have political democracy, then cultural democracy logically follows. You make pictures available to people who aren't rich enough to buy paintings."

Marzio talks fast, with a lot of emphasis, and writes fast as well. He has written a book on the drawing manuals of the nineteenth century by which fine artists attempted to teach everyone to draw. Their motto was: Anyone who can learn to write can learn to draw. "Well, it didn't quite work out that way," says Marzio. "So the next idea was that anyone could at least buy a lithograph." Marzio wrote a book about that, too. When he came to write the 670-page catalog for *A Nation of Nations,* he ended up with such batches of text and photographs, he loaded everything into a supermarket pushcart, wheeled the cart onto the train to New York and right into the office of the publisher. "It cracked him up."

Unlike many people who came to museum work through an all-consuming interest or hobby, and then took the university work they found they would need, Marzio collected his degrees early: a BA at Juniata College ("doing a lot of sports, nothing serious"), an MA in communications a PhD in art history and American history from the University of Chicago. Along the way he worked as a carpenter. For a time he did some college teaching. "But I never felt at home there. I never came away from the classroom with a sense of elation. If a job isn't fun I can't imagine how you do it.

"With museum work I felt instantly at home. My approach and thought processes were so compatible with it. Museum work is fulfilling beyond belief. There are times, when things are going really well, I can't believe I'm getting paid to do what I do here." Marzio checks the flow of his inspirational speech, grins, adds as an afterthought, "Things don't always go so well."

 **CHUCK ROWELL**
Restoration Carpenter

Carpenter Chuck Rowell, who puts his days to hammer-and-nails work—pencil behind his ear, folding ruler in his back pocket, pipe in his mouth—claims he has the best job of anyone at the Smithsonian including the Secretary. He dresses for the job in workpants, sweatshirt, and hard-toe boots. "I like to be comfortable," says this medium-height relaxed-looking person with thinning fair hair and a quiet, deliberate way of talking. The job which suits Rowell so well takes him about the country in the wake of a curator. The period rooms and sometimes whole buildings selected by the curator he dismantles and then reassembles back home in the

Museum of History and Technology. In his time he has installed a California rancher's kitchen abandoned for forty years, a New York City automat, an 1890s drugstore, an overstuffed Victorian library, a butcher shop, printing and machine shops, colonial bedrooms, a grist mill, a rural post office. "Officially I'm listed as historical restorer. No," he corrects himself, "historic restoration specialist. But if anyone asks me, I say, 'I work with wood.' "

Before its Bicentennial opening, Rowell worked on *A Nation of Nations*, the museum's biggest show ever, which was being mounted, walled off from public view, on an acre of the second floor. Rowell was assigned to "Shared Experiences," the section of the show demonstrating how immigrants from many nations eventually became Americans, more like one another than like their ancestors in other countries. His job was to put a shape to experiences and attitudes the immigrants shared—public schooling for one, the Army for another, a fascination with sports, and a desire for the American dream house. Under Rowell's hammer the concepts emerged as a classroom, a barracks bunkroom, a baseball park ticket booth, and four rooms of mass-produced furniture which were the pride of a 1920s working-class family of Italian origin.

The classroom seen today by museum-goers through a glass front was an actual room which Rowell took from the 1883 Dunham public elementary school in Cleveland, Ohio. Dismantling room #201 just before the school was torn down, Rowell took oversized windows, the door with its door frame, floorboards, wainscoting, and blackboards. He took radiators, pictures from the wall, maps, erasers, and chalk. The old building superintendent came around to verify for him what the original color scheme had been — blue and yellow — and the original paint company mixed colors to match. On an earlier visit while the room was still in use, a camera recorded the look of an ordinary day — all the writing on the boards, the paperwork tacked on the walls.

Rowell trucked everything he'd collected back to Washington. He drove the truck. He loaded and unloaded every item himself. "I lift up an old board I know I need and I put it down gently. Somebody else thinks it's just an old board and throws it down," he says. "And it breaks."

Just as wreckers were about to go at New York City's Yankee Stadium before its remodeling, Rowell seized examples of box seats, grandstand seats, the visitor team's bat rack used from 1923 to 1973; he acquired a fanciful eight-sided, red, tin-on-wood ticket booth resembling a small pagoda. He took them just in the nick of time, too, as police caught vandals running away with the ticket window grill only hours before he arrived.

It was a different story with the barracks. "There at Fort Belvoir, in Virginia, the Army people hoped we'd cart away all of their 1940s buildings," Rowell explains. "They wanted to be rid of them. We had to tell them we could only use parts of one bunkroom and one latrine. All we took was the woodwork, three sets of upper and lower bunks, the fire extinguisher, two basins, one laundry tub, two toilets and a urinal plus all the pipes. The paint shop here," he adds, "had to research 1940s paints to get the pipes back to the right shade of Army green." In the end he had to bring in a substitution urinal from Camp Pickett. Because he wanted to show only half the latrine, the Belvoir one was too big. It would have dominated the room. Substitutions of that sort are rare, though, with him.

People often ask Rowell whether it really mattered all that much to use the actual wainscoting from the Dunham school and the actual pipes from Fort Belvoir, and Rowell always says, yes, it did. It was important, he tells them, thwacking a hand against a supporting post, to use the original posts and joists and floors — "not something new or beat up to look old. This wood is warmer somehow. It makes you think of the people who put it up and used it. It has the touch of history on it, which after all is what a museum is all about."

To emphasize his point Rowell walks visitors to the 1861 post office from Headsville, West Virginia, which he installed on the museum's first floor. It's a combined country store and post office. It stands in the museum just as the postal history curator found it, after a 10,000-mile search — with the original postmaster's desk and sorting rack, and stocked, as it was then, with jars, tins, high-button shoes, fly-papers, coal scuttles, horse collars. When Rowell took down the building he saved the old stickers on the windows, notices on the walls, names carved and scribbled behind the shutters by Civil War soldiers passing by (the old graffiti are coated now to preserve them, even if new graffiti and fingerprints must be washed away).

A board across the outside wallboards of the post office advertises Birdsell Wagons. Below it there's the ghost of another board, which must have slowed the weathering of the wood under it. Pointing to the shadowy strip, Rowell says, "That's a bit of history you don't want to lose. By numbering the boards as you take them down, you get them back in the right order. Bushes leave round patches in the same way. You preserve evidence like that."

An exception to Rowell's usual practice is the Italian-American home in *A Nation of Nations*. This is not the home of a specific family but a reconstruction of a typical 1910-1925 home. In this case, working with new materials, Rowell simply made sure that the floorboards were standard width for the times (3 1/4 inch, yellow pine), that the trim around doors was "sanitary trim" (3 1/2 inch, plain), that the cross-section of the walls showed rough-cut studs and plaster on wood lath, that the light switches were pushbutton and not flick-type, and that the wallpaper was correct for the period, as was the icebox, and the card in the kitchen window requesting delivery of 25 pounds of ice.

In his basement workshop, labeled "Chuck's Room," Rowell keeps a good stock of wood and supplies to help him with such jobs — windows, door frames, radiator covers, "the kinds of items that aren't easy to come by when you want them." He has stacks of old bricks under his workbench, drawers of period hardware and light switches, a coffee pot filled with hand-wrought nails, and coffee cans of old machine-made nails. "People laugh. I sweep up the trash where we dismantle, pick out nails and splinters. But the old nails are hard to come by and splinters can be glued back. They say it's easier to buy new. But if you do that, you might as well make models. That's not museum work to me."

A recent assignment very much to Rowell's liking took him to an abandoned home built in 1852 near Chicago. He dismantled it and installed it in the museum as an example of a "balloon-type" framed house. "People at the time said it would blow up and be carried away in a puff of wind," Rowell explains. "They were skeptical because the advent of pre-cut lumber and machine nails made it possible to erect houses quickly. They also still advocated much heavier structures — like the Ipswich house, which we installed in the museum some years back. That was built between 1690 and 1750 and had enormously heavy corner posts and beams. The balloon house uses thinner materials. Its corner posts are two two-by-fours nailed together. Its studs run from the sill on the foundation all the way up to the roofplate, without the heavy beams."

Rowell spends several days a week on two ongoing assignments. One is the redesigning of the museum's storage sheds in Maryland, putting up garage stalls for the collections of automobiles, streetcars, and wagons. He is also adding balconies of openwork metal so that cigar-store Indians, dentist chairs, boat models, and looms are accessible, without first having to move other Indians, chairs, boats, and looms out of the way.

His other assignment is to work in an "upward mobility" program, training members of the janitorial staff to handle "technical aide" positions. He trains them, gives them practice in removing glass display cases, using suction-cup apparatus, and in handling and cleaning museum objects.

Rowell himself attended high school in Milwaukee, Wisconsin, and in Arlington, Virginia. In World War II he did cabinetwork with the Seabees in the Aleutians, and at Pearl Harbor fixed wooden truck beds. He worked with his father, a carpenter and contractor, for a number of years. At one time he had what he calls a "quarter-horse" business of his own — turning out bookcases and carports. His first job at the Smithsonian was to help install early American rooms.

Rowell says all his building and cabinetmaking skills he learned as a boy from his father. "I didn't get any of it from courses or colleges. My father was a hard man, hard on me," he says. His expression is sober. Then, amused at himself, his eyes light up as he transfers the corncob to his workpants pocket and takes up his hammer again. "I'm beginning to appreciate him, you know. Of all the jobs here at the Smithsonian I'll take mine. I happen to like it."

 ## VIRGINIA BEETS
Registrar

Registrars are charged with keeping track of everything and are expected by outsiders to know exactly how many "things" the Smithsonian possesses. Registrars think 100 million is about right, though it doesn't bother them to say they don't know. Virginia Beets, registrar for the History and Technology collections, doesn't at all mind rummaging through her files for a time before she comes up with the figure of 18 million objects for her building. "Counting is just an inventory," she says briskly as if to put it in its place. A small woman, seated at an executive-size desk, she speaks in a soft, Mississippi voice, rapidly, precisely, and with authority. "In counting so many problems are involved, you don't have hands enough or brains or time enough to solve them all. There is just so much more important work to be done."

Beets ticks off rapid-fire some of the snags in counting, to finish off the pesky subject. "For one thing," she throws a question back at her questioner, "How are you going to count the pot and the lid? One item or two? How will you count three scrapbooks containing 6,000 pictures? If you're in photographic history, you might count them as 6,000. If you're in agriculture on the other hand and all the pictures are of Jersey cows, you might count them three. A cup and a saucer, since they function pretty well independently, are apt to be counted as two. A four-piece tea set could be one item, but if a piece, say the sugar bowl, is missing, then you might count the teapot, the cream pitcher and the tray one by one."

Never mind the grand total. The important thing to a registrar is that the number she assigns to an object is the vital link between it and its records. "If someone comes in asking to see his Aunt Nell's needlepoint footstool or her collection of grasses, or wanting to know if the Smithsonian winkled him out of his rightful inheritance by taking it, I should be able to handle the matter and satisfy him. I should be able to put my hand on the file for the object containing all the legal papers—the deeds of gift, loan agreements—all the letters, the photographs, the condition reports on how the object looked when it was acquired by the museum."

The numbers assigned by registrar Beets are accession numbers. She gives out 1,200 to 2,400 new numbers every year. That doesn't mean that the acquisitive collectors in her building are taking in only 1,200 to 2,400 new objects in a twelve-month. They do, in fact, take in hundreds of thousands. The figure 1,200 to 2,400 refers to the number of separate transactions. If 175,000 stamps are acquired from one source, they receive one accession number. The accession number refers to the lot and is the same for each of the stamps in it. Another accession number may apply to 17 hats accepted from a single donor on the first of May. Still another number may refer to one wheel.

Beyond accession numbers, objects have catalog numbers, assigned by the divisions the objects go to — like postal history or political history or engineering — and a catalog record. It's the cataloging phase of her work that Beets finds intriguing, because it's here, she says, that she gets into the soul of things. Speaking on this subject which so appeals to her, as opposed to counting, she becomes animated — the blue eyes an even deeper blue — and intense. It's been challenging to her, a game, to have compiled a list of the 500 aspects which apply to every object in her building and which it is important to record. Beets and the small committee who worked to produce the basic list of what they call cataloguing descriptors can't help saying they're proud. It was exacting work but worth doing. "When you're cataloging, you're getting at the history of an object," says Beets. "You're beyond counting, where a bucket is a bucket. You're going a step farther, where a bucket may be a milk pail."

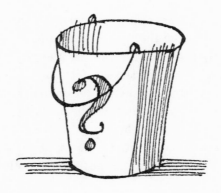

The list of categories has taken her eight years of work, with a committee guided by the mathematics curator. The list still has its boggy patches, but the museum people who have adopted it are pleased. They find it applies to every possible object. And if, in fields like printing or optics or textiles, they want to be even more specific, they can add their own descriptions beyond the basic 500 — to refer to pages or prisms or types of decoration, in the way most useful to them.

The 500 basics begin with what the object is, its name or names, its foreign names, its misnomers. It includes information on the donor, previous owners, the maker or inventor, the manufacturer, the collector; information on its weight and dimensions and materials, its component parts, its decoration (colors, though, are still a problem — how many choices does one offer the computer?); information on its importance (traditional? sentimental? or a first step in cultural or technological change?).

"A bread-slicing machine came up for consideration — should it go into our collection or not? It made quite a difference," Beets explains, "to know that this was the *first* bread-slicing machine, it was developed by an individual, and it revolutionized the food industry."

The day-by-day workload for Registrar Beets was extremely heavy in the time leading up to the Bicentennial. She had never before handled the sheer volume of objects moved into and out of the museum during the preparations for the three major shows. *We the People* had 5,000 objects in it; "1876" had 8,000; *A Nation of Nations* 7,000. "We had to borrow safely, rapidly, in volume and from all over the world. We had to be able to say: we'll take care of your object from the moment it leaves your hand till it gets back." To do that, Beets set up a uniform system to get blanket insurance for everything coming in or going out. As an extra precaution she set up staging areas for each show and put assistant registrars in charge, on the spot.

For *A Nation of Nations* the exhibits, on immigrants in

America, Beets used a vast space on the third floor. It was the size of a playing field and blocked off from public view. Working under Beets' direction over a period of more than two years were two young museum technicians, Frank Roche and Sally Richner. Roche and Richner stockpiled all the objects as they came in. There were even more than the 7,000 which wound up in the show, because curators tend to over-collect—taking more than they need—to give themselves and the designers some choice. The two technicians stowed securely—on platforms and on rows and rows of shelves—clothing on racks, small valuables in a locked room-within-a-room, oversize items standing free, among them, a voting booth, an Ellis Island bench, a stagecoach, a traffic stop sign.

A safe, uncluttered work space was set aside in the back of the staging area. Designers used it to plan layouts. They spread out arrangements of objects—like tools or tennis racquets and ice skates—and then photographed them from the top of a ladder to see how they would look on a wall. Conservators used the space for working on documents—for mending passports, citizenship papers, report cards.

In the staging area all the paperwork was done for each item as it came through the door, including each one of the hundreds of military dogtags and each one of the thousands of campaign buttons. One numbering system covered the things on loan. The number for all of them began with 308987. Thus 308987.530 went to the 530th loan they took in, which happened to be one woman's birth certificate, while 308987.531 was her naturalization paper and 308987.532 her marriage certificate. The biggest batch of numbers was assigned to a Washington doctor whose family had saved just about everything. He was able to lend furniture for the exhibit's Italian-American home, plus pots and cakepans, sausage grinder, icebox, wine bottles, religious pictures, doilies, a rolling pin.

Still another numbering system covered the "props" that were the property of the show, either because they were picked up for the taking, like political posters from telephone poles, or because they were bought or donated, like a clawfoot bathtub or a 1920s mattress. Props don't get accession numbers unless, at the close of the exhibit, the museum decides to retain them for its permanent collections. The only items for *A Nation of Nations* to receive no numbers at all were the five 200-pound crates of dirt, which were brought in for the bed of the railroad track. They just got fumigated and dumped into place.

Recordkeeping, in the staging area by Beets' system included seeing to the deeds of gift, the loan agreements, the insurance forms. It included photographing and it included filling out condition reports. The condition report for a set of city street-cleaning equipment, for example, indicated that the cart, shovel and broom were on loan from the District of Columbia bureau of solid waste collection, that the loan extended through 1981 and could be renewed. It indicated that the cart, in good condition, lacked one reflector light; the shovel, in fair condition, had corrosion on its pan; the broom, in fair-to-poor condition, had its binding string broken.

In many cases the registrars in the staging area arranged for transport. Roche organized the travel of the Akan drum, lent by the British Museum; it came by air, insured for $50,000, on a seat next to the gentleman accompanying it. Roche went by train to pick up other items, carrying them back to the museum in cardboard boxes which he always hoped looked inconspicuous and uninviting. By the time the designers were actually mounting the show on the second floor, he and Richner were trundling the objects down to them on padded carts.

Quite as important as the staging areas for maintaining Beets' serenity through the year 1976 was the fact that she got her "objects processing area" in the basement. She'd been agitating for it for a long time. The engineers took some convincing, she says, that she knew what walls ought to come down and where new ones should go up, but in the end she got the setup she thought the museum needed — right off the loading docks. "I wanted one space for objects coming in and a separate space for objects going out. And I wanted the area where we worked on things to be under inspection at all times, so that we'd have visibility within total security." It's the only such facility, she thinks, in the world.

The work that was to go on there, she explains, was first-rate packing and unpacking. Beets sent out a job description to museum people all over the country to find just the person who could pack not just art objects but objects of every kind handled by a history and technology museum. In the end she hired Ken Bush, a cabinetmaker for 25 years, who was teaching in the Washington schools. "Though he'd never worked on museum objects, he was totally conscientious about their sanctity," she said, and she arranged a training program for him of visits to commercial packers, factories, other museums. Bush set up his work space with tools, padded work tables and padded storage shelves, with air hoses to carry away dust, with an ample stock of foam rubber, anti-tarnish, acid-free, static-free papers, polyethylene bags, foam spaghetti, with hardware and woods. He has turned out, ever since, crates that are not just six-sided boxes but complex structures designed to protect contents from shock, from inner movement, from humidity—from stresses within the package and from without. Among his first assignments were crates for skis, scientific instruments, a toy train

and a set of very old, fragile, irreplaceable saddles. Beets is proud of his work to the point of being smug.

Her own work began at the Smithsonian 27 years ago when she was hired as a clerk. "I was in insects," she says, "a nice little country girl from Prentiss, Mississippi (that's a cotton and sugar cane and watermelon county) with not enough money to finish college. I came to Washington because I heard it was clean and like a small town. I was determined to work at something with some intellectual appeal and I went down to 85 pounds before I found it." From insects she moved to a job with the committee planning for the new History and Technology building. She found herself writing budgets to win appropriations from Congress.

Along the way Beets has learned quite a bit of mathematics, though she still thinks of herself as a history-literature-drama person. "I'm a person to whom numbers are not necessarily the most appealing means of communication." Her job in fact is much more people-oriented, she claims, than anyone expects it to be. "Take the accession letters that we file for each object. There's tremendous nostalgia in them. You read in them the strong emotional ties people have to the things they're giving—things that have come down in their families, traveled with them as they moved and resettled, things that matter so much they want to preserve them by giving."

She especially likes the letter, written with sentiment and a sense of history, sent by a teenager from New Jersey along with the blue jeans her mother threatened to throw out. The young Brigid thought her jeans were an item of history fit for a museum. And indeed they wound up in a clothing exhibit called *Suiting Everyone*. Brigid wrote, "my favorite jeans will be three years old this spring; they are thin and worn; patched with remnants of clothes i've made. i wore them to a rock festival and a Janis joplin concert, bicycling, canoeing, every where." She said she bought them on sale for $4.50 when she was a seventh-grader but was not allowed to wear them to school because an "archaic dress code" forbade wearing pants. She said she wrote to the American Civil Liberties Union for legal aid in defending her right to wear the jeans to school, her school reversed its ruling, and she felt good about it as a matter of personal freedom.

The clothing division, on receiving Brigid's package of jeans and accessories, assigned a six-digit number to the transaction. Four cards, with photographs, carry the descriptions. Beets knows from them that the jeans have "copper studs, fly-front opening, gingham, printed and knit patches, bumblebee and American flag patch on front right leg." The sneakers catalogued with another number are: "white canvas, crepe sole, shoe strings not original, ink marks, quite worn and discolored." The socks: "knee high, stretch knit, somewhat discolored." And the shirt: "Sears Roebuck, boys' size 16."

Brigid can't borrow back the jeans now that they are museum objects, but she or someone else who wants to study them can always find them by looking under Brigid's name or by locality (New Jersey) or by subject, filed under: women's clothing, sportswear, Twentieth Century.

 ## WILLIAM HENSON
Restoration Machinist

It took two and a half years for William Henson and his machineshop staff of ten to restore to working condition objects for the "1876" show in Arts and Industries, commemorating the Philadelphia exposition of that year. The job, to be completed by 1976, involved hammers, generators, presses, ice plows, an Otis elevator, one big steam-driven Linde Wolf ice machine with an eight-foot flywheel, guns, scientific instruments, and telegraph equipment.

The Tech-Lab staff worked under a full head of steam, taking six weeks just to set up their work space in the basement of History and Technology, bolting together shelves and work benches, placing machinery, ordering supplies and planning out their horseshoe-shaped assembly line. After that, they worked on each individual piece of machinery, not only restoring it to good condition but giving it a new shiny look as well. The goal was to show machinery as it was marveled at 100 years earlier.

Using a monorail with an electric hoist, two people did the cleaning — dipping into a hot caustic soda solution the engine and machine-tool parts, the pistons and connecting rods, nuts and bolts, to remove rust and layers of paint. Two others sanded and primed. One replaced missing parts. Others re-assembled and repainted. Then they installed the finished pieces on the exhibition floor and looked on, pleased, while machines, their voices silent for years, now filled the building with great whirrings punctuated with ticks, stops and knocks.

Henson figures that 25 percent of his time was "actual doing." The rest was figuring what to do and keeping good records each step of the way for each piece, with photographs and tracings, for example, to document the early paint jobs — the skyblues and the greens, the elaborate stripings, and, on the Linde Wolf ice machine, the painted bouquets of daisies and roses. He reserved as a treat for himself the painting of the two big Rodman guns, one with a 15-ton barrel, the other with a 25-ton barrel. Henson stayed late nights to paint the undercoat on the guns as far as they'd been sandblasted and cleaned. Then on a Saturday morning he brought along 35 Boy Scouts to share the fun of finishing the barrels. "We took one and a half hours to do it and three hours to clean up." As someone who likes doing a job more than supervising one, Henson is happy to say "I had my hand at least halfway in all of our projects."

The son of a gun-factory machinist, Henson grew up building things — wagons, boats — making motors out of old clocks to run little elevators. "I always knew a machinist was what I wanted to be." He was a machinist's mate in the Navy during the Korean War, with four years of service in Engine Room #4 on the battleship *Wisconsin*, learning steam engineering and how to disassemble turbines and pumps.

After the war he built toy-size metal models of aircraft

and submarines for Naval research, and put in four years on-the-job as an apprentice to become a journeyman machinist. "For 18 months I also went four nights a week to George Washington University. I could see I was smart enough to be a college man. But then I kept thinking: what am I doing here? The answer was: getting tired. I decided I'd better pick what I wanted to do and give it my full attention. I'd better do one job and do it the best I could."

Henson presented himself at the Smithsonian in 1960, as a machinist and a good mechanic, who could set up a machine shop and run it, service tools, replace parts, build machines. "One of the first things I was given to do was to restore a piece of old machinery. I said I didn't know how to do that. The curator said he didn't either. In a shop there's usually one older person to turn to, but I had no one. I called chemical companies and paint companies and everyone I thought could help me. You need the sense to know when to ask questions," he adds, "and not just to blunder ahead."

In time, trying different solvents and techniques, Henson worked out procedures for machinery restoration. He has written about them and lectured about them. He thinks he has the safest methods now for removing rust and keeping it from reappearing. "The idea," Henson says, "is to remove the corrosion that will deteriorate the metal further and stop the dry rot in the wood. You're stabilizing the object, holding it the way it is. Maybe you go a little further, into the business of restoration. But cautiously. Old machinery should look like old machinery. A 125–year–old tool should look like a 125–year–old tool."

Some things he thinks are under-restored, like the big pin-making machine he cleaned recently, a circular thing resembling a merry-go-round. Henson wanted to take it apart and work on it piece by piece. He thought it might deteriorate further otherwise. "But that's the curator's responsibility," he says, and the curator decided it should be left in a 'relic state.'

Being a party to over-restoration can be worse. During

the rush of work for "1876" Henson was cleaning a wood-shaping machine, "a black thing about the size of my desk," he describes it. "I was starting with the mildest solution — soap and water — because I wanted to record what the original paint looked like. And I came on this American eagle on the side. It was raised in a casting, painted with gold leaf, on green. It was beautiful. I decided we shouldn't lose it. There was no way I would allow this eagle to be sandblasted or put in a caustic bath. I wanted to save it. But how? I followed the best advice I could get, from the conservation lab, which was to put a barrier coat on top of the green and gold. We stabilized the old paint first, then put on our barrier coat as a water-soluble film and painted on top with oil-base paint. We went through this process to satisfy the needs of the show — for machinery to look new — and to satisfy my feeling for history. When the show is over, we can remove the new paint job and reveal the original."

A chart above Henson's desk lists the jobs the staff is currently working on, including a batch of 200 telephones for a telephone exhibit as one item. His chart doesn't list on-going chores, like training the men and women volunteers who run the machinery in exhibits. And it doesn't list servicing the machinery in the power hall, where operating specimens wear out parts as they hammer and bang. "We call ourselves specialists," Henson says. "In a sense that's true. Among us we have one expert on clock faces, one on telephones, one on heavy machinery, one on scientific instruments. But we all have to be diversified. We all clean machinery or clean floors around here if that's what is needed. I don't think there's a degree in the bunch," he adds. "And when I interview people to work here I'm more inclined to ask if they've ever torn their bicycles apart or if they change the plugs in their cars than I am to ask how good they've been in math."

When he retires, Henson, who is getting some gray in his sideburns, would like to teach manual arts in a high school — "if they'd have me without any degrees and if they'd get over the idea that only dummies take shop." He has already taught a university seminar for manual arts teachers. "I wanted them to incorporate in their teaching the whole fantastic history of machine tools and the fact that only the machine tool can make an exact duplicate of itself. A printing press can't make another printing press and a telephone can't make a telephone, but machine tools can reproduce themselves. I can take a lathe, a milling machine, grinder, drill press and shaper and build another lathe, milling machine, grinder, drill press, shaper."

"With what we have here in our $100,000 shop plus a grinder we could make a steam engine or copy a Remington .44. We couldn't build a space capsule, but the only thing stopping us is the tools."

Now that "1876" preparations are over, the Tech Lab has revamped its space to meet the needs of the museum's restoration projects. Henson is grateful for a slowed-down pace. "It's back to the dirt and grime for me," he says, showing off his grease-blacked hands. "After a lot of desk work, I'm back at home, doing what I like best—building missing machine parts so vital in the art of restoration." He's also willing in emergencies to fix a fellow-Smithsonian employe's eyeglasses.

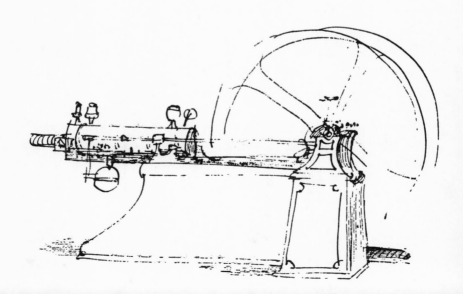

3. People in Science

ROLLAND HOWER
Freeze-drier of Animals

The time to visit Rolland Hower in the Natural History Museum lab where he freeze-dries animals is on a day when he has an "opening," that is, when he swings open the round door on his big nine-by-five-foot vacuum tank to check if his specimens are "done" and ready for exhibit. It happens only once every few months. As he opens the door Hower looks in on a jumble of animals. Neatly stacked, birds, beasts, and fish are posed, motionless — some of them stalking, some feeding, some coiled to strike. Coot and coyote look out at him with glassy eyes; lizards, too, from the dark tunnel, bobcats, bunnies, robins, foxes.

On any opening day Hower — who gets most of his specimens from road kills and TV tower deaths — removes and checks each animal to decide whether it needs more time in the tank or not. By the time the tank is emptied, every surface in the lab itself, already crowded with apparatus and pipes and finished specimens, is covered with animals. The newcomers to this strange and disorderly zoo are muscling aside the old, some of which already swing from the lighting fixtures or pace along the uppermost ducts.

Up there a Pallas cat stalks a sea turtle. An opossum, treed between condenser and air-return, bares its teeth at a tabulated tortoise. Shearwaters are nesting in the bookcase alongside starlings; little rodents are capering on the file cabi-

net; a hawk dives from a ceiling light. One praying mantis shares the Out box on Hower's desk with a trio of cowbirds, a gecko, and a black widow spider. And a three-foot Australian monitor lizard, hanging over a nail, has its jaws clenched on a rat (a local product, caught in a Smithsonian trap). These animals and birds seem alive — much more so than the stiff fauna mounted by a taxidermist.

Freeze-drying animals and birds to prepare them for exhibit is a process Hower pioneered. The traditional way of preparing animals, by taxidermy, is slow and messy. It requires eviscerating the animal, preparing the skin, and rebuilding a structure inside. For freeze-dry, on the other hand, the animal is positioned, then frozen quickly, and put into the tank where its moisture is removed under vacuum. "That's all there is to it. The nice thing is that the anatomy is all done for us by Mother Nature," says Hower, "and we can concentrate on realistic positioning."

Preparing a turtle may take a taxidermist three days to three weeks, Hower explains. "It's a long, slow, manmade process. Freeze-dry is long and slow, too, but not in terms of human work-hours. A turtle, depending on its size, may be in the chamber from one month to four. But it takes only one person-hour to prepare it — to wire it into position and insert the eyes. And the idiot vacuum machine doesn't know it's working 24 hours a day."

Dried at room temperature, an animal will shrink and shrivel, its cell walls collapsing as the water evaporates. Freeze-dried, it does not shrink. The ice crystals in its tissues are transformed directly to vapor, bypassing the liquid state. The cell walls stay rigid. And the animal looks essentially as it does in life.

Hower rates his small mammals and birds the most successful products of his freeze-dry technique. They emerge glossy of fur and feather, requiring at the most a little touch-up of color in faded membranes around the eyes and mouth (and a bit of tick and flea spray before they go on exhibit). Also successful are his amphibians and reptiles, which come out from the tank properly mucoid and scaly. His larvae and furred insects come out fine (so do mushrooms); crustaceans and smooth insects somewhat less well. Jellyfish have been a flop. Likewise Luci Johnson Nugent's wedding bouquet, which was an experiment—and embarrassing. Hower has freeze-dried some fish successfully, "but they're not our favorites."

Weight, volume, and structure of the animal affect the time it takes to freeze-dry it, and Hower has worked out the math for calculating the proper vapor pressures. Small fatty subjects take longer to freeze-dry than larger specimens without fat, desert animals longer than Eastern woodland animals. So do freshwater animals, which have a fatty layer just under the skin.

Hower can prepare a song sparrow in one and a half weeks and a robin in two. A frog takes two weeks, also, but a toad, which is a little oilier, takes three. A mouse will be ready in two weeks only if its tail has been punctured to speed its drying. Otherwise it takes an extra two to three weeks. Gerbils take one month, turtles three, bats four, Gila monsters six. A crocodile head, which went in at 65 pounds and came out at 30 pounds, took nine months to freeze-dry satisfactorily.

All through 1976 the space in Hower's biggest tank was dominated by an 8 1/2-foot Komodo dragon, which had died at the Zoo. "If I were doing it again," says Hower, a relaxed and genial man, "well, I wouldn't attempt it. Anything that takes that long—a year and more—is really beyond reasonable feasibility. It's no longer economical." As it was, he mounted his dragon on a large board with its head raised and its tail curled around behind and he put a frame over it on which to stack other specimens like hawks and raccoons.

Hower's card file indicates that at the same time another, medium-sized tank was working away at two armadillos, one woodchuck, goose, horned owl, some doves, ducks, flickers, an immature pilot black snake and a slimy salamander. The smallest chamber had two gerbils, a box turtle, a tufted titmouse, a pair of cardinals, and one orange, which, Hower says, probably will never dry because it's surrounded by little cells filled with oil.

Hower makes his own reptile and fish eyes, because there's a metallic look he likes to get. Beyond that he settles for ready-made eyes he can buy. A chart tells him what size to use—size six on a frog, size four on a toad. And he can often improvise. A moose eye, for example, turned sideways, did nicely for his Komodo. As well as his eye files, he has spare parts drawers. They're filled with extra wings, legs, paws, and claws, not so much for patching as for sending around to schools where students use them in science classes to consider means of locomotion, perching, or gathering food.

So far most of the freeze-dry work has been for exhibition purposes. Hower would like to see it used more for research. He has freeze-dried many organs for medical research—hearts, livers, brains, which in the past would only be available for study pickled in formaldehyde. Lung material has been difficult to freeze, Hower says, because outer layers insulate the inner layers. There has been trouble, too, keeping the color in the blood-filled organs. "It's been exciting work," he says, adding, as scientists do, without seeming to mind, "by the way, we've failed in that particular experiment."

He also freeze-dries worms. When someone brings in to him microscopic nematodes suspended in water in tiny glass dishes, Hower tucks them into his smallest chamber and promises to return them done the next day.

Hower grew up in Bowling Green, Ohio. As a boy, by tagging along with a birds man who was studying the ring-necked pheasant, he came to learn the birds of the fields, thickets, and woodlands around his home. His academic studies were in art and engineering, both of which — though he couldn't know it at the time — were good preparation for what he would do at the Smithsonian. "I took a lot of little courses all over, most of them non-credit, at Case Institute of Technology and the University of Toledo — things I wanted to know about like math and metallurgy, and history and English and how to cast metal objects." For some years he had his own commercial art studio. Now he's working on a PhD, which he says will pull all of his "scrappy-looking education into order."

The first freeze-dry experiment Hower made at the museum, at a time before freeze-dried foods were commercially available, was in 1959 with an Eastern woodland hare. "It shrank a bit because we had no idea of the temperature to use. We learned a lot just by doing." By now he has done 3,500 animals, plus a load of garbage that was needed by the exhibits people for an urban display. His animals have replaced a lot of turn-of-the-century specimens on exhibit that were beginning to look tattered and lacklustre. And he has presented to view a number of items like spiders and snakes and an octopus which formerly were seen only as plaster casts or floating in jars of alcohol.

Hower also, some years back, became the smells man for the museum. He rather enjoyed that task and he built up a fine assortment of chemicals to work with. He made a lavender-and-old-lace smell, which was wafted through the First Ladies Hall. He had a leather and oil smell going in the machine shop exhibit and an apple pie smell in the California kitchen, compounded of eight ingredients including oil of rue, cinnamon, and a touch of oil of tangerine. He was just getting somewhere with his farm-stable smell (hay and ma-

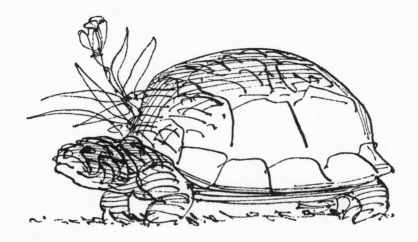

nure) and with his seashore smell, which included just a
whiff of dead fish, when it was decided to shelve the whole
project. "We began to think that some of the oils we used as
a base for the smells might be harmful to the museum objects. It wasn't worth the risk."

Hower has several freezers of animals awaiting his attention, including an albatross with a five-foot wingspread
which, because of its fattiness, he hasn't yet figured how to
handle. There are a lot of droppers-in to the lab. It's partly
because people are curious to see what he is up to and hope
they'll catch him at tank opening. It's partly, they say, because he is "just so darned helpful." On a given morning, an
illustrator, stumped by a problem with his fly-eye drawing,
comes to consult him. So does an insect-zookeeper, stumped
by finicky eating on the part of her mosquitoes.

Hower runs from time to time a course on exhibits
techniques for people from small museums all around the
country, quite a few of which now have their own freeze-dry
labs. He has written a manual on his process, including
graphs and charts for times, temperatures, and pressures, in-

formation on vacuum pump systems and how to build them, tips on mounting animals and making eyes. He wrote it in response to all the visits he gets and the hundreds and hundreds of letters of inquiry. "I also got a poison pen letter from a fifth-grader. He thought I was freeze-drying live animals and he told me to cut it out."

 ## JAMES BUCKLER
Horticulturalist

Because his job takes him into flower beds and drainage ditches James Buckler, 29, the museums' horticulturalist, keeps a tin of boot polish in his bookshelf. Two of his special projects, though, he can look at from his office, located on the balcony of the Arts and Industries building, and he doesn't get his boots wet, let alone muddy. Out his window he can see the new Victorian garden which he created in the Bicentennial year in front of Arts and Industries and the next-door Castle. Through his office door, six feet from his desk, he can step into the new indoor garden he created to suggest the extravagant plantings at the Centennial fair in Philadelphia. Buckler designed both gardens to enhance "1876" — the exhibit which fills Arts and Industries with its gleaming engines and other wondrous inventions.

While the gardens were in the making the shoe polish was used constantly. Buckler went in and out a lot. Under his direction bulldozers leveled the ground and work crews laid paths and cut scalloped borders for the beds. One elaborate flower bed, 200 feet long, called an embroidery parterre, was patterned like a piece of stitchery, and Buckler filled in the pattern with swatches of color from 35,000 bushy little plants of Joseph's Coat from his greenhouses — in cheerful yellows and bronze and red.

For the indoor garden, spotted about as clumps of green among the "1876" objects, he brought in truckloads of tropical trees — 150 of them, 12 to 25 feet tall, some with 20-foot wingspreads. He muscled them into big tubs he had ready for them — his orangerie boxes. And he added hundreds on hundreds of big palms, lantanas, ferns, and weeping figs — all the greenery he needed to give a lush and and leafy look to the building.

Buckler checked over lists to make sure he used the exact varieties of plants used in the 100-years-ago exhibition. He even borrowed from Philadelphia the oval marble fountain to be the central feature of the show in the rotunda. Never mind that the fountain weighed three tons and was fragile and awkward to ship and install. He positioned it satisfactorily and made sure his greenhouses kept it surrounded with a constantly changing show of color — lilies, poinsettias, daisies, dahlias. Visitors might not notice or realize that he changed the colors. Employees would. He wanted to surprise them in the mornings as they came in.

It was nip and tuck to do everything before "1876" opened in May, 1976. Close to the deadline workmen with jackhammers still drilled into cement in the garden, installing lampposts. Other workmen moved the last large palms indoors. Buckler built a mobile unit for beaming light onto trees and plants during off-hours to keep them healthy. He also lined up volunteers to mist the plants and wash them.

Buckler, looking younger even than his 29 years, with reddish hair and mustache, a nimble person and cricket-quick, is in charge of all the green and growing things at the Smithsonian, inside and out. He's in charge of the splashes of spring color from 150,000 tulips and the lawns that are trampled by 23 million people, and all the beeches and bushes and elms — their planting, cultivating, watering, spraying. He supplies the shiny-leaved plants and potted trees for all the gallery corridors and the floral decorations for events and special visitors — the wreaths, the six-foot shrubbery kangaroos, the chrysanthemums to honor the visiting Japanese Emperor (yellow, not white, which he learned the Japanese consider funereal).

The *Discovery Room* in the Natural History Museum requires a regular supply of live grasses from Buckler, for children to experience how corn, wheat, rye, and barley grow, and rice and sugar cane and bamboo as well. The *Insect Zoo* in Natural History wants greens from him, too, as healthful cricket and grasshopper food — free from insecticides. And the radiation laboratories have a standing order with him for cockleburs and winter barley, which they use in time-study experiments.

Buckler is designing also a mini-garden for the blind. He'll put in it herbal scented plants and textured plants — to touch — with signs in braille easy to reach on a nearby wall.

To make sure everything moves along at a good clip and is done on time, Buckler keeps a pocket notebook with a program for each day. Paperwork he gets out of the way first. Then a tour of the grounds. He checks edging, pruning, drainage in flower beds, jots down which trees are doing poorly and may need soil tests, which hedges have been tunneled into by rats in spite of his border of sharp-edged yucca plants called Adam's Needle, which shade of pink he will never plant again or at least not without a yellow border to tone it down.

Exteriors of buildings he views from a historic and aesthetic point of view. "You plant in scale and feeling to suit the purpose of the building and the architecture. A clover-shaped flower bed repeats the quatrefoil carving over a window in the Castle. Flowers in shades of blue do well by Arts and Industries, because of its designs of blue-glaze brick in amongst the red. Oriental shapes suit the Freer. Trees that have figured in American history and the trees of the States are suitable for History and Technology. The dawn redwoods, evocative of exploration and distant places, are right for Natural History.

For interiors, he asks the designers what size and number and color and texture of plants they want for their shows. He must take lighting into account, too; most plants have to be rotated out of dark corners every four to six weeks. He suits plants to objects. "I wouldn't put a bamboo by a portrait of George Washington, for example," he says. "Tobacco

plants are just right for Thomas Jefferson." When he saw
how bad white plastic flower pots looked in the Castle
lounge, with its dark carpets, marble pillars, and gilded picture frames, he discarded them in favor of terra-cotta pots.

Buckler schedules research time for himself before
noon. Early afternoons he is at his greenhouse-nursery complex, conferring with the manager, planning moves of the
carnation and mum crops, checking moisture in the propaga-
tion house (when it's too moist the seedlings rot). He counts
it the best part of the day for him when he's working on his
topiaries—shaping them up with his very sharp pocket knife
and with the shears he wears in a holster at his belt. Buckler
is pleased with his ball-on-ball shaped bushes, his ducks,
geese, and swans. It takes four years to make a proper six-
foot kangaroo from a shrub, but he can turn out an "instant"
one in four months by stuffing a chickenwire kangaroo frame
with moss and planting it with thousands of ivy or creeping
fig cuttings, which grow out quickly and hide the wire.

Back at the office, he writes his log for the day, copes
with orders, money, work plans for 26 full-time gardeners,
18 temporaries, 25 volunteers. "Planting seasons just don't
conform to bureaucratic schedules. You need to buy ahead,
order seeds one year ahead, bulbs one or two years. You need
to buy lead time to get seven-foot rubber trees from cuttings.
Besides, if you can't afford to spray trees when they need it,
you lose the trees."

Buckler sometimes goes on collecting trips — to Florida for fishtail palms, Australian tree ferns, Norfolk Island pines. Once on a speechmaking trip to Tulsa he found just the varieties of Joseph's Coat he needed and brought them home in his arms by plane, along with half a bushel each of burr oak acorns and black oak acorns scavenged from a park. "The back seat of my car always has a layer of bark and potting soil from spills," he says, "from the plant life I cart about." Mail brings him, from a network of the Smithsonian's friends, giant sugar pine cones, eucalyptus pods, teazles, gumballs, Kentucky coffee beans. They are all items he uses at Christmastime.

Buckler seems to have as many plans as he has acorns and seedlings. They pop up everywhere in his conversation. He wishes he had charge of the Mall between the museums. He'd like to turn it back into curving, shaded walks instead of straight sidewalks under hot sun. He wishes he had a hall of horticulture. "I'd like to show how gardening is related to the economy through food crops and fibers, and to the development of farm tools, how it's related to man's inner pleasure and to the decorative arts — how the rose and tobacco motifs are used in porcelains, how bell-flowers are used in furniture, and acanthus leaves in capitals. I'd like to go into Flemish and Egyptian flower arranging and show the history of the glass house, or conservatory. There's no end to what I'd like to do."

He wants to be sure he is delighting and educating and not just cutting the grass. For now he practices the educating on his 26 gardeners, "most of whom," he says, "come from poor backgrounds like mine and find the study as mind-opening as it was to me." Buckler regularly brings the whole crew together for two-hour sessions. "It amounts to a lot of lost work time, but it's important. Otherwise I get complaints from the gardeners: all they see of me is my coattails flying. We need to talk about what we're doing — like why we did a Victorian garden at all — in order to feel pride in the work and what we're presenting.

"The gardeners were fascinated by the old pictures of

Horticulture Hall in Philadelphia. We couldn't re-create that hall. It was a whole separate building at the Centennial. But we took our planting scheme from it. We all studied pictures I took of what's left of it—the foundations and some of the old trees and the brick 'necessary buildings'—the outhouses. The gardeners were fascinated by old pictures of the iron garden benches and the wickets for edging flower beds. We could see that some benches and wickets I had found in Philadelphia, in an antique shop, were identical. We cast more of them, just alike. Now I stand back when visitors ask questions and I hear the gardeners give them a good lecture."

Buckler grew up on a southern Maryland tobacco farm, without electricity or running water. By age 13 he was already self-sufficient, working as busboy and cashier, then digging in a cemetery. Graduating from a vocational high school, in agriculture, he wanted to be an accountant, but he was bored by numbers and dropped out. He worked in a bindery—stapling—but found that noisy and he couldn't get used to a basement. On a lab job he ruled out biology as a career because of the smell of formaldehyde. "Then I took a course in botany and I found it fascinating. I even liked memorizing lists of Latin names. My professor suggested I go into horticulture. It was the first time I heard the word. Ever."

While he was still an undergraduate, Buckler spent a summer at the Longwood Gardens in Pennsylvania, doing practical gardening and taking courses. "I'd never seen gardens, never knew there were such gardens. It was a marvelous mind-blowing experience. It set the tone for the rest of my life." He did his graduate work there at Longwood. "I was like a great big sponge, finding out what horticulture was, what the world was. I worked in private gardens all the time I was studying. I met people who helped me and directed me."

Buckler was 24 when he was hired as the Smithsonian's first horticulturalist. "It was a fight at first. I had to battle until people understood what a garden is and why it's important and why you can't buy plants off a shelf and why you can't bulldoze over tree roots. Now I'm spending 95 percent of my time on administration, bookkeeping, budgets. It's almost as if I'd become an accountant after all. But I can see results in terms of living, growing things. And five percent of my time—as well as weekends—I'm still gardening.

"There's one thing about growing up on a farm," Buckler says. "I've enjoyed catching up ever since. Well, there's more than one thing. I hated tobacco, hate it still, a dirty, grimy crop. But I learned the seasons from working it and the whole cycle of planting, weeding, transplanting, hoeing, fertilizing, harvesting, cutting, drying, stripping. I learned there isn't anything too hard or too menial for you to do if you're going to have a garden. Besides, I love going out of doors and barefoot." He still loves being out of doors, even in shoes; and polish takes care of appearances.

EDWARD S. AYENSU
Botanist

In his office botanist Edward Ayensu has a moss-green carpet on the floor. He has photographs of orchids on the walls, shiny-leaved miracle berry plants hanging about, an impeccable white lab coat on a hook next to an impeccable suit coat. The setting is green, tidy, and gleaming clean. Out in the field, though, Ayensu sits under a tree with bat urine drizzling on his shoulders.

Ayensu's study of the interactions of neem trees and bats, which puts him in this damp situation, is a study he has been conducting for a number of years, during rainy seasons and dry seasons, on the Accra plains in his native country of Ghana, in West Africa. The neem tree was imported to Ghana from India some 60 years earlier as a quick-growing fuel wood by the British who found it wasteful to continue burning up Ghanaian mahogany. The neem tree flourished. Its fruit proved to be very attractive to bats, who dropped the seeds on the grassy plains as they ate. The trees soon multiplied. The well-fed bats multiplied as well. And Ayensu set himself to monitor the situation. It causes him some alarm because the vegetation is changing—from grassland to forest—and because he thinks the bats may be carrying disease.

His practice in the field, Ayensu says, is to watch the bats' comings and goings for four and five days at a time, from a kind of blind he fixes for himself out of bushes. That way he gets a sense of the bats' biological clocks. He knows that at sunset they begin to fidget on their roosts, hover a bit, and then take off in a mass for an hour's feeding. They never feed in the neem tree where they roost, though other bats, roosting elsewhere, may come to feed at it. Ayensu can count on their feeding again at three in the morning. He follows the flights by truck, capturing specimens in a mist net. He studies their stomach contents and the parasites in their fur. Then he moves on to a different population.

In his office, mounted, are specimens of a number of the bat species the botanist is working on. "Pleasant and beautiful animals," he says of them, "if temperamental." He claims not to understand why they arouse such antagonism in people. "Well, the hammerhead *is* a little ugly," he admits, adding quickly, however, "but look what nice teeth it has."

The field work has some disagreeable aspects, the bat urine in particular, with its high ammonia content. The sardine and bread diet. And the insects. But bees in the early morning and moths at night are of considerable interest to botanist Ayensu. And the heat, he says, never bothers him. "I was born in the tropics."

Gardening was compulsory in elementary school in Ghana. "We had prizes for raising cassavas and plantains. And we all knew about collecting cow dung and spreading it to get better produce. We knew that our tropical area is fragile though it looks lush, that we have poor topsoil and the red clay directly under it is as hard as a table." In high school Ayensu became interested in nature on field trips led by a teacher from Chicago, an avid snake biologist. He did his undergraduate work in America and his doctorate in botany at the University of London.

He chose to work on the yam for his doctor's thesis, attracted to it because it was an economically important root food, an important component of medicine, with a curious and interesting structure. Ayensu has worked a great deal on orchids as well. He spends several hours of each day in the lab upstairs from his office, examining cross-sections of orchid stems or leaves under a light-microscope or studying photographs taken with the electron microscope (it magnifies 1,000 to 10,000 times, blowing up starch grains in orchid root cells so that they look like bunches of grapes).

Ayensu is writing—early and late. He comes back to the office at night after dinner and arrives again at dawn. He looks calm, cheerful, and clear-eyed, however, and says three to four hours of sleep are quite enough for him. He writes on airplanes, too, traveling the world over—to visit the herbarium in Leningrad, to study plants in South America and Africa and Sri Lanka, to lecture at Oxford, to attend, every three weeks, biological meetings in Paris. On a first trip to China Ayensu looked at rice, sorghum, and wheat crops, and at bonsai trees. He asked to go again, to the eastern part of the Tibetan plateau, to see the relics of ancient plants, destroyed elsewhere under Ice Age glaciers. Now he has a book in the works on China as well as books on the anatomy of orchids, the biology of orchids, and fruit bats.

A team headed by Ayensu has brought out a fat volume listing 3,000 endangered and threatened species of native plants of the United States, including Hawaii, and mapping their whereabouts. The team continues to tabulate reports from the field, adding plant names to the roster and subtracting names, too, as new counts come in. The work is leading to protection of the plants' habitats and a crackdown, Ayensu hopes, on commercial exploitation. He is outraged by people who trundle away truckloads of wild plants, such as the rattlesnake orchid, the Venus flytrap, butterworts, the Dehesa beargrass of California, and by those who show off in their homes or offices a rare cactus, dug from the wild. "It's just ridiculous to buy a $350 Arizona barrel cactus. I'd like to see the day come, soon, when it's considered as bad form as making a coat from leopard skins." He wants to bring out posters picturing endangered American plants and urging people to protect them. A nice touch, he thinks, is that the endangered list includes a rock-dwelling plant called "live forever".

For five years, through 1976, Ayensu put his workdays at the Smithsonian to running the botany department. The job of being chairman rotates among the botanists as it would in a university department. At the Natural History Museum it involves a lot of supervising and the housekeeping of a collection of four million grasses, pine cones, bamboo culms, roots, and pods. It involves answering requests from artists, students, and from the Army Corps of Engineers for grass to stabilize sand dunes, from lawyers and agriculturalists who want information on narcotics, from the FBI wanting an analysis of leaves or pollens found on some car bumper.

Materials have to be shipped to the field—plant driers, presses, blotting papers (there was once an SOS from a team in the Marquesas Islands when it ran out of newspapers for pressing its plants). Bundles of incoming materials have to be fumigated. Whole collections of specimens on deteriorating paper need to be remounted—a job which keeps five women constantly at work. Like members of a sewing circle, they stitch along together companionably in sunny rooms. They stitch plants to 100 percent rag paper, using double loops of #8 white cotton thread, or they tape with gummed cloth, or they glue with plastic glue bands. Broken fragments they tuck into pockets attached to the page. As experts they welcome the challenge of bulgy and prickly specimens. There is nothing, these women say, to mounting a flat trillium, for example.

The department chairman also keeps track of research, conducted by his colleagues in the offices that rim the central storage range. It's research, Ayensu says, which he would not be able to judge properly or even to understand if he were not doing regular scientific research himself. The other botanists are working on mosses, lichens, dogwood, ferns, cactus, palms. There's Joan Nowicke, a palynologist, studying the pollen which blows through the air and causes hay fever. She has photographs of pollen grains enlarged to fantastic balls textured with wrinkles or bumps or prickles or puckers. Botanical illustrator Regina Hughes reproduces them in sketches.

There's an algae team, husband and wife James Norris and Katina Bucher, who study the marine algae from the Baja peninsula off California — algae which they think have great potential for food and for medicines. They collect and dive together, and collaborate on their writing. In their files they have stacks of papers onto which they have floated the lacy shapes of the red algae, which they say have the potent chemistry to be used as a natural pesticide.

By winter of 1976, his term as chairman ended, Ayensu was able to keep a date with his Ghanaian bats. He was glad to be off in the field again with his nets and his machetes and his night vision equipment to magnify the night light 20,000 times without alerting the bats. "You develop a keen eye in the field," he says. "All the while you are under the tree, watching and making notes, your brain stores away information. And later, as you sit down to write, this amazing amount of information you never knew you had comes to you. And you put the pieces together."

KJELL SANDVED
Photographer

"I love moths. I love to be in a cloud of moths, to have moths crawling all over me," states Kjell Sandved, Natural History Museum photographer. "They can't sting. They can't bite. No other form on earth has so much diversity of color and shape or is so marvelously interesting. They've been overlooked," he says, though not by him. He calculates that he has taken some 20,000 moth portraits in the past 15 years, on a Malaysian mountaintop near the South China Sea, in New Guinea, Thailand, Venezuela, Brazil. And he has covered possibly 3,000 of 100,000 species.

Flipping through the packs of pictures stacked on his tables, Sandved fans out colorful examples of the camouflage, the mimicry, the deception that has enabled moths to survive. He has pictures of moths that look like bark, moths that look like lichen, like bird droppings, like twigs. He has moths that look—and act—like fluttering leaves—not just leaf-colored but veined and spotted like leaves as well and imitating states of leaf disease and decay. He has moths with enormous, startling, fake eye-spots at the tops of their wings, to frighten away birds and lizards or at least to deflect their attack from vital areas.

Sandved flips out the picture of a moth holding its leg in position to make it look like a spider. "Pure bluff," he says admiringly. "They assume positions to look like tarantulas or cockroaches or beetles or flowers or a yellow leaf in a spider web. Here is one, he says, putting it out on the table like an ace in a game of solitaire, "sitting on its wings as though saying, 'This is nothing edible here, just a little stick sticking out, something that fell from the forest canopy. Pass me by.' " Sandved knows *he* passes many by, deceived himself, especially during the day, when the moths sleep in their contrived poses. "I have to maintain a snail-slow pace through the jungle, as I examine bark and moss. If I find three moths in a single day I count myself lucky." At that, once while photographing a moth as it slept on its head he reached out to move a twig from the picture and the twig crept away. It was a Notodontid moth he was too startled to photograph.

This bulky middle-aged Norseman is in a state of boyish excitement whenever he is packing film, socks, his strobe lights, and "Owl Eye" portable night-light amplifier for a trip, such as the ones to Ghana with botanist Ayensu to photograph fruit bats. In his cubicle of an office he already hears in his head the rushing wings of the bats. "It's a strange and elegant sound," he says. He sees their eyes as they show up at night from his infrared light source "like car lights on my lens." Sandved is agitated until he is in the field. Once there, however, he is patience itself, able to sit motionless for days or nights, high up on scaffolding swathed in veils or net, or in water, or on an ice floe, so that he will be able to record with his cameras the behavior of moths, bats, spiny sea urchins, and seals.

"Extraordinary, wonderful behavior" (he pronounces it *won*-derful, with a long, gliding emphasized first syllable). "Animal behavior is weird and awesome. You get such respect and love for animals. Animal behavior surpasses everything. Especially that of moths, of course."

The oversized photographer talks in a hushed whisper,

contorting his body and describing intricate movements in the air with his big hands, to show how weaver ants use larvae as needles to weave leaves together, how leaf-cutter ants carry flowers to their underground chamber to grow fungus, or a mother stink bug watches over her babies on a lower leaf; how crickets in a ritual fight throw one another over a shoulder, the victor then trampling on the vanquished, who crouches in concession of defeat.

Sandved pantomimes the bats he has watched while on a field trip with Ayensu, describing how they move along a branch hand over hand like a sailor on a rope. He mimes the spiny sea urchin, making for a sand dollar buried in sand, lifting it, nibbling it around the edges. From his high-speed photographs he found that the sea urchin passes sand, grain by grain, along its thousands of spines as it moves. Sandved even tries to mimic movements like that.

Sifting through yet another pack of pictures, he shudders to describe how the newborn seal pup, ice crystals on its fur, shivered on a slippery, dirty ice shelf. Sandved had awaited the birth for three days before he was able to photograph it. "The males are always a bit angry," he says, "but the female seals are docile, except for one that kicked my legs from under me with her flipper. My gosh, it hurt, and all she said was 'aahh.' Penguins are more fun—*won*derful, *won*derful walking feedbags, those penguins. They turned their heads, chattered at me, and nibbled at my shoelaces." Sandved acts out the rough cat-and-mouse game the leopard seal plays with the Adelie penguins. "One time I arrived at Antarctica in early February, and caught the penguin chicks' first rush to the sea, 3,000 of them. The air was filled with their feathers, and so was my sandwich."

Sandved never actually studied photography. "It never interested me really. I never went around with cameras dangling. I'm still only interested now in cameras for how they record significant facts of animal behavior or relationships between animals and plants. As a boy, he says, growing up on the Oslo Fjord, he had a little rowboat which he took out for fishing and looking at marine life. Close to his home were woods where he played Tarzan and Indians. For a time he repaired radios to make a living. Then he became a publisher and brought out an encyclopedia of music and one of art. "When I wanted to do an encyclopedia of natural history I came to the Smithsonian. And the more I looked, the more I saw what gaps there were in the photograph collections. I wanted to fill them myself, but it took me years to find out how. Man," he says, of his self-taught skills, "I learned photography the hard way."

Now he has the equipment he likes, quite a bit of which he makes himself. Working with Ayensu on the bats he has used the snooper scope, originally designed for night warfare, a device that magnifies light without the aid of any artificial light source, and the newer and more powerful "Owl Eye." For attracting moths at night he has invented a rig of two stroboscopic lights, with strong emissions in both long- and short-range ultraviolet rays. At the top of a 25-foot bamboo pole he hangs one lamp, with a sheet of aluminum directly beneath it to diffuse the light on all sides and to keep it from shining below. Five feet from the ground he hangs a low lamp, under a banana-leaf roof. Moths are attracted to the high lamp. After circling it, they drop below the shield. They're attracted then to the low lamp, and from there they settle onto low vegetation where he can photograph them. For his underwater work he has learned to simulate sea conditions in tanks and to capture the behavior he wants with the

use of mirrors, plastic sheets, and of multiple cameras placed directly above and below and at oblique angles.

Sandved hoards his vacations and goes right back out to the places he liked best on assignments — to the Upper Amazon and the slopes of the Andes or to New Guinea or Java, where he finds the most species and the most diverse forms of animal life. Or he goes to the Philippines. "You find some of the nicest beetles in the world in the Philippines, they're just like jewels," he says.

"I love to be in the tropics and sweat. I never stay a minute in the city if I can help it." And he never heads out at the time of a full moon either. He learned by experience that even his lamps are powerless to attract insects when they're competing with a full moon.

Sandved recently went to Sumatra, drawn there by word of the largest flower on earth. An endangered, *mar*velous flower, he calls it — three feet across — the "whale" of the botanical world. He photographed it, a mottled orange and brown flower, as it grows on vines on the jungle floor. "It has no roots, no leaves. It's a parasite. Very, very little is known about its biology. And it was only my looking for it that showed it to be extinct now in two of the four places it grew. Perhaps something can be done to save it. I was thrilled that I as a nonprofessional could discover an important event like that."

Sandved, whose pictures appear in articles, in books, as illustrations to lectures, and in exhibits like the museum's *Insect Zoo,* travels around the country showing his films and explaining how he takes them. "I don't lecture on The Ecology. That can be a waste of breath. I show my pictures of the wonders of creatures. People step on them, kill them without thinking. But when they see them enlarged, they have such a respect for them." He shows his pictures of the surface of a moth wing, magnified to look like a deep-pile carpet, or more highly still to look like a forest of Christmas trees. He shows his series on wasp nests — hanging nests, round ones, the ones in cracks of trees. And he shows his series of fly eyes — the horseflies with the straight color bands, the deerflies with undulating ones.

"If you inspire people's love, they'll want to do something. Millions of creatures are destroyed by the mercury lights on our highways. One summer day we'll see a scrap of paper blowing in the wind but no more butterflies. It's such a gradual thing. They will just fade away. It's terrible."

Sandved has a minor complaint as well as his cosmic one. It's the photograph he has to wear around his neck on his Smithsonian badge. He dislikes the mug shot of himself ("I'd rather wear a number") showing a glum face with a blue cast to the complexion. It's a bad picture, he thinks for someone who wakes up "jumping for joy every day. I *like* my job. What's best about it is I'm always working with scientists, collecting data with them, using my cameras as research tools, documenting things you would never see in their normal size or at normal speed. Things which happen very fast you have to take at high speed; most things happen slowly and you take them at time lapse. All my work is focused on biological events or concepts. There's no gimmickry involved. And not too many people walking around and talking, either. There's a special atmosphere about a museum — the books, the specimens, the people. It's like a university — stimulating."

 ## DEVRA KLEIMAN
Zoologist

Fellow workers entering Devra Kleiman's office at the National Zoo's animal health building are often greeted with "Watch your feet" instead of "Hello." They're used to it. They know that once again she has bottlefed a small animal through the night at her home, brought it back to her office with her, complete with heating pad, formula, roll of toilet paper, and medical chart, and is letting it run loose on the floor while she works.

"It can be heartbreaking," she says, "sitting up with newborns that die, having to cope with death on a daily basis, and also with your own lack of knowledge. I become attached to the animals I work with. Most people do. Losses are a major problem, especially if you could have prevented them. You have to live with knowledge of human guilt and error."

Kleiman came to her job as reproduction zoologist, in charge of breeding programs, in 1971, at a time, she says, when zoos were becoming very much aware of their long-range responsibilities. "The time came when we saw we would no longer replenish our stocks from the wild. If people were to be able to see these animals 50 and 100 years from now, then we would have to perpetuate active colonies. To breed animals successfully in captivity we would have to know a great deal more than we did — about social behavior and nutrition and medical care."

That's why the Zoo acquired a big new breeding farm, away from public view, for the purpose of developing herds of threatened and endangered species, such as the Scimitar-horned oryx (a prized antelope with 40-inch curved horns) or the Pere David's deer (an animal, now extinct in the wild, with deer antlers, a horsy muzzle, and a tail like a mule). These days the Zoo rejoices more than ever over births — of a bald eagle chick or a 125 pound rhinoceros calf or a Bactrian camel calf or a string of lesser panda kits and infant pygmy hippos.

Kleiman has been spending much of her time and energy on the Zoo's marmoset project. The marmosets, housed down the hall from her office, are small golden monkeys from Brazil, so diminished in numbers that as few as 400 remain in the wild. It has been a triumph for the Zoo to have the marmosets breed well and into the second generation. With 28 animals, the Zoo has the largest colony outside Brazil.

Marmosets are monogamous — have but one mate. They reproduce once or twice a year, usually twins. The male carries the young on his back and helps to rear them. The older juveniles help also, and it seems, Kleiman explains, that the experience is important to them. If they are deprived of helping with the child care, moved away from the family before the next infants are born, they may reject their own young — abandon them or kill them.

On her wall, along with rhinoceros baby pictures and children's poems, Kleiman has an impressive chart — the kind historians use to tell the family histories of kings. It is an occupancy chart for five cages of marmosets, listing each animal, male and female, by accession number and diagraming each move it has made since 1969. It notes when the marmosets were paired, what issue they had, and what became of the young. A file card on each animal goes into greater detail. It gives parentage and statistics and it lists the important happenings in the animal's life, including fights, injuries, illnesses. Still another file contains information on all the other marmosets in other zoos.

"For now," Kleiman explains, "we have to breed every marmoset we can, just to get our numbers up. But if marmosets survive in zoos, most of them will be derived from six or seven females. This really isn't enough for maintaining heterogeneity of the species. It's not ideal for a colony to be derived from a small number of animals. We're conscious of that problem and have to be very careful as we raise our animals and trade them with other zoos."

A second major project for Kleiman is a comparison of

the social behavior of three species of South American ca-
nids — maned wolves, which are solitary animals, crab-eating
foxes, which live in pairs, and bush dogs, which live in small
packs. As an undergraduate at the University of Chicago
Kleiman carried out a study of wolves — seeing whether adult
wolves could be socialized to human beings. That work led to
further studies of dogs and wolves at the London Zoo, and to
a PhD from the University of London.

She has used both her marmoset and her wolf observations in a recent paper on monogamy. In it she describes
similarities found in widely different animals, which all happened to be paired animals having only one mate — like the
marmosets and the wolves, as well as beavers, dikdiks, dwarf
mongooses and acouchis. "It pleased me," she says, "to find
any generalizations. I found two. One: the males and females
among these animals are not very different from one another
in size or behavior. Male and female wolves share in such
rituals as scentmarking and howling to defend their territory.
Two: the males are heavily involved in caring for the young.
The male marmoset carries the young. The male wolf shares
in regurgitating meat to the young around the time of wean-
ing.

"Every time you see a biological pattern that clicks and
makes sense to you, it's a very exciting thing," says Kleiman,
who enjoys writing up her observations. "All that you learn
is relevant to management in zoos, but useful only if written
and circulated. It's exciting, too," she says "when you develop

a program that works. You've logiked it out, put together something that succeeds. And there's just nothing more satisfying than that."

Kleiman is in the cages and dens when she needs to be — to check equipment, to introduce a new animal, to catch one for the vet. She works out the animals' environments — the woodchip ground cover for the marmosets, the temperature, the humidity, the height of the nest boxes, the visual isolation of groups from each other, the trees where monkeys can chase each other, leap from branch to branch, wrestle. For the maned wolves she works out gate systems to get the interactions she wants. When the vet has a cheetah anesthetized she is invited into the operating room to examine the ovaries by laparoscope. "Now that's an eerie feeling," she says, "seeing into a cheetah's belly."

Much time goes to supervising the Zoo students' research. Some are working on the vocalizations of the very vocal marmosets, some on how the marmosets develop pairbonds. With one student she goes over the videotape of a maned wolf birth, with another the videotape of encounters between the giant pandas from China, Ling-Ling and Hsing-Hsing, who disappointed Washington by failing to produce a kit for the Bicentennial. All through the weeks of the panda encounters, while the female is in heat, Kleiman observes on a six to ten A.M. and five to eight P.M. schedule, talking her data into a tape recorder.

She is involved with lesser panda breeding as well. The lesser pandas, which look like red raccoons, have been breeding successfully at the Zoo — ever since the keeper noticed that the mother, following the birth of a litter, required three secure nests for moving her kits about. Two would not do. With one nesting box and one hollow log, she still looked nervously about. With a second nesting box as well she seemed to be at peace.

Types of enclosure are important. The cheetahs need running space during courtship. Certain waterfowl need fenced-in territory to establish and defend, since they won't breed amongst lots of other species. Diet is important, and that's where Zoo people get a direct payoff from field work in the wild. "If we learn about feeding habits of howler monkeys in the wild — what parts of leaves they eat, what kinds of minerals they get — maybe we can alter diets here so that we will be more successful with breeding howlers in the Zoo."

Kleiman's complaint is that her time is fragmented. "I can't carry on a sustained series of observations on any one thing. I may spend a night with a pregnant bush dog. But then I have other appointments to keep. There's no solution," she says, pushing a batch of dark hair back from her face, tucking a stray shirttail into her patchwork skirt, "unless you're willing to be a hermit."

 ## BELA DEMETER

Lizards Keeper, Herpetologist

Bela Demeter is the National Zoo's keeper of lizards. He is 29, wears one earring and a bright green day gecko tattooed on his right arm. "I just happen to like everything about lizards," he says. "They have neat faces. They're alert, much more so than snakes. They have a really nice expression, and they have the most elaborate adaptations. The gliding gecko, for instance, has flaps like a parachute and if a snake or shrew is after him, he'll sail off on an angle, then scurry away. The tokay has four pinholes in the pupil of his eye that give him a really sharp image — better day vision because of that adaptation than other nocturnal animals."

Demeter came to the Zoo with a degree in psychology from the University of Florida. At home he kept cobras, rattlers, boas, and pythons. After a year of junior college training as a zoo keeper, he applied to zoos with reptile collections and ended up at the Smithsonian. Now his only housepets are two rosy boas. When Demeter started work, he found that literature on lizards was too skimpy to be of use to him in keeping his specimens healthy and breeding. He began carrying out his own observations and behavior projects. "I recorded my findings, and seeing that the Gila monsters and tegu lizards were dying off young, I switched them off their diet of cat food mixed with egg yolk. Perhaps they were gaining too fast. I tried them on whole mice, but they wouldn't eat that. It was only when I chopped up the mice to the same consistency as the food they were used to, and dribbled egg yolk on top, that they took to it. Then they began to eat really well. Simple," says Demeter, his eyes lively, amused. "But it took me some time to think of it and work it out. Reptile husbandry is often a touch and go thing, but by writing down my successes and failures I figured it maybe wouldn't take me three months to get a Gila monster to eat the next time."

Some of Demeter's findings, on how to induce "herps" to feed and breed, go into a column he writes called RAP (Reptile Amphibian Potpourri) for the newsletter of the American Association of Zoo Keepers (he is a board member). "It's just more difficult to breed lizards than other reptiles, because so little is known about them," he says. "It's no big deal to breed pythons. No big deal to breed giant day geckos either, with healthy specimens from the wild. But it is unusual to breed them, as the Zoo does here, into the second generation."

The close watch on diet helps with the successful breeding. So does Demeter's watch on the animals' weight. Tuesday afternoons he gives his meat-eating lizards their weekly feeding of the suckling mice, called pinks. Opening the cages along the lizards' line, he offers some of the pinks by hand, others by long tweezers; still others he throws, fast, to the Jamaican anole, a known escape artist.

The baby leopard geckos, not yet a year old, need their pinks cut up. The adults, gravid females about to lay eggs, haven't much appetite. Nor does the male Gila monster, which hasn't eaten for a month. Demeter removes the female from the cage to let him take his time over his meal. On down the line, the water dragons manage the pinks nicely. He hears them crunch the bones. The three European glass lizards he calls "pigs" for taking two pinks at a time, but he kindly leaves them a dozen, and nine for the Salvador's monitor, a dramatic-looking New Guinea tree crocodile with bright green dots, which gorges at one meal and then fasts for a week. Demeter weighs the monitor in the scale's metal pan, where it twitches about with a sound like popping corn. In the 30 months since he got it as a juvenile it has gained weight, from 68 to 247 grams.

At the sink Demeter mixes up a quick batch of food supplement — calcium, vitamin D-3, touches of honey, molasses, yeast. It's the closest he can duplicate the nutrients lizards get by licking sap out of acacia trees. As a general pick-me-up it may keep gecko bones from going soft, especially while the geckos are producing hard-shelled eggs.

Twice weekly Demeter feeds crickets to the insect-eating lizards, and coats the crickets with a vitamin-mineral mixture, too. The twice-a-week salads for the grass-eaters — of kale, oranges, apples, sweet potatoes, bananas — he sometimes fortifies with cut-up hard-boiled eggs, including shells.

Demeter records behavior regularly — vocalizations like clicks, chirps, and barks. He lists movements during courtship like "lateral head swaying" or "tongue flicking." If something special seems to be happening he calls down Dale Marcellini, research curator in reptiles, who has advanced degrees in zoology and whose office is just above the lizards' line. Together they film and tape interactions — "like if the gliding geckos are doing some weird movement I haven't

seen before, waving their tails over their backs or the male approaching with a jerky motion, rubbing his nose along the red streak between the female's eye and nostril." Demeter laughs. "It sounds absolutely insignificant, but these animals may be close to extinction and every little thing we can learn may help us to get new generations of them.

"Curators can't know all there is about the collection. Sometimes you just have to dig a lot to find the key to breeding." He and the curator still have to learn how many lizards can be put in a cage, and what proportion of males to females. Lacking data on the number of eggs one female lays in the wild, they think it "prudent" to limit a female's egg-laying to once a year, so that she replaces her calcium and continues to reproduce over a four-year period.

Demeter's day begins with the traditional keeper chores of sweeping the floor and cleaning the glass. He inspects down the front of his line as visitors would see it. Then he works the line behind the scene with a disinfectant bucket and a long spoon for removing feces. He cleans the cage walls, scrubs the rocks, bleaches the pools where they've grown algae. He checks the sand and looks in the hollows for eggs — which he takes.

Leaving eggs in the cage is not too successful, he has found, because the cage may not be moist enough. Eggs tend to do better in damp sand or gravel in a heated aquarium. Demeter writes detailed notes about collapsed, poorly calcified eggs as he finds them. Pairs of perfect specimens laid by his geckos he calls "beautiful, terrific" eggs.

Working the line, he handles each animal, noting signs like bad color or a limp or sluggish behavior, raspy breathing, bubbles from the nostrils. If the blue-tongued skink is off its feed, he takes a fecal sample and sends it to the lab. If the vet prescribes worming medicine, Demeter does the worming and follows up two weeks later with another sample. If the animal isn't feeding at all, he may have to forcefeed it with a premature-baby feeding tube and perhaps send it to the hospital for X-ray.

Afternoons Demeter works on his cages. He digs gravel and decorates — which he considers important. "Lizards need more than water and a rock on which to shed their skin. Some, like the gliding geckos, need a lot of visual cover. They freak out if they don't have barriers. They're distressed. Attack each other. The barriers give them security, a place for the female to hide. And the public needs to get an idea of the environment, whether rain forest or desert. You don't find herps out on a piece of newspaper or on a rug. You look under logs for them. They're very secretive."

Then there's the paperwork — all the records to keep. Demeter says he doesn't think of his charges by their five-digit numbers as he has them on the charts. He tells one from another by the way the toes have been clipped (differently, for identification purposes) — Number Seven having the seventh of its 20 toes clipped. Or he tells them by the different scaling on the tails. Or he keeps the hierarchy in mind, thinking of the most aggressive female as Number One, the next Two, then Three. "I don't think of them by names," he says. "I like them a lot but they aren't people."

LUCILE ST. HOYME
Physical Anthropologist

Lucile St. Hoyme, physical anthropologist, makes a quick circuit of her lab, her long skirts swishing about her and her ponytail bobbing. "People think bones are cold and hard and silent. They say how can a lively person spend a lifetime on bones?" She taps a fibula here, a few femurs there, with her ballpoint pen, getting a thud from a bone that was never buried, a twang from ones that were, and a fine chinking ring from a knobby specimen that, from the sound of it, must have been buried close to the sea. "Silent, indeed! The sound of bones, like their smell, feel, even sometimes their taste (I run a moist fingertip along their surface) is a clue in the great game of sleuthing we play as physical anthropologists."

St. Hoyme was 17 when she began work in 1944 as a typist in the very office where she now conducts her research. "I was hooked within weeks," she says, her cherub face beaming behind spectacles. "I still have the first building pass I was issued then. The picture on it is of a grim, humorless-looking girl. I was completely lacking in high school biology, unprepared for work in anthropology except by my early exposure to cultural differences—I grew up in an Irish, Italian, Greek, and Jewish neighborhood, with blacks nearby, in Washington. I was allowed to play with anyone I chose, that was the important thing. I did wonder why, if ancient Romans spoke Latin, why the family next door, who came from Rome, spoke Italian."

St. Hoyme doesn't think the 13 years at the typewriter were at all wasted. "I'd never thought about where books come from, but here I was, typing a book which began with someone's looking at a bunch of bones on a table. The shock of discovering books were written by people has never worn off. And from that typing over the years, I got an idea of what constitutes good research and reporting, and what is rubbish." During this period she spent her nights on work for degrees and her summers in digging up skeletons. "People may think the study of archaeology is romantic. But there's something about digging with a six-foot shovel in a ten-foot-square hole in July on a treeless farm in North Dakota that dispelled any remnant of that notion, as far as I was concerned." St. Hoyme went on to get her doctorate from Oxford University, working on pelvic bones. "One assumes they grow uniformly, the way a picture of Mickey Mouse on a balloon expands as the balloon is blown up. Actually, the growth after adolescence is at certain growing points."

Now St. Hoyme works in her office and lab, and in the skull stacks (the library of skulls) right outside her door. Her movements are brisk as she pushes a ten-foot platform ladder on wheels, gathering up the specimens she wants. The stacks are impressive in extent—aisles of row on row gray drawers, fourteen drawers high, containing a reference collection of about 27,000 skulls. Climbing the rolling stepladder nimbly (she wears Keds at work), and standing on the top step to talk, St. Hoyme hauls out a 40-pound drawer. Reaching overhead, she extracts in a wide-fingered grip one skull that she places under her arm, another for her left hand, and a third for the right.

The lab where she conducts skull examinations is sunny, cluttered, with green leafiness at the window boxes and a pleasant jumble of teacups — and the occasional skull — in the sink. The room is busy with traffic, with students taking measurements of XII Dynasty Egyptian leg bones. There's the click of a camera, the tap-tap of calculators, a gentle domino-clatter of bone against bone. "Museum people learn to concentrate in a hoorah ... no matter what is going on," says St. Hoyme. "The mother who has raised ten children would fit right in here."

St. Hoyme works rapidly, turning and tilting a skull to observe brow, chin, mastoid form, all of which tell her its sex, and the fusion of sutures that tells its age. She records the number of missing teeth, the numbers and severity of cavities, and the crown-height measurements which she gets with her calipers. It's part of a dental study she's busy with — of four prehistoric American Indian societies. In fact, she has opened up a whole new field — dental anthropology. And it is presenting the first evidence that there is a significant sex difference in dental disease. "You could almost assume there would be," she says, "since there was a division of labor by sex in most groups and with it would go a difference in diet. Women and children may have collected berries and nuts, while the men hunted game. There would also be another kind of sex difference due to hormones."

She has also found that regional differences show up in teeth. "The enamel of teeth is the only part of the body at age 70 that was there at age four. Everything else has been replaced. The enamel will reflect what you were doing at the age it was deposited — what minerals you got from the water you drank and the plants you ate." From analyses for 11 minerals in samples of tooth enamel, she is finding very clear, definite variants by region. "That will be a fantastic tool for archaeologists, who will be able to plot the movements of populations by this kind of analysis. It's wild," she says, explaining that she finds quite different results from her Southern Illinois Indians and her Potomac Indians. "Most of the tribes got their wives from some place else. By the tooth enamel we can tell from where — or anyway make some astute guesses backed up by other evidence like pottery and such."

It took four years for St. Hoyme to decide how to take records and what to record. "It sounds dull and stupid to take that long, but otherwise at the end you'll find you recorded garbage. Then it took a long time to pick the right Indian populations to work with — ones for which we have enough skulls. We wound up with four. Then we sat down and took observations and spent hours punching cards and taking the bugs out of the computer deck and going over and over the stacks of printouts to make head or tail of them. You can never predict where your pay dirt is going to be. We've been ten years at it, my dentist collaborator and I," she says, grinning, "and, you'll pardon the expression, it's been like pulling teeth."

One of the surprising finds St. Hoyme made along the way was a jawbone from A.D. 600, containing the first known example — by 1,000 years — of fillings. The tooth cavities were filled with a creamy cement of, by her guess, crushed fish bone. She had only the jawbone, the left humerus and the right clavicle from that skeleton, clues enough, though, to indicate that the individual with the fillings was a woman, five foot three inches in height, and 35 to 40 years old when she died.

In the same way St. Hoyme can riffle through a box of what looks like bony odds and ends and describe a whole community — what its supply of game and fish would have been, its infant mortality rate, its adult illnesses. Her assurance in making these statements comes from years of han-

dling bones — washing mountains of them as they come in to the museum from the field, mending them, and inscribing them with six-digit accession numbers.

It was the kind of unhurried apprenticeship, she says, that built a mental file for her of thousands of remembered bones against which she automatically measures any single bone today. "It was as a technician that I acquired 90 percent of my expertise," she says. "Technicians who keep their minds open and their wits about them know far more than the college student who hasn't handled bones. It's a bad thing to put too much emphasis on formal work in class."

Though she claims she still has a third of the 6,000 skull drawers to investigate, St. Hoyme gives whirlwind tours through the skull stacks for visitors. She brings out Pueblo Indian skulls deformed by cradleboards, also flat-foreheaded Flatheads, and New Guinean skulls that are decorated all over and have cowrie-shell eyes. For medical and dental researchers she finds evidence of diseases they want to see.

Like all Smithsonian scientists St. Hoyme is at the disposal of the telephoning public. Farmers or construction workers call to find out whether they have hit on a prehistoric find or the remnants of someone's barbecue. Students and parents call about science fair projects. "Mummy transmitting junior's question usually gets it all mixed up. I tell her: have junior call me himself. If he's in sixth grade he probably wants me to send everything I have on evolution. A high school senior narrows it to evolution of the brain. When

I'm asked about the evolution of the hand in catarrhines then I know I've got someone who's serious."

Some questions are practical. They come from people designing seatbelts or baby caps who need measurements. Some are to settle bets over whose skull is the thickest. "I wind up by telling them an adult white male has a skull five times thicker than a gorilla's."

About once a week cardboard cartons of bones arrive at the lab for identification. They're carried over by an agent from the FBI across the street. A Perry Mason fan, St. Hoyme rather enjoys helping with that chore. Forensic osteology it's called — the kind of detective work which enables someone to say of a given skeleton from a roadside ditch: this is a girl, white, under 20, a homicide victim, and, to judge from the quality of dental work, more likely a local farmgirl than a hitchhiking college girl.

St. Hoyme once testified in a Montana court that the bones in the pocket of an admitted cannibal were indeed the finger bones of a victim. She also remembers when a small skeleton found in a bag on a riverbank was brought to her. The police were suspecting kidnapping and murder. "It arrived with each bone wrapped separately in yards and yards of toilet paper. We unwrapped juvenile rib after rib after rib, then forearm bones. They didn't look quite right. Then we unwrapped what seemed like millions of vertebrae and short arm and leg bones. Only then at last came a canine jaw. We decided it belonged to a dachshund."

By now the FBI is so used to calls about child mutilators during the hunting season that it doesn't even bring around the spare bear paws it gets. Hunters, St. Hoyme explains, toss away bear feet in people's garbage cans as they pass by, and the panicked homeowners conclude someone has been murdering children. "The dead giveaway is that the 'big toe' on a bear is the shortest and the 'little toe' is the longest, so the right hind foot of a bear looks like a left foot on a right leg."

As new boxes arrive from the FBI, the students in the

lab egg her on, and often St. Hoyme gives in to the temptation to sort through the contents right away. On one occasion they turned out to be bleached bones, but lacking a skull. A monkey? queried one student. But a very un-monkeylike elbow, replied St. Hoyme. Sheep? Goat? Could be, but for the foot bones, and she lined them up in her hand. "Perhaps," she said, "a very large dog. In any case, not human. Not a murder. We can tell them that much."

To students and volunteers in the museum St. Hoyme tries to communicate both the "enormous excitement" of her work and the "enormous amount of scut work and drudgery." That's pretty much the message, too, of her colleagues, up and down the neighboring corridors—such as an anthropologist who, for example, found his first arrowhead in Wyoming at age six, had a collection of 200 at age seven, was attending historical society meetings at age ten, and soon after was assisting university professors on summer digs. Today he goes to bison kill sites, teaching himself ancient butchering techniques by studying the bones he finds and by making his own tools with which to hunt, kill, and skin.

Another neighbor down the hall is sorting through 20,000 prehistoric animal bones, determining for each bone whether it is from a sheep or a goat, a male or a female, and of what age. He talks about the excitement of the work combined with the tedium and unpleasant conditions. His evidence—that the huge majority of the animals used for food are young males—is pushing back the date for the start of domestication of animals by something like 6,000 years.

"My basic technique with students," says St. Hoyme, "is to say, 'Here is a bone. Explain it. Don't give me philosophy or poetry. Give me evidence that can be poked or prodded, looked at or sniffed. Theories change every five years. If you concentrate on the evidence and not on interpretation you can change with the times.' "

At her home St. Hoyme does her own carpentry. She repairs her own appliances. She creates the copper jewelry she wears in abundance along with a watch and a chain of keys around her neck. It annoys her to see women discriminated against in science. It annoys her that women scientists have often been taken on field trips only to do the boring camp chores. She has done field work in the Caribbean, in Poland, and most recently in Ethiopia, where she was measuring heads and shining a flashlight into mouths to examine teeth. Earlier, though, when she found it hard to get such assignments, she set up her own field study at home — on a free society of cats, documenting their litters and their shared kitten care. She learned a lot, but when the numbers reached 70, her neighbors complained. St. Hoyme is down now to six adult cats, which get special treats from her on Sundays served from a silver spoon.

"I just can't help questioning," she says blandly, "why a skull has to be called Zinjanthropus *man*. From the fragments we have there is no telling if it's man or woman. Minnesota *man*," she adds, implying that anybody should know it, "is a teenage girl."

 ## TOM SIMKIN

Geologist-Volcanologist

On a January morning in 1973 museum volcanologist Tom Simkin was airborne over Iceland, circling the roaring crater erupting below and the endangered village of Heimaey close by it. By afternoon he stood at a prime viewing point on high ground. "It was an awesome display," he says now, describing the fountain of fire, the pulsating din, the spill-over of lava burying farmland and threatening to seal off the fishing harbor. "Awesome to absorb and to document, and yet not unlike a winter campfire where you toast in front and freeze behind."

It wasn't intuition or some finely tuned sensing apparatus in the museum that alerted Simkin to the blast thundering up through a mile-long rift the night before. He read about it in his morning's Washington *Post*. Following a race to the airport ("the greatest hazard as far as my work's concerned") he was on his way. All the next afternoon, until nine at night when the wind swung around and began depositing ashfall on the town, he was absorbing the spectacle, filming it, taping the roar, that sounds like nothing else on earth, and shouting his field notes into a recording machine.

Throughout that night he collected specimens of falling ash and cinders from village streets. He sieved and weighed them and measured their accumulation. Cinders pinged on his hardhat and crunched underfoot. And in the deserted streets of early morning they piled up like black snow against the buildings. Some were removed with snow-removal equipment. A long 24 hours after his arrival in Heimaey he was being evacuated by boat along with other scientists. "I looked back and saw first one home and then another catch fire."

Simkin is always prepared to fly at the shortest notice to places like Iceland, or to the island of Fernandina in the Galapagos, places apt to have the kind of spectacular geophysical "happenings" that interest him. He shows a photograph of himself digging on Fernandina, with mockingbirds perched on his hat. "Here I am," he says, "back in the sandbox after 22 years of formal education." In the photograph Simkin, 42, bushy-bearded and ponytailed, is digging out a 13-ton boulder. He did it, he explains, to estimate from its weight the force of the eruption that had projected it more than 2,000 feet into the air.

Simkin is a Smithsonian curator of petrology ("that's rocks not oil") and volcanology. He arrived at the Galapagos volcano in July, 1968, some weeks following the major eruption but before the dust had settled from the collapse of Fernandina's big caldera, the round depression at the volcano's top. In this case, after the volcano blew, the caldera floor dropped more than 1,000 feet. Simkin and his wife, a high school math teacher, reached the rim of the crater as avalanches were still sending down great rumbling, grinding rock slides. "And some of the rocks were the size of houses."

The inner slopes of the crater which had been thickly

vegetated, the habitat for numbers of animals including the crested lizards called iguanas, were covered with rock and ash. The lake had shifted from one corner to another of the caldera floor. In a lecture which Simkin gave on his return called "Can Thousands of Nervous Iguanas Find Happiness on an Unquiet Mountain?", he explained that the reason for the special "unquiet" at Fernandina was that the island is new—spewed up from the ocean probably within the last few million years—and that it is located near where three of the tectonic plates of the earth's crust are drawing apart.

On a return visit two years later Simkin and his wife made a survey of the altered lake, finding that the volume of water had increased ten times. "Because we backpacked our gear for two days to the lake, we used the world's lightest hydrographic survey kit—an inflated raft and a marked nylon cord to which we tied a rock. I paddled a straight course on a marked range and took the soundings, which I signaled to Sharon with wags of the paddle. She was seated 400 feet up, on rock, watching me through binoculars. She took compass bearings to locate my position and wrote down the depth."

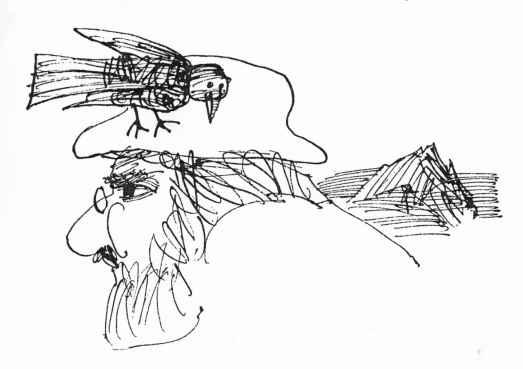

The lake, he remembers, looked better than it tasted. "It mixed disastrously with our dehydrated minestrone, with just about everything we had, in fact, except the butterscotch pudding." Walking on volcanoes has its hazards, too. "Ash is pleasant underfoot. It's even pleasant when you're hiking through the water-cut gullies in 30-foot piles of it. It's like being in an alley. But blocky lava terrain you never get used to. It can be like a loose cinder pile where the cinders are from snowball to snowman size. You're always fighting for your balance and when you fall it's hard stuff to land on. It's hard on your boots. One geologist in our group wound up walking down the mountain on his notebook covers."

Camping on the rim of the volcano itself is grim and gritty, unsettling with the sound of rock slides. By contrast, camping on the island's coast is breeze-cooled and pleasant, with views of cormorants and pelicans and scarlet Sally Lightfoot crabs, scrambling over black rock. "Penguins woke us in the early morning with their barking."

Simkin always counts it a hardship to return from the field to the steaming heat of Washington, even if his trip took him to the equator. The Galapagos is surprisingly cool. But satisfying open-air exertions like digging up a boulder or making field notes with mockingbirds perched on head or notebook are just one aspect of a volcanologist's work. Ten and eleven months of the year lab and office chores keep Simkin in the Natural History Museum.

He has a collection to help curate — 100,000 rocks, for which he's computerizing all the data. He also uses the computer in compiling a directory and history of all the world's active volcanoes, and in the analytical lab work of his research. One recent report describing less than a thimbleful of Apollo 16 material yielded a yard-high stack of computer cards with the analyses of its contents. He used an electron microprobe for the work. With this device it is possible to measure nine elements in ten seconds on a spot so small that 1,000 adjacent analyses can be made across a one-millimeter grain.

Part of Simkin's job is also to insert some geology into the museum's exhibits. He wants to remind visitors in as many ways as possible that "man's arrival on earth is the most recent one thousandth part of earth's history. On a 30-foot timeline, it shows as the latest one-sixth of an inch." To dramatize this, he exhibits vertebrae and sharks' teeth to show that Washington was under the sea 20 million years ago, and a dinosaur footprint to show that dinosaurs "walked the streets of the Capital 200 million years ago, at a time when our continent was still connected with Africa."

Simkin monitors volcano activity in distant parts of the globe—like Cotopaxi volcano on the crest of the Andes. Friends in Ecuador alerted him in September, 1975, that it was heating up. He kept track as it increased in vapor plumes and in tremors, knowing from its history that the 33 years since its last eruption was an unusually long period of repose. Before that there had been activity every five or ten years.

"It did look as though something were going to hap pen." Simkin says he tried to see that the people wh help the most were doing the right things. "We sent a seismograph to Ecuador—to act as a stethoscope on the heart of the patient. It was kind of a sobering experience," he recalls, "since Cotopaxi has kicked out volcanic mud flows in the past which have gone roaring down the mountainside and kept flowing on across the fertile, populated valley. In 1877 mud flows did substantial damage for 70 miles and killed several hundred people. Probably ten times as many people are living there today. It was a threat."

Simkin also beat the drum, he says, to get a U.S. Geological Survey team of volcano disaster specialists to go down there. As it happened, Cotopaxi didn't erupt, though another nearby volcano—Reventador—did. The team left behind its volcano risk maps, so that local authorities would have plans to go on the next time Cotopaxi heated up.

Simkin's interest in geology dates from the years he spent in the Northwest working for the U.S. Coast and Geodetic Survey. He came to know the Cascade Mountains in those years as well as the geologists who climbed them. Before that he'd been an engineering student at Swarthmore College, where, he says, few of his courses distracted him significantly from football and lacrosse. Later he went to Princeton for advanced degrees in geology and he worked on the ancient volcano that is on the Scottish island of Skye for his PhD dissertation.

These days he keeps in shape by bicycling to and from work at the Smithsonian. And his preferred recreation away from a volcano's roar is listening to rock music played by the likes of the Grateful Dead, Little Feat, and the Rolling Stones.

 ## FAROUK EL-BAZ
Moon Geologist

"What we've learned from going into space—that's what I'm here to find out," says Farouk El-Baz, moon geologist in charge of the Center for Earth and Planetary Studies at the new National Air and Space Museum. Through the years of the Apollo programs, El-Baz trained the astronauts in geology, photography, and visual observation—showed them how and where to photograph and how to describe what they saw.

A visitor to his office today finds him scrutinizing a filmstrip from the Apollo-Soyuz (American-Russian) Test Project, which photographed the earth from its orbit in space. Looking like someone at a penny arcade, El-Baz bends over a machine to peer at the strip of photographs he is hand-cranking into motion. Glasses discarded, his eyes practically touch against the zoom stereoscope, as he cranks jerkily along until he reaches the frame he is looking for. Not the barrier reefs off Australia. One more twirl and he comes to it. "Ah, here, Lake Chad to Egypt." He points out the distinction between red desert and yellow desert, the red being the old, the yellow young, with dunes. From the shape of these dunes, El-Baz demonstrates which way the desert is moving, building up within the lake, taking it over.

In his brightly colored offices, in big black cans and in albums and drawers, El-Baz stores a complete collection of the film shot from space. He has a staff of nine, referred to in the museum as "El-Baz's harem" because seven of its members are women, among them three geologists. He has also a team of 40 specialists from the United States and elsewhere helping him study every aspect of the pictures. Much has already been discovered from them, about the advance of the deserts, the drainage patterns of snow cover, the movement of land masses and of tides and ocean currents. So much that El-Baz talks in a torrent, his face, with eyeglasses resettled, animated with pleasure he seems scarcely able to contain. He waves his hands in frustration, trying to conjure up a description of the photographs in his care. In spite of his scientific training in his native Cairo, and Germany, with advanced degrees from the Missouri School of Mines and Massachusetts Institute of Technology, he settles for just what a layman or a child would say: "They're fantastic!"

The most significant findings from the pictures, he thinks, are related to the deserts. "Before Apollo-Soyuz I thought they were relatively simple geologic features. Gee whiz, they're not! We know very little about them. We don't know how they were formed, how to account for the different kinds of dunes. Now at least we can assign an age to them, because from the weathering of the iron we know that the older the desert is, the redder it becomes. From the pic-

tures we can map the zones of desert growth. The shape of the dunes tells the exact direction. It could mean a lot for countries stricken by drought and desert growth to be able to plan ahead accordingly."

From his desk drawer El-Baz pulls out a color wheel he devised for the astronauts — a color doughnut he calls it — with 54 colors for the deserts on one side, and 54 for the oceans on the other. "Even the best color film isn't entirely accurate. With this, the numbers recorded by the astronauts can later be checked against the color processing of the pictures. Astronauts are very accurate," he adds, "twice as much so as the most highly sensitive photometer.

"We're learning about the oceans, too," he continues. "No one thought we could see currents from space, because it's water moving within water. But the temperatures give the currents different colors. The colder ones are loaded with nutrients, plankton, a lot of chlorophyll. They show up as definite green strips. We've known before that the Gulf Stream carries trash from New Orleans to England. Now we can map the exact lanes. That's important for shipping and for fishing.

"And we've found a weird ocean phenomenon called internal waves. We see the waves, twenty miles long and two or three miles across, not on the surface but down below. There are bands of these off Spain visible in a very dramatic way, and we're finding new locations, too."

The El-Baz team is making finds in hydrology. Pictures of the snow cover over the Himalayas and other mountain regions give an idea of the extent of snow. Drainage patterns can be mapped for use in planning irrigation and flood control. The team is making finds in meteorology. Apollo-Soyuz flew over one developing storm, over Florida, and one dissipating storm over the Atlantic. "We're clueing in to the shapes of storms, the topography of clouds within them. The eye of a storm, for example, is turning out to be a cone, not a cylinder."

El-Baz and his staff are making finds in geology. "We

used to think of the Red Sea rift as the result of a rip-apart motion with the ground ripping away where tectonic plates migrated apart. Now look—here and here and here—from the forks of these three fractures we believe there has been a rotating motion, anticlockwise, from a point in the Syrian mountains. The tension created by the motion has something to do with earthquakes developing in the Middle East." He illustrates the effect by shoving a piece of notebook paper into a pileup of folds.

Perhaps most exciting to El-Baz is what has been learned from photographs of the moon itself. When El-Baz lectures from time to time on the moon photographs he lines up his wife and four little daughters in the front row—to cheer him on, he says, in case no one else comes. His precautions aren't necessary. Non-scientists have discovered that this scientist is remarkably eager to make complex material understandable. And he's good at it. His opener is to say: "People with good eyesight or access to a telescope have for centuries observed dark and light areas on the moon. Now we have sent six missions and 12 astronauts. They have brought back black rocks and white rocks. And, lo and behold, what do we know? We know there are dark areas and light areas on the moon. And we're also beginning to understand why."

He clearly knows a lot more that he is brimming over to show and tell, though in a fashion that is comforting to the layman he continues to refer to the left eye and the right eye of the man in the moon. Audiences come away having seen on his pictures the little lunar golfcart, called the Rover, not more than six feet long, and its tracks, taken by a camera that was 70 miles above. They come away knowing, at least momentarily, that the white areas surrounding the dark basins (the eyes) are older material, the product of impact craters, composed of rocks high in aluminum. They know that the near side of the moon has a lot of dark material; the far side, very little. They hear that the moon isn't a perfect sphere. The near side is depressed by two miles; the far side is higher and rougher.

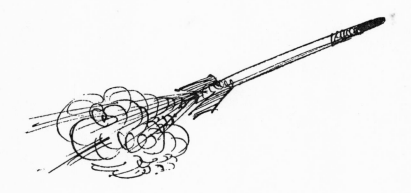

"It's all important to us," says El-Baz, "because we can use the moon as a window on the early history of our earth. There's nothing weird about it. They're very similar. The earth and the moon must have formed at the same time from the same chemical elements and evolved with much the same volcanic episodes. The difference is that the moon stopped evolving three million years ago, while the earth keeps changing. Down here we don't have a single rock dating back to the time when the earth was formed. We have all new young features. To pick up our early history we have to go to the moon, where the internal engine has died. From there we can begin to interpret the things we're seeing on Mars, Mercury, Venus. Comparative planetology is what we'll be involved in next."

Mapping the moon and assigning names to its features are ongoing duties for El-Baz, along with photo interpretation. To help him he has designated one of his researchers as a toponymist. He laughs but adds, "It's in the dictionary. Well, toponymy is (it's the study of place names). Toponymist Anne Adams never expected to become that or to attend meetings on lunar nomenclature.

"A person really qualified for my job wouldn't be interested in it," she says. She, on the other hand, is. An English student who left college without a degree, Adams is learning as she goes along the geology, the photo interpretation, the science history, and the computer skills she needs in her work. "Plus I'm doing just a lot of checking to make sure we don't duplicate our crater names."

There were some 1,400 names on the moon before she began her lists—a bank compiled from earlier maps. Some date from Johannes Hevelius, who in 1647 mapped the moon as a mirror image of the earth—the boot of Italy here, the Alps there, and Constantinople yonder. Some date from 1651, when Giovanni Riccioli named moon features after illustrious persons, many of them his contemporaries. By 1976 the moon had 2,000 names on it. Sixty were added in 1964, in the extreme limb regions, the very outside edges of the near side of the moon. These include the craters named for Goddard (Robert), the father of rocketry, and Bohr (Nils), the atomic physicist. Five hundred were added in 1971, after the far side of the moon, which is peppered with craters, was photographed. That's when craters were named for the cosmonauts and the astronauts, for Bell (Alexander Graham), for Carver (George Washington), for Mendel (Gregor), Marconi (Guglielmo), and Pavlov (Ivan).

"A myriad more could be added, but I rather hope they won't be. We want to keep the moon from becoming cluttered," says Adams.

Based on some ground rules set up in Sydney in 1973, people from politics, the military, or religion can't have craters named for them. That's why Franklin (Ben) is a moon crater. And Edison (Thomas). But George Washington is not, DeGaulle is not, Lenin is not. Writers Longfellow, Balzac, and Tolstoy got on the moon that year, at least tentatively, but Adams is confining her candidates to scientists, dead scientists, to fill out the roster that began with Archimedes, Copernicus, Galileo, and Paracelsus, and moved along to such a modern figure as Einstein. One of the few living scientists whose name went on the moon was the Smithsonian's fifth Secretary, Charles Greeley Abbot, now dead, who had a crater named for him when he was 100.

Adams seeks out possible people to honor by going

through physics and astronomy journals and Polish and Russian encyclopedias. She has made a file of biographies to go with the current list. Some of the recent names can be a puzzle. "Which Stewart do they mean? Which Banerji?" she asks. She takes special interest in some of the women on the moon. There's Sklodowska crater for Madame Marie Curie. (Her maiden name was used to distinguish her crater from the Curie crater, honoring her husband, and the Joliot crater for her son.) There's Hypatia crater for a female Alexandrian mathematician, and Clerke crater for Mary Agnes Clerke, an Irish astronomer. According to Adams, the craters on Venus will probably have women's names. Those larger than 100 kilometers across will have names drawn from mythology; the smaller ones will have names like Maud and Agnes and Anne.

Since no one has yet given her interplanetary toponymy duties, Adams hasn't begun listing goddesses for Venus, or classical figures for Mars, or artists, writers, and musicians for Mercury. She figures she has her hands filled with the moon. As part of her duties she prepares moon maps for NASA. Working from big muddy-brown photo-mosaics, she lines up two pictures of an overlapping territory under a stereoscope and then outlines the features on a plastic overlay and transfers her markings and names onto a worksheet. New craters are very distinct, she says, but old ones, more eroded, might be missed if it weren't for the three-dimensional effect of the stereoscope.

For purposes of mapping the moon has been cut up into bands, she explains, like the peel of an orange — into 144 regions more or less equal in area. Each region, named for its most prominent feature, is divided into 16 provinces and each province into A,B,C,D. Adams can't map all 144 regions because she has to work from straight-down photographs, which exist for only 20 percent of the moon's surface. Oblique photographs won't do because of the perspective problem. And she can't proceed by numerical order because scientists with urgent needs for information assign priorities for the mapping.

Since 1974, when she began, Adams has mapped, among others, all of Region 102, named Gagarin; all of 101, named Fermi; much of 66, Mendeleev; much of 82, Pasteur. She is mapping regions which include in their boundaries the landing sites for Apollo missions. Region 41, where Apollo 15 landed, near Rima Hadley, is named Montes Apenninus for the mountain chain bordering Mare Imbrium (Sea of Rains). Region 78, where Apollo 16 landed, is named Theophilus after a fourth-century astronomer-bishop, and Region 43 between Mare Serenitatis and Mare Tranquilitatis, where Apollo 17 landed, is called Macrobius after the fourth-century grammarian who wrote about the moon, sun, planets, and the Milky Way.

Toponymy is indeed an education for her, says Adams. She approves of the international decision to retain the Latin names for geographic features, which date from the time when the dark portions of the moon were taken to be water. Thus there will still be the large ocean called Oceanus, the seas (Maria), the valleys (Valles), rilles (Rimae), mountains (Montes). In future, humps will be called Dorsa and crater chains Catenae.

"A rose is a rose is a rose to me," Adams says. "I'm really not that concerned with whose names go on. I'm much more concerned that we have a logical and consistent scheme which is simple and clear to the users." Names assigned by the moon-walkers themselves have to be incorporated into the scheme. Astronauts from Apollos 11 through 17 have added such names as Snowman, Old Nameless, Weird, St. George, Spot, Gator, Baby Ray, Cochise, Tortilla Flat, Spook, Stubby, and Bear Mountain. Though they are still pretty bewildering to Adams, they are as familiar to El-Baz as the street names of Washington. He intends to get to know them even better by checking them out at firsthand.

Cheerfully, his voice permitting no contradiction, El-

Baz says, "I am going to the moon whether *they* know it or not." No one on his staff doubts that he will, though not one, including toponymist Adams, expects to tag along.

 ## AL EFTINK
Special Effects Man for the Spacearium

"It helps to be an amateur astronomer," says Al (for Aloysius) Eftink, who is in charge of special effects for the Albert Einstein Spacearium shows in the Air and Space Museum. "Beyond that you just have to be electrically, electronically, optically, mechanically inclined. And you have to keep up with your housework, lubricating the big projector, checking the gearing when a planet seems to fade too fast, cleaning the lenses so that a clot of dust doesn't erase a star."

Eftink makes it possible for a scriptwriter to write directions like these: put up the stars, make Saturn and rings arise, show Pioneer II approaching Jupiter as seen from Jupiter's moon Europa, show Pioneer II barely missing a collision with a giant rocky asteroid.

The stars are easy. Putting up 8,900 of them is standard work for a Zeiss Model VI planetarium projector like the one in the center of the 70-foot-in-diameter space theater. It throws the night sky onto the domed ceiling and lets sun, moon, planets, and stars play out their movements in speeded-up time. Showing the surface of Jupiter is another matter, though. It goes beyond what the planetarium instrument can do. So does simulating the view from a spacecraft, especially when the spacecraft has to zoom in on a planet and rotate as well. Al Eftink can do it all. He does it all the time. Building equipment to fit a scriptwriter's wild descriptions — or wildly windmilling arms — is even an agreeable challenge to him. "Putting script ideas onto the dome is my job."

For a single Spacearium show Eftink has 200 projectors set up in the projection cove around the circumference of the room. The projectors are out of sight, beaming out their special effects through a narrow slot under the dome. Twelve of them project a landscape 360 degrees around the rim of the dome, encircling the audience with a scene. One such scene is Boston harbor on a summer evening, 1776. Another is a farm in winter with snow on the fences. Others are the surface of Mars and the surface of the moon as a Mars-walker and a moon-walker would see them.

To set these scenes Eftink invented a distortion gig with which he photographed each landscape painted by an artist on twelve panels. "That way you get the image distorted on the film so that it's projected evenly for the viewer. You're compensating for the slope of the dome. Otherwise you get a keystone effect: the buildings and mountains look as though they are toppling in on you."

Eftink's 200 projectors are labeled with their functions, as described by the 200 diagram cards tacked up on the story board for the Spacearium's show. Each projector has its control box and switches below it. One projector, chalk-marked "Copernicus", puts up the sun with the planets circling around it. Others play out the cartoons — still projected onto the sky — of a spindly *Flyer* gliding through the air to make history at Kitty Hawk, the *Spirit of St. Louis* putt-putting to Paris, and Professor Goddard lofting a crude rocket. Still other projectors flash onto the sky the portraits of pioneers in rocketry and spaceflight. Or they send a beam of light across a galaxy. Or they demonstrate such concepts as pulsars and quasars and black holes.

Eftink has always been a tinkerer and good at it. As a boy in St. Louis, he rummaged through the neighborhood trash cans early Tuesday and Thursday mornings before the pickup, taking out clocks, radios, and sewing machines. He repaired them when he could and sold them. When he couldn't he broke them up for parts. After high school he studied electronics at a technical school, drove dump trucks for the city, and was a motor pool sergeant in the Army, where he serviced Company B's vehicles. Before coming to the Smithsonian he worked for planetariums in St. Louis and Hartford, Connecticut, where he learned his astronomy by having to sit through the shows over and over again.

Whenever the Spacearium show is on, Eftink has the sound piped into his shop, at low volume but audible enough to alert him to trouble. If something is out of synchronization he is at the source with a few strides. The time at a packed performance when the stars refused to come on, he managed to get them up manually, the whole skyful, including, he boasts, the Milky Way. It's what anyone would expect of a man who has never had a repairman in his home for anything—washing machine or furnace—and has never had a mechanic for any of his 100,000-mile cars.

Not everything Eftink does at his job is beyond the layman's understanding. It's reassuring to his co-workers that this big, jovial, optimistic, emphatic man with the oversized hands still creates some of his special effects with Christmas-tree light bulbs and coffee cans. But he buys parts now at sewing-machine shops instead of searching for them amongst the trash.

HERNAN OTANO

Electronics Specialist

A museum devoted to the air and space age was bound to feature radios crackling with pilot talk, hot-air balloons rising, films, pushbutton wind-tunnel experiments, sounds of shellfire and takeoffs and landings—all sorts of flashy effects that are invitations to malfunction and signs saying OUT OF ORDER. Two years before the National Air and Space Museum opened, Hernan Otano was hired—as chief of the audiovisual and electromechanical unit—to make the space-age exhibits possible and to keep them running. He did it by devising a system in which everything operates from one wire.

Otano is a quiet fellow, but quick, on the alert, with straight-line eyebrows that dart up and down as he talks. The

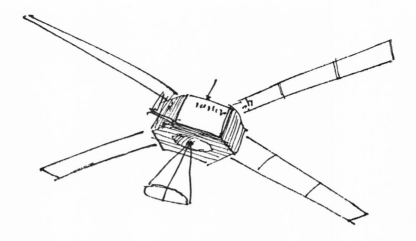

eyebrows are down, apologetically, when he gives the complex name for his system — "bi-directional multiplexing." They're up again as he explains, "It's just what we needed — keeps everything simple."

Otano pretty much thought up the system on a DC-10 flight from Washington to Los Angeles. "I was bored. I knew the DC-10 had multiplexing — so that lights, call buttons, audio all worked off a single wire. I took apart my seat to look for it and I found it." In California on the same trip he observed an experiment on bi-directional computer-control cable TV. "It demonstrates how you can push a button at home to buy things from a store, or to vote, or to give an alarm and get a response."

Putting these two systems together, he says, he came up with just what he wanted for NASM. Therefore he was able to install and operate everything the exhibitors dreamed up, and was ready for them to dream up more. He was able to light the airplanes, the spacecraft, the Skylab Orbital Workshop and to rig an alarm on the moon rock for alerting guards when someone not only touched but picked at it.

With a conventional hard-wire system, he would have had a whole bundle of wires, bigger — he indicates by reaching wide with his arms — than he could ever fit into the building's ducts. Instead, he is able to run everything off one wire, no bigger around than a toaster cord. And one console in a little basement room of this building (which is really a wired cable-TV city) monitors and controls it all — one gently bleeping console with pale lights and a steady tap-tap from its typewriter.

This console monitors and controls a dozen TV channels, hundreds of audio channels and projectors (except for the ones in the Spacearium). Second by second it taps out its report on what is happening with the equipment. A film has torn at 15:36:30 (3:36 P.M.) in gallery 107. A lamp has blown. A cockpit has gone dark. A puppet is out of synchronization. The sound has gone from Julia Child's cooking lesson on mixing Primordial Soup from cosmic elements.

The main problem isn't fixing exhibits when they break down, says Otano. That's easy. The main problem is knowing what went wrong in which far corner of the building and knowing it fast. Sometimes the repair is just a matter of substituting a back-up tape in the tape deck right in the control room. More often, Otano or a member of his crew — six men, one woman — must be off and away to the trouble site somewhere else.

The fixing goes quickly for them, since they installed the equipment in the first place. They put the circuitry in the puppets, synchronized the puppet movements with voices and with a slide-show projected over their heads to illuminate their thoughts. As a crew they rigged the heat element and blower under the hot-air balloon. They put the shellfire and flash and sound into the World War I hall. They mounted the 35-mm projectors (as big as ones used for drive-in movies) — one in the ceiling, one in a wall — to show fighter planes taking off and skidding in for landings on the primary flight deck of a Navy carrier.

During the time they are free from the ills that happen to a wire, Otano and his crew piece together new projects. Now they're working on an overflight sound for the forward airstrip near Verdun — the sound of planes buzzing the field — and another overflight sound for a squadron of B-17 bombers. They're also modifying equipment from Link training planes, to get flight simulators out in the exhibit hall, where the public can try its hand at flying.

Otano, who was in the Argentine Navy, came to the United States in 1959 and to the Smithsonian in 1973. He was at Cape Canaveral for the Apollo 11 launch. "It seems funny," he says, "that the Apollo 11 pilot, Michael Collins, should later have become director of this museum and that he should hire me. At that time I still thought museums meant dead insects on pins and curators at desks. Now I know a museum is a place where everyone pitches in to push a P-40 down the corridor.

"It's also a place where you wear out your running shoes," he adds. "Sure, you plan. I planned until six months before we opened. After that there was no more time to plan. I just ran." Slight and nimble, he still runs. When the walkie-talkie on his belt bleeps as he's racing, full-tilt forward, to visit a repair shop of ailing projectors, he pivots on a dime and makes it back, fast, to the control room.

E. J. THOMAS
Airplane Mechanic

"I didn't like the idea to start with—hanging planes," says airplane mechanic E. J. Thomas, who supervised the hanging of 21 planes in the great glass bays of the new National Air and Space Museum prior to its opening on July 1, 1976. "It didn't seem right to me. Planes have always been displayed on the floor. But now we've done it, I think it looks good. At night with the clouds forming outside and the lights on in the planes, you look up and you think: Hey, the Three really *is* flying—all those planes are flying."

The Three is special to Thomas—the Douglas DC-3. With its 95-foot wingspan it was the biggest of the airplanes to hang. It was the heaviest—17,500 pounds. It was the second one to go up, right after the tri-motor Ford, in the spacious pink marble and glass gallery—one of the three largest—with a 62-foot-high roof of plexiglass bubbles. "We brought the Three in at night," Thomas says, "at 2 A.M. when the Washington streets were empty. We retracted the wheels and towed it with the center section supported on a dolly. Rolling on its own wheels, it wouldn't have gone under the overpasses. We moved it into the building from the street on a path of timbers, assembled it on the floor — wings and tail — and picked it with the crane by special cables attached to pulleys on the overhead pipe trusswork. "Riggers always say 'picked,'" he explains, "rather than 'picked up.' It took three people on the floor to hold guide lines and three people in a cherry picker to tie it off. We picked it in a day, and the whole thing was finally cinched off in three days."

The particular DC-3 in the Smithsonian means a lot to Thomas because he was the last mechanic to service it when he worked for Eastern Airlines. That was in 1952. "The air frame of the Three had its maximum hours on it," Thomas recalls. "It was out of time, going to the boneyard with metal fatigue. I never dreamed then it would be in a museum. Never expected I'd be in a museum either." Now it pleases Thomas that his name was the last one on the DC-3's log book — he found it there — and that the log book is in a pocket in the cockpit, where it ought to be, to the left of the captain's seat.

Raised on a Maryland farm, Thomas went to a Washington high school, worked at a gas station, and when he was in his early twenties, applied for work at Eastern Airlines on the suggestion of one of his customers. "In those days you started out as water boy, believe me," Thomas remembers, "cleaning the windshield and greasing the propeller with a handgun." During World War II he signed up to take a mechanics apprentice program, got an aircraft and engine license, and was sent around the country by airlines to work in Miami, Detroit, Chicago. Thomas came to the Smithsonian in 1965 and became supervisor of the preservation and restoration shops for the airplanes. When the new building was up, he took on his new duties. "Anything that moved into our building," he says, "I saw that it was done in proper fashion."

Most of the big airplanes were brought in at night and

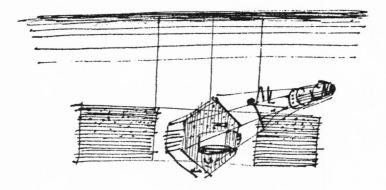

hung in the same way as the DC-3, though each presented a different set of problems. "You can't just put a chain around a plane and hoist it. No way! You have to know what the overhead trusswork will take and at what points. You have to know how much clearance you have. You have to know the pickup points on the plane. It's a question of matching the hard points on the roof with the hard points on the planes. Of course you've got blueprints to go by and you might have some notes you scratched to yourself. But the important thing is that you have it all figured in your head—how you're going to pick your plane, how high, how you're going to tie it off when you get it there."

Hanging the first plane in each bay is easy, he says. And the second. It gets harder with a roomful—like plotting the elements of a huge, nicely balanced mobile. Thomas's boss, Walter Boyne, the museum's curator of aeronautics, calls it "a challenge to rigging and to geometry." Hanging the Boeing 247-D in the Transportation Hall was such a challenge, not just because it was brought into the building on the night of a blinding rainstorm but because its cables had to be threaded past the bulky form of the DC-3.

The Pitcairn PA-5 *Mailwing*, one of six planes sharing the gallery with the DC-3 and the 247-D, was a "breeze" to hang—with clear space around it. Thomas took a special pleasure in hanging it because the pilot, John Toth, "was here with us when we raised it." Toth had flown the *Mailwing*—sitting on a packing crate—through 950 hours of crop-dusting. He had put in 400 straight days of restoration work on the plane to get it ready for the museum. "I serviced many a plane for him in the past when he was a test pilot," Thomas recalls. "He'd write up the squawks in the log book and I'd have to clear them. The *Mailwing* was an old sidekick for Toth. He put a lot of pains into it."

Hanging *Sputnik* was easy. The little satellite orbited by the Russians was empty and weighed only ten pounds. The *Spirit of St. Louis* at 2,000 pounds was easy, too. But the Wright brothers' Kitty Hawk *Flyer,* though it weighed a scant 300 pounds, was the most worrisome plane of the lot to hang. So old and fragile, it seemed to sing and moan at the slightest touch. "We couldn't push it into the building for fear of accordion-pleating it. The workmen had to make a box that fit it like a glove. We treated it with kid gloves, too, believe me. The *Flyer* is a one and only."

Moving the cylindrical Skylab into the building was easier than it looked. Skylab, where three teams of astronauts lived and worked for months, was "a lot of bulk but empty and not a lot of weight. We just lifted one section on top of another." The lunar module LEM, back-up for the one that landed astronauts on the moon, would have been easy, too, Thomas admits, "if it hadn't all been new to us and everything on it needed such a close fit. When we got into the job, though, we found it took only a few small special wrenches besides our standard tools."

Assembling *Soyuz* was the Russians' problem, not his. Thomas and his crew of riggers just sat back and watched as the *Soyuz* was assembled, identical to the Soviet spacecraft which docked with the American Apollo in 1975. "The Russian workers who came here used the same techniques we did, I didn't see anything different. It was frustrating not to have the same language. But they're used to working with their hands. And so are we. They'd measure something and gesture. And the funny thing is, we pretty much knew what they wanted."

Missiles were tricky. "We'd lay them flat on the floor, put cables on them, and then work the base down into our 15-foot-in-diameter well and set them up and bolt them to the floor. Jupiter-C misses the ceiling by inches." The riggers could hang the German V-1 buzz bomb, which Hitler launched against England. The larger V-2, which was built to reach America, they had to stand on the floor.

The X-15 rocket-propelled aircraft, which flew higher and faster than any other airplane in history, was awkward, heavy, and hard to hang. So was the D-558 Skyrocket. Anything that had to be maneuvered up through the stairwells to the balcony was extremely difficult. The gondola of the zeppelin *Hindenburg* (the replica of the gondola, that is, made by Universal Pictures) had to be lifted that way. So did the F-1 rocket engine from the Saturn booster.

"That F-1 was nine tons of dead weight. There was practically no overhead clearance. Because it's right up against the ceiling we couldn't use a crane. We had to use three chain block-and-falls. And then we had to attach the engine to a steel upright so it cantilevers out over mirrors to give the idea of a five-engine cluster. Of course we had diagrams to go by, for how they anchored the engines at Cape Canaveral before positioning them for a launch. But it was a challenge for us."

The pressure was off, for Thomas, once the installations were completed and the museum was open. There were always changes to be made, though, and new artifacts to hang. There was the Pioneer he had to put up—the prototype of the Pioneer which sent the first photographs of Jupiter back to earth. There was the Ranger, not the very one that transmitted TV pictures of the lunar surface (it crashed on the moon), but a Ranger made up of parts from test vehicles. There was—and always is—routine maintenance. Thomas regularly cruises the balcony, checking through field glasses for any changes in airplane position. He hasn't seen any, although planes move, he says, from 1/8 to 1/4 inch with temperature changes in the building. And the *Spirit of St. Louis* rocks a little every time the air-conditioner comes on. Every three months Thomas rolls along the bright blue carpet in a "cherry picker" (the same one used by the cleaning crew with their long-handled dusters). He's checking cables for stretch, and also checking the fittings.

A lot of visitors seek Thomas out. Some are riggers from the New Jersey company that was hired to hang the planes with him. Thomas, now 61, likes walking through the building with the men, admiring the handiwork in which they shared. He relives with them the late-night hauling of planes into the building during rainstorms. "It seems like 90 percent of the time we worked in bad weather," he recalls. "We talk about the awful suspense of moving the *Flyer*, quarter inch by quarter inch, all of us holding our breaths as it creaked. We were a genuine crew," he says.

4. People in the Arts

LYNDA HARTIGAN
Fine Arts Historian

The Throne of the Third Heaven of the Nations Millennium General Assembly is a bright, shining, surprising thing that fills an entire room — a kind of church setting of throne, pulpits, altar table, offertory tables, plaques, pedestals, all of them covered over in layer on layer of gold and silver tinfoil and embellished with a multitude of angel wings and crowns and orbs, foil-covered as well. Other embellishments are tiny writings, some in childlike capital letters, some in a secret-looking script, and the words FEAR NOT written, large, above the armchair part of the throne itself. When Lynda Hartigan started work at the Smithsonian's National Collection of Fine Arts in 1973 she chose the Throne as her research project. She was 23 years old. Through the next few years she studied it, cared for it, wrote about it, traveled with it. She became totally absorbed in it and fiercely protective of it.

At the start she didn't know what to call it. A sculpture? An environment? An assemblage? She still doesn't know. No one else does either. The Throne's 180 pieces have to be set up by a floor plan. It is an elaborate puzzle.

James Hampton, creator of the Throne, was not a professional artist. He was a night janitor in Washington government office buildings. After his job, he worked on it alone during the midnight to early morning hours in an unheated garage close to his boarding house. It took him 14 years. He

143

used foil—from liquor bottles, packs of cigarettes, rolls of kitchen aluminum foil. He probably found the old furniture and light bulbs and In and Out boxes and drawers in the office trash. Some of the desk blotters decorating his tabletops show telephone numbers jotted on them. The cheap drinking glasses that became vases in his scheme he may have collected in his croker sack, the burlap bag he carried on scavenging trips.

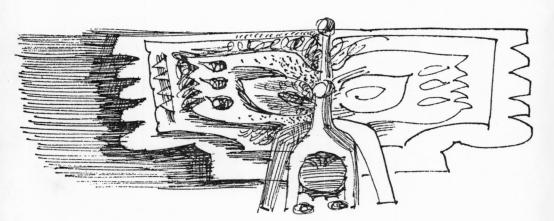

When Hartigan began her detective work little was known of Hampton beyond the fact that he died in 1964, aged 55, before he was quite finished with his work. No one knew what he intended for the Throne. Hartigan still doesn't know for certain. He may have intended it as the setting for a store-front ministry, because he conducted services in the garage, alone, for himself. On his blackboard there he wrote "Where there is no vision, the people perish."

As it was, the whole thing might have been pitched out if the National Collection hadn't moved decisively. That part of the story was well known. Anyone in the museum could tell Hartigan: how assistant director Harry Lowe received a letter from a friend enclosing a newspaper picture of the Throne taken in the garage just after Hampton's death, how the friend wrote, "I guess you're going to save this now," how Lowe answered, "You're damned right I am. I've just been to see it. It's great, a sensational thing." There was no competition for the Throne. The landlord wished to rent the space it took up. Hampton's family seemed embarrassed that he should have spent a lifetime crinkling up tinfoil.

The Throne was thoroughly photographed in place, then moved out by museum people, who took every scrap of it. This included notebooks written in secret script and signed "St. James," scissors and pencils, and the cardboard cartons of extra lightbulbs and spare silver wings.

By the time Hartigan visited the garage lit by six naked bulbs hanging from wires, the primitive building had been abandoned: it was full of rubbish and about to be torn down. A broken refrigerator gave her a leg up to climb into the loft. "I found nothing, up there or below. That garage bore no traces of Hampton. But it did give me a sense of the space in which he worked — 16 feet by 27 — and the distances there must have been between his objects."

She looked up Hampton's landlady and his doctor but neither one could recall having heard anything about his project. "There were so many dead ends, it was frustrating," she says. From Army records she was able to learn only that he was a private, drafted, and that he served on Saipan and Guam during World War II. She couldn't locate any of his Army buddies, and, although he wrote once of having attended Dunbar High School in Washington, Dunbar had no record of him. Hampton's brother in Elloree, South Carolina, a deacon in the Baptist Church, old, very deaf, recalled his working on silver stars during summer visits but he didn't recall any talk about it. He did tell Hartigan that Hampton's father had left the family at one time to become an itinerant preacher and gospel singer.

She thought she might have a clue from a reference in Hampton's writings to A. J. Tyler, a Baptist minister in Washington who was known to have said that in this city of monuments there was no monument to Jesus. Perhaps Hampton intended to fill that gap. Another clue came to her from a woman who used to bring food to Hampton while he worked, who heard about Hampton from a taxi driver and struck up an acquaintance. She remembered his talking to her about his fondness for the Book of Revelation in the Bible.

"Eventually I felt I had enough knowledge, enough feeling for the Throne, to write about it. I based my writing on my observations of the pieces themselves and what I could track down from the sources and what I was coming to understand about black fundamentalism—the literal belief in a Second Coming, the real attachment to God that is not ceremonial but a real one-to-one attachment. And then I used my imagination."

Her imagination and research led her to believe that Hampton's version was based on the passage from Revelation describing "the lamb of God on the throne of God surrounded by fluttering wings of angels in gold and silver raiment."

When the Walker Art Center in Minneapolis asked to borrow the Throne for a show, *Naives and Visionaries,* Hartigan wrote the article on Hampton for its catalog. She selected the pieces to go and she hovered over them while art conservator Tony Konrad prepared them for travel. The Throne, they agreed, is a conservator's nightmare. The materials are poor—pulpy cardboard, old dry wood, fragile lightbulbs, and construction paper that has faded from purple to gray. Hampton was an inexperienced carpenter, who connected the parts with cardboard hinges and tacks, or with tin strips cut from cans.

Konrad considered it unethical to alter Hampton's system—by replacing the cardboard braces with wood or by replacing the tacks with screws. What he did was to clean all the pieces—an inch by inch job over the crinkled paper, with cotton swabs. He replaced lightbulbs that were broken in storage, and stabilized some of the structures. Tightening up the casters on the furniture bases at least prevented further damage from vibration and wobbling. At first Konrad worked from detailed photographs. Later, familiar with Hampton's system, he felt he could trust his intuition.

When the 44 pieces went to Minnesota they were packed in crates, each piece braced at its strongest points, and the crates were loaded, one deep, onto quilts on a 40-foot truck. Hartigan flew out and spent four days unpacking them. Since then the entire Throne—all 180 pieces, two trucks' worth—has gone to the Whitney Museum in New York and the Boston Museum of Fine Arts, always in her care. She wants it to make a trip to the South and then to come "home," never to travel again.

Hartigan hopes the Throne will be on permanent show soon in its own room in the museum. "It's a curiosity if you display just bits of it; one object alone looks like a piece of junk sculpture. It doesn't convey the symmetry, or the organization by which all the objects on the left side relate to Jesus and the New Testament, and all the objects on the right side to the Old Testament and Moses. The obsession with symmetry is mind-blowing when you look at the Throne part by part, swirl by swirl. Hampton didn't present himself or imagine himself as such but we look on him as a talented artist with a wonderful grasp of decoration and pattern and possessing a vision. Bits and pieces of the Throne don't convey the extent to which he realized that vision. The Throne needs its own environment. And then you sense it whole."

Hartigan, who has an MA in art history, juggles her research on the Throne with other duties on the twentieth-century painting staff. But she finds the Throne has opened a whole field of modern art to her. She is seeking out modern folk art now and reading about it. And she is still puzzling over interpretations of Hampton's work. She'd like to decipher his secret script, which she finds as graceful as it is baffling. And she'd like to know why, on the stand labeled Elisha, he wrote: Moses appeared in Washington April 11, 1931. "The Throne means an awful lot to me," says

Hartigan. "I've tried to get as close to the heart of it as I can."

 ## MARGERY GORDON

Educator

Margery Gordon, educator and tour leader, set up the one-room *Explore Gallery* of the National Collection of Fine Arts especially for children. A tall flamboyant person who walks with big strides and gestures a lot with her hands, Gordon encourages those she leads around the gallery to react physically to what they see — the works of art in the collection. She has them moving in imitation of the lines of a picture, forming shapes like statues, making sounds to match colors. In the *Explore Gallery* she introduces children to this kind of approach. A hole in the yellow door leads to a ramp inside, right away inviting children into motion. The rug underfoot is a patchwork of colors that range from cool to hot, while wind chimes overhead are at heights to be batted or blown into sound. In a crawl space under the ramp, there's a light show. Colors, shapes, textures, are repeated throughout the room. A stripey knit boa constrictor, for example, hung close to the ceiling repeats the stripes of a large painting by Gene Davis. Jazz flute music takes turns with bird song. A line-up of portrait paintings suddenly surprises with a mirror that distorts, like one in a fun-house. Stuffed birds look very real, while others of corduroy don't pretend. In a small indoor garden plot are statues made of warm, carved wood, cold stone, and bronze cast to be smooth or rough.

The *Explore* room makes museum guards nervous, because most of the things in it allow touching. They fear it will become habit-forming, that young people will feel free to explore by touch in the rest of the gallery. Gordon, who is a former teacher and painter (who loves to backpack in Europe, and carries a roll of drawing paper sticking out of the pack), says no. "It leads to talk about museums, and I explain that, except in this room, you touch with your eyes."

Only one child tried to take her advice literally. He thought he was supposed to apply his eyeball to a painting and didn't much like the idea.

Gordon trains volunteer docents in the techniques she uses. The active tours are a kind of improvisational theater — inventing on the spur of the moment whatever is suggested by works of art. She takes groups of these future tour leaders out on the gallery floor with her, to be her pretend class of children. Often they start at a George Rickey sculpture inside the front door, called "24 lines," a tower of stainless steel that shifts mysteriously as its 24 nicely balanced shafts respond to the breeze from two electric fans. Each "child" chooses a shaft to represent and sways as it sways. Together they form triangles by leaning toward each other, shift and form others. They give the sculpture new names, such as "pins," "swords," "snowtree," "TV antenna," "needles."

In front of a Gene Davis stripe painting each of them chooses one of the colors to be. They invent the sound their color would make and the feeling it inspires. They carry their private color like a balloon on a string down along the corridor, taking note that each patch of lemon yellow in paintings along the way or each patch of green or skyblue is theirs. Stopping before a red, white, and blue abstract painting they dream up the kind of music they would play to accompany it and on what instruments.

They trace lines in the air like the lines in paintings and prints, and ponder the qualities that go with them. Zigzag: sharp, nervous. Curvy: relaxed. There's tension in a diagonal and strength in a solid line. If the broad slash of green is what Alexander Liberman's *Green Diagonal* is all about, then what is the little patch of purple doing there, and the white?

The students circle a piece of sculpture to see how the shapes and shadows change as their own positions change. Was it modeled first from a great wad of clay, this part pulled out, this part punched, like that and that? Was liquid metal poured into a cast like gelatin into a mold? The piece can't be touched, but there is marble on a nearby pillar that can be, and granite on another and plaster and cool stone floors.

Gordon and her class study the oversized statue of a colonial figure holding a scroll. Could he be a messenger? Why not? What makes him look so important? How does it feel to stand the way he stands? Taking an imposing stance herself, Gordon flips her straight black hair behind her ears and faces her students. All of them stand ramrod straight. There's the cloak to consider, too. And the wig. And the buttons on the bulging middle, which hints at prosperity. The label confirms the identity of General Washington. A bit of detective work, where the statue has been nicked, shows the General was not made of solid bronze. Plaster shows under the bronzed surface.

Gordon shares her pleasure in the Lincoln Gallery with the students. This great room with its vaulted arches she peoples with ghosts from its past. At one time the building was the old U.S. Patent Office. Later, a makeshift hospital. During the Civil War soldiers lay on cots between the glass cases of patent models. Both Clara Barton and Walt Whitman served there, nursing the wounded. For Lincoln's second inaugural ball, Washingtonians flocked to it to dance. Torches and bunting decorated the halls on that occasion, and the bands played. Treats for the banquet included enormous spun-sugar replicas of the Capitol and a battlefield of the war just ended.

Gordon teaches her student leaders that tours can be organized around themes, such as the sea, the opening of the West, or the occupations of women, including as an example the work of nineteenth-century painter Lilly Martin Spencer, whose husband did the housework. Tours can be organized around faces or feet, or almost anything. Eyes — just looking into them, thinking oneself into the personality within. She stands her group before George Catlin's Indian portraits. What did those eyes see? What were they thinking about the white man who came to live among them with duffle bags filled with canvas and paints. The eyes in the self-portrait of painter Benjamin West; how did West look to himself? To

you? Or 88-year-old John Adams in the portrait painted by Gilbert Stuart. Why do the rheumy eyes still intimidate? You are certain this man would not budge an inch, but why are you? Leaders must use an approach they feel comfortable with, Gordon teaches. "As a painter I tend to organize tours around lines, shapes, around color. The important thing is to get people into really looking, into a direct personal encounter with the painting. Adults," she adds, "are apt to look at the labels first."

Invited to read a paper in Yugoslavia about her innovative approach to museum tours, Gordon panicked when she realized she couldn't employ her customary warm-up exercises. "The audience was wired to headphones for translating and of course they couldn't get up without the headphones falling off. All I could think of was to ask them to shake their hands vigorously, so that they'd feel the blood rushing to their fingertips, the tingling and the heaviness. It did achieve something, it got me their attention, and they came alive, alert to me, alert to the subject."

Winning attention in that way, with adults or with school groups, is ultimately tiring. "All of us who use this approach put out so much energy. We share, we get excited. It's like a shot in the arm when there's a real exchange, between us and adults, us and children. But it's draining. We're exhausted at the end, from responding as we do."

Gordon finds her own painting suffers, that evenings she

is often too tired to paint in her own studio. "But if the museum job has done that, it has also made my eyes stronger, more critical, more perceptive. And I learn, too. I once hated *Green Diagonal*. But seeing it with kids, working with it, watching them as they play it out, now I think it's terrific."

Just working in a building (the National Collection of Fine Arts) of such size and history strongly affects her, she says. She's glad for the excuse to wander through it every day, up and down the curving staircases, along ironwork balconies, over mosaic floors, in and out of the park-sized courtyard. "The building has a real flow, an openness about it. Even if it's grandiose, you can really have a personal relationship with it, you're not overpowered by it, not even by the vaulted ceilings that send back an echo from your voice. It's partly because the space is broken up and used so creatively. You never walk in and see things all in a row. Things are hung in a way that makes you think about them. Partitions guide you around into little carpeted areas into corners with hidden spaces to explore.

"It's a learning situation, and fun, to work in this building. I like the politics and the marvelous fights over, say, the colors for an exhibition. There must be 20 people on this staff who are painters. Designer Val Lewton came up with wild colors for the *Made in Chicago* show. For the Barbizon School of landscape painting show called *American Art in the Barbizon Mood,* he used greens and golds that looked like a pasture. Soft. Quiet. You could hear a cow moo."

Best of all Gordon likes prowling through the basement cabinet shops and workrooms and talking to the people there. When she is asked by schools to honor young people — for good work in the arts — she skips the prizes and takes them on a "backstage" basement tour instead. "I use my special key and walk them through the tunnels that are almost like catacombs. I take them in to see the framer, Oliver Anderson, who lets them feel the velvets he uses for his linings, hold the mitre while he gets a perfect corner on a frame, and blow on his gold leaf. The kids are mesmerized watching him pick up his fine brush — from inside the pages of his dictionary — and slip it across his hair before he lifts the gold leaf and lays it on the frame. They watch him blend in the gold and polish it with his agate stone. He shows them how he patches the decoration on a frame — rebuilding bits of rope trim or flower garlands or lamb's tongue, how he makes a cast in clay and a mold in plaster and paints it. There's something about his low-key, deliberate way, his pride in his woods and his tools that gets to the kids. There's an earnest feeling in him."

Gordon takes her young people past all the crates stacked in the hall to meet Burgess Coleman, cratemaker and packer, and into the silkscreen shop to meet Ralph Logan, as he turns out a new batch of posters onto drying racks. She introduces them to Will Adair, framer for the Portrait Gallery, who shows the patching mixture he uses on a frame — rabbit-skin glue mixed with a little clay. Adair tells them the old Italian formulas for mixing egg tempera paints, which give the proportions of glue to water to egg and even specify whether the egg should be country-size or city-size. Gordon, as a painter, is interested in his recipes.

"There's a huge difference between working here and in an office building; it really gets to you," says Gordon.

 ## ELLEN MYETTE
Registrar

"The traffic here can be like a downtown rush hour," says 30-year-old Ellen Myette, assistant curator in charge of all the comings and goings at the Renwick Gallery. This small museum, kittycorner across Pennsylvania Avenue from the White House, was designed in 1858, when galleries tended to be sumptuous. It was later turned over to the U.S. Court of Claims, and finally, fallen on hard times, to the pigeons. When the Smithsonian acquired it in 1972 and restored its opulent appearance — overstuffed and plush (even to plush-

covered handrails on the staircase) — the Renwick itself became a museum piece. Some of its rooms are now loaded
with draperies and fringe, palms, urns, and paintings hung
row on row up to the ceilings. The other rooms have been
stripped bare, and are used for transient exhibitions of American crafts, the decorative arts, and design.

Because workspace behind the scenes at the Renwick is
tight while shows move through there on an extra-heavy
schedule, it's no small matter for Myette to prevent tangles.
There was a week or two at the end of winter, 1976, when
she narrowly averted head-on collisions. "This is crunch time
for me," she said then.

The *Craft Multiples* show was on its way out (the title
meant the craft items were not one-of-a-kind; they were
mass-produced, at least to the number of ten). Packers were
in the building dismantling the cases and packing the 132
craft objects, text panels, and labels, to be sent on tour. The
Signs of Life and Symbols in the American City, a new show
containing 450 objects, was just coming in, arriving in batches,
and including such bulky items as sofas and hi-fis, billboards, flashing-light marquees, and antique shop signs.
Within a few weeks two other exhibitions were due to close
and would have to be packed up — one called *Man Made Mobile,* on the Western saddle; the other on the decorated boxes
and bowls made by American Indian artists from the Haida,
Tlingit, Bella Bella, and Tsimshian tribes. For future shows
catalog copy had to be prepared. And still on hand, taking up
storage space and blocking the aisles, was *The Designs of Ray-
mond Loewy,* a show on the work of the well-known industrial designer. Its objects should have been packed and returned to the lenders long since, but tour plans for the show
were still uncertain.

At least the automobile from the Loewy show was gone
from the premises. The luxury cream-colored Studebaker
Avanti II, featured as a prime example of Loewy's streamlined work, was a production to move in and out. Because
there's no loading dock at the Renwick, the car, in a specially

designed cradle, had to be carried through the front door on its side. (Cost for the round trip, sidewalk to sidewalk: $3,,300.) The rest of the Loewy-designed objects, though in the way, were of manageable size — his bathroom scale, Lucky Strike cigarette packets, space suit, plus models to represent his design of the Presidential airplane *Air Force One*, and the Greyhound Super Scenicruiser bus, and a photograph of the crew quarters he designed for Skylab.

Working in a small gallery, Myette does a greater variety of jobs than she would in a larger museum with more staff. She is part registrar, part writer of catalogs and labels, part art handler. And more. Her registrar duties include preparing loan and insurance forms for objects the Renwick borrows, unpacking objects herself, or supervising their unpacking, assigning temporary loan numbers to them and writing reports on their condition. On the job and through courses given at the Smithsonian, she has learned to examine objects thoroughly and to write about them in conservators' vocabulary: she refers to cracks in wood as "checking," to waviness on the surface of paper as "cockling," and to the presence of roundish red-brown spots on paper as "foxing." "Cleavage" on a painting means the paint is flaking. "Blooming" means there's a white haze on the varnish. She knows that watercolor paintings, even protected with the plexiglass, which filters out harmful light rays, need a rest in storage after being on exhibit for six months; she makes sure they get it.

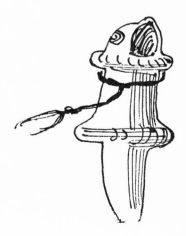

Of her art handling, Myette says, "There's an awareness you acquire on the job along with the common sense of it. You move one item at a time and you map out your moves before you make them. You never lift an object by its handle or its neck. You use a padded cart, taking care not to overload it with objects or to let any part of an object hang over the edge of the cart. You move slowly, plan ahead. You avoid bringing an object into a gallery while the gallery is being prepared for an exhibition because you don't want a hammer or a pylon to fall on it. You just take care to handle objects as little as possible because the more they are handled the more risk there is of something happening to them. You wear gloves for handling silver or porous stone to protect them from perspiration, oil, and grease."

From packing and unpacking, Myette has learned a lot about crates. First-rate crates—many of them made for the Renwick by Burgess Coleman at the National Collection of Fine Arts—are as small and light as safety will allow. Their lids are sealed with screws rather than nails, and they are lined with waterproof paper. They contain silica gel: salts which act as humidity stabilizers. Inside the lid are packing lists and photographs or diagrams to indicate contents and just how the items are packed. Some crates, for shipping ceramics or glass, have special foam cutout nests, which secure the objects in place with plenty of support.

Myette has come to be scornful of sloppy packing,

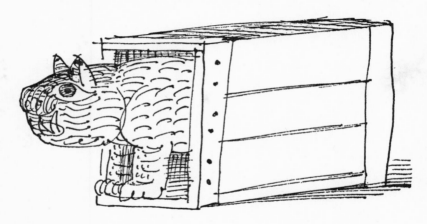

which brings objects to the gallery damaged — whether from insufficient support or padding or too little space provided for the object to "float" when the crate sustains a shock. She couldn't help feeling crabby when a crate arrived from a lender with a big metal and glass antique illuminated soft-drink sign — smashed. It had been placed in the bottom of the crate with very little protective wrapping and three other metal signs on top of it.

The need to fumigate objects on arrival she learned the expensive way, after a wooden sculpture from South America, a religious figure, released a swarm of termites whose hundreds of pairs of white wings showed like snow against the dark blue felt setting. "We had to fumigate the whole building."

In preparing catalogs Myette has to keep her wits about her — to write clearly, concisely, to pull it all together for the designer and the printer, who are on a pretty rigid schedule. She prepares pictures, picture credits, captions, and texts. She proofreads galleys for accuracy. In effect, she's her own publications department.

Writing labels for the objects on exhibition is demanding, too, but more of a game — a word puzzle — in which she tries to keep the labels as short and easy to read as possible while packing in information. For *Craft Multiples* Myette figured people would want to know not only the materials used by the craftspeople but also the techniques. The format she chose worked well for the variety of things in the exhibition. Her label for the Christmas-cookie ornaments read: SALT DOUGH, WIRE; HAND FORMED, BAKED. The rolling pin label read: BIRCH, WALNUT; LAMINATED, TURNED, OILED. The label for the kitchen pot rack read: MILD STEEL; HOT-FORGED, WELDED, PUNCHED, TWISTED, TEXTURED, WAXED. One sentence for each process would have made a lengthy paragraph. The goblets label read: GLASS; OFF-HAND BLOWN. The same label format would not necessarily work for another exhibition. With each new exhibition, the format has to be rethought.

Before the packers came to take away the *Craft Multiples* show on the first lap of its three-year tour of the country Myette had to write catalog numbers on the objects — the lacquer and ink routine, she calls it. It took her three full days to paint the small lacquer patches, then to write on them in ink, and paint over the ink with lacquer as a sealer. It was a finicky job which had to be done neatly and unobtrusively, especially when on clear glass.

A fine-boned, small person who is high-spirited in spite of her finicky chores, Myette says: "I'm always learning new things here. It's not dull, like standing on an assembly line in a tuna factory. Not dull at all. But hard, demanding. The glamor, if you call it that, comes from working with fine and beautiful objects. And from presenting exhibitions." An art history major in college, Myette did her graduate work in museology at George Washington University. She feels her affection for objects suits her to her work, along with liking detail and having a head for it and being comfortable with juggling a great variety of responsibilities.

Even when the *Craft Multiples* objects were moved out of the gallery Myette kept her eye on them. She stood watching, on the curb outside the Renwick between two woodcrafted items as tall as herself — a modern grandfather clock and a library ladder. She had stayed with the packers in the gallery, checking items on the master list as they were wrapped. She wanted to be there until the last of the large items were loaded. Clock, ladder, and a wooden bathtub would travel, quilt-wrapped, until crates were built for them in New York. As she waved off the van, a circa-1900 fire hydrant was on its way into the Renwick. It was placed on the curbside elevator for its descent, to the gallery basement — to become part of *Signs and Symbols*.

Myette appears to shift to the concerns of a new show as easily as she flips back her long hair. Within minutes she is leading Washington *Star* reporter Ben Forgey through the *Signs and Symbols* area that is still under construction. They skirt ladders and wires and paint buckets to watch the silkscreeners applying text to a white wall and to admire a neon sign (advertisement for a plumber) with faucet and droplets, flashing off and on — drip, drip and splat. There is a gaping hole where a billboard is to hang. Some truck driver, Myette explains to Forgey, is still on the far side of the Rockies moving east with it. Loud complaint comes from a member of the workcrew, irritated because someone has once again tidied away his beer can. Myette explains that, too. The beer can is there intentionally, on a table, and as part of the exhibit.

 ## SCOTT ODELL
Restorer of Musical Instruments

A bell-pull out in the hall with instructions to play it *adagio ma non troppo* (slowly but not too slowly) activates a piano mechanism in a high corner of Scott Odell's workshop which causes a hammer to strike a bell. In this way, restorer Odell hears he has visitors. His workshop in History and Technology is an inner box of a room at the back of a large, locked storeroom containing pianos and mechanical music machines under plastic sheets. His shop's walls are lined and double-lined with brass instruments on pegs, with spools of wire, mallets, chisels, clamps, with shelves of chemicals in bottles and tins. Odell at the center of it all is apt to be totally absorbed, bent over an organ bellows, a grand piano, or a harpsichord, and not hear anything. But the sound of the bell, played *adagio,* does break into his concentration.

The bellows, which Odell fixed in 1976, was part of an 1876 organ he restored to playing condition for the opening of the Smithsonian's "1876" show. He repaired its cracked windchest. Then he found its bellows had split, the leather rotting. So layer by layer he removed the papers glued to the wooden ribs and to the old leather hinges of the bellows. They were bits of Paris newspapers and old bills. He washed them to remove the acid, lined them with thin, non-acid paper, and put them on again — the same newspapers, the same bills — though he replaced the old sheepskin hinges with new.

Odell thinks he copied the old workmanship exactly. In any case he photographed and wrote down what he did step by step, so that "the record is there — in the likely event someone will have to do the job again in another 100 years."

The fat-legged grand piano Odell worked on, soon after, required complete restringing. While he was at it, Odell painted a clear lacquer patch as protection over the message pianist Paderewski had written in ink on the piano's cast-iron plate. The message read: "I played this piano in 75 concerts in America in 1892-93" and was signed with Paderewski's name.

A harpsichord Odell had in the shop at the same time called for study — and admiration — as much as for structural work. "Unbelievably fresh and untouched," it was almost 300 years old, he said. Its name batten was lettered: JOSEPH JOANNES COUCHET ME FECIT ANTVERPIAE 1679 — made in Antwerp. It had its original padding on the keyboard and even tiny fragments of its original wire, caught under its pegs — enough of it for Odell to analyze. That instrument was remarkable, in that it showed so few of the ravages of time, weather, woodworms, and the overenthusiastic repairs that regularly afflict harpsichords. To Odell it was special, too, because he had flown to California to identify it after thieves stole it in Maine and trucked it across the continent.

Odell, who has restored to playing condition some 100 antique musical instruments in the museum's collection, always stresses that he does as little as he possibly can to the looks of an instrument. He tries to make it look cared for. Nothing more. Where a private restorer might strip the instrument down, repaint, and varnish, to make it as beautiful as the day it was sold, "a museum's concern is with history. We want to retain evidence of how an instrument was used. All the traces of the maker's hand are important to us — his clamp marks, his gauge lines, which tell about the way he worked."

Wanting his repairs to be visible, Odell initials and dates any pieces of wood he puts in as replacements. He uses materials that are reversible — glues and paints which are dissolvable — so that what he does can be undone. He uses old-type materials where he can — goose quills, for example, instead of plastic picks, for the plectra that pluck harpsichord strings. But he doesn't make a fetish of it. When people tell him the early instrument makers might have been glad to use plastics and synthetic glues if they'd had them, he admits they might have. He just prefers to use them very, very sparingly on the chance that they might make a difference in the sound.

"I started out using nylon fishing line for the springs in the harpsichord jacks. It's handy. You buy 100 yards at the hardware store. Carpet beetles aren't going to eat it. But I came to find it wasn't reliable. It acquires a set and loses its springiness. I had to keep re-tensioning my springs. So the next time I was in Paris I bought a bundle of Chinese hog-bristles at a shoemakers' supply store." He tosses them out on his workbench — a dozen and more little packets of white wiry bristles tied up with red thread. "I've had no trouble since."

Sound is something Odell prefers not to compromise about. "The harpsichord we work on," he says, "should be as mechanically reliable, as quiet, as pretty to hear as it ever was, so that a professional feels comfortable performing on it. It used to be common to hear old instruments played out of

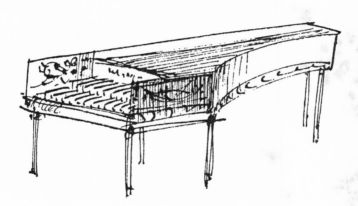

tune. People had the notion squeaks and squawks were acceptable in them. But eighteenth-century standards were no more slack than our own. We want our instruments to be a testimony to their makers' intentions, to do justice to the original sound."

Restoring the sound is worth doing because he has a good chance of keeping it restored. His shop has stricter humidity control than the rest of the building. An alarm goes off if the humidity goes above 55 percent or below 45, though if he's in the building Odell detects the change first, by the way his instruments go out of tune. "The touch becomes two and three times as heavy. The notes don't go off ding ding ding with a nice interval, but all together."

Odell, who is bearded, merry-eyed, a wiry-looking person, came to the Smithsonian in 1963 to plan the restoration shop, "which today we'd call a conservation lab." He counts his work a "funny combination of traditional craft skills, like woodworking, and an awareness of modern scientific ways of doing things." His background he considers a funny combination as well. He got a degree in philosophy at Middlebury College and took quite a bit of chemistry, too. He's still taking courses. Woodworking he learned through a job with a boat builder. And he learned a great deal, he says, about respect for objects through a job with a harpsichord maker—"a man who felt the harpsichord has a courtly tradition of 300 years and it doesn't need as much improvement as people think."

 ## W. THOMAS CHASE
Conservator

At the Freer Gallery of Art when two goddesses needed treatment recently—one for bronze disease, one for woodrot—the person who took care of them was W. Thomas Chase. Chase, who has degrees in conservation from Oberlin and New York University, is head of the Freer's technical laboratory, a world-famous center for research into ancient oriental crafts. Chase does scientific analyses of objects. He treats objects. And he does research on materials to see how they age and how they react to treatment.

A portly, genial fellow, Chase has a vague expression behind his wire-rimmed glasses that belies the precise way he goes about his work. In his analysis of Chinese bronzes — weapons, mirrors, ceremonial vessels — he determines the amounts of copper and tin and lead and iron and zinc in them. And he determines, to the ten-thousandth of one percent, the trace amounts they contain of some 15 other metals. In a single object, a Chou Dynasty weapon from 450 B.C., for example, there was more than one set of findings. One alloy of metals was used for the center of the blade and a harder alloy was used for the edges.

Chase also analyses particles of earth on surfaces, as well as the clay that remains inside from the time objects were cast. "You get spiky quartz crystals," he explains, "from the famous Chinese yellow earth, or *loess*, which give you a good idea that the object was made. or buried, in the central part of China." He also finds particles which he identifies as airborne dust that was dumped on China from Turkey.

It is this preoccupation with materials which has involved Chase in years of concentrated study on two weapons — one a broad axe, the other a dagger axe. He was able to date both weapons as 3,000 years old. His dates placed them in a period before the Chinese knew how to make iron, yet both had iron in them. Tests proved to Chase that the date and the materials were not inconsistent, that the iron in the blades had come from meteorites. Nature had done the smelting for the makers.

For years Chase has worked on a collection of 159 Chinese bronze belt hooks, from between 350 B.C. and A.D. 100. "We do this for the same reason people do any kind of historical study — to illuminate the past. A lot of it consists in examining documents — the written word. Objects, though, give a different slant. We're interested in the objects and their history. Part of their history is what they're made from and how they're made and where people got the materials. If you can determine this sort of thing, well, it's interesting."

Chase's study of materials leads him to gather and save a surprising amount for his museum's study collection — of logs, pipes, nails, ingots. "We have some rather amusing junk that's useful," he says — iron that's rusting, wood that's rotting. He picks up pieces that look "interesting." Some bronze drainpipes on a downtown Washington fountain interested him especially, because he thought the caps on the pipes were corroding very much the way Chinese bronzes corrode. "The corrosion wasn't crusty or scaly at all but a thin, shiny green patina."

Chase expressed such interest in those drainpipes that a hard-hatted construction worker arrived at the museum one day with two of the pipes under his arms as a present (they were being replaced anyway). Once Chase picked up a ten-by-ten wooden post and brought it himself into the museum in his car. The post was one of a number of stout "balks" blocking traffic near his suburban home. He liked it for the very reason that it was being discarded. It was well rotted. It made a sample for him on which to test treatments.

Chase's study collection also includes a piece of copper from the Capitol roof — "nicely sulfated," he says — and a drawer of twisted and scaly-looking ingots. These are tagged with the names of shipwrecks at which they were found — a copper ingot, covered with green and white crusts from a wreck off Turkey in ancient times, a piece of iron from the ship *Wasa*, which sank off Sweden in 1628, pieces of silver from the Spanish treasure fleet sunk off Florida. Shipwreck materials are ideal because they can be dated. On a recent trip to China, Chase also collected a little bottleful of earth in Sian from a roadside near the Green Dragon Temple in order to have a sample of earth from a very specific locality.

The technical lab where Chase works looks strictly like a place of science with very little in it to suggest the world of art. It is a room of microscopes, burners, scales, lamps, fume hoods, and — lining the walls — record books and bottles

of chemicals with eyedroppers. As Chase entered it on a recent Monday morning, tying the strings of a white coat about
his middle, his immediate question to conservators Ilona
Benet and Lynda Zycherman was, "How is she?" The
woman scrutinizing the arm of a three-foot statue through
a magnifying glass, answered, "Worse!"

The figure on the examination table was a tenth century
goddess from South India, solid bronze weighing 156 pounds.
Her situation came to the attention of the lab in a highly ir-
regular way, through a note left between the statue's feet by a
museum visitor. The note said: This statue has bronze disease. And the visitor was right. The telltale bright green dots
from the disease were visible in several places.

Chase went back over his records. His hydro-
thermograph records showed there had been ten hours in the
past year when the humidity in the room was more than 70
percent. That would have been quite enough, he says, to start
up the disease. His notes also contained drawings made from
time to time of the patterns of corrosion on the statue, which
he had been watching with some concern. Quite soon after
the visitor's note, the corrosion crust was bubbling up, notice-
ably, even just over a weekend.

Not unusual, says Chase. Such an object, once buried,
has chlorides, usually from salt, reacting with its copper. The
chlorides sometimes remain unnoticed for decades and
then flare up in humid conditions. As someone whose advice
has been sought by the Thai government on how to protect
and treat its national collection of bronzes, he knew what to
do. "It is just the kind of thing," he says, "one is hesitant to
treat unless one absolutely has to."

He started by removing the wax finish with solvents,
down to but not including the green patina underneath the
wax. Then he and Zycherman removed the crusts on the figure by hand with fine dental picks, he standing on a stool
with one foot planted on the examination table. They then
covered the figure in a plastic bag, vacuum sealed it, and with
the help of one more pair of hands, lowered it into a box to
soak for a week in 30 gallons of alcohol containing a chem-

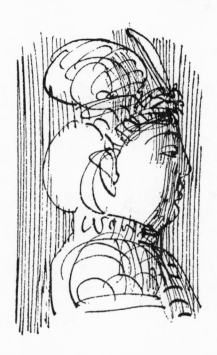

ical called benzotriazole. The treatment was successful. It stabilized the goddess's condition without destroying her prized green patina.

At the same time Chase had treated the other patient—a larger-than-life-sized painted wooden Goddess of Mercy, a thousand-year-old Kuan-Yin. This one, because of her size, he examined in a large storage room for stone sculpture. Here she was laid out across a pair of sawhorses padded with quilts. This goddess had rot in her feet—quite a bit of it—from termites that must have got into them when she stood on temple floors. To prevent the feet from caving in and toppling her, Chase had to fortify them by injecting plastic from syringes into the holes, though he first had to build a box, fitted with a padded yoke, in which to stand the figure on her head. As part of the treatment he also coated the painted surfaces with diluted seaweed glue to fix the paint to the wood and prevent its flaking.

Chase at the same time removed from one foot a sliver of wood which he sent out to be carbon-dated. That was a shipment out of the museum which he felt he could make without violating the will of Charles Lang Freer, who gave his art collections to the Smithsonian, stipulating that no object was to leave the premises.

In the same spirit Chase also ships to Oxford (England), where there is thermoluminescent-dating apparatus, these tiny fragments of clay core which he extracts from the handles or legs or feet of the bronzes by drilling through the metal to reach them. The actual handling of objects — through treatment and study — is a highly satisfying part of his work, Chase says, and it makes for a feeling of kinship between him and the craftsmen of thousands of years ago. Chase also feels kin to the three Japanese craftsmen at the opposite end of the building from him. They work in spacious, sunlit quarters quite unlike his lab, with methods quite unlike his own — mounting and restoring oriental paintings in the traditional, ages-old ways of the *hyogushi*. The master restorer among them, Takashi Sugiura, was already working at the Freer when the technical lab opened in 1951. He is so skilled that Japan, the country he has left, lists him as one of its national treasures.

It was to capture the extraordinary skill of these three men — and share it with other conservators — that Chase some years back made a film on the art of the *hyogushi* as practiced at the Freer. "We wanted to get across the remarkable way they handle very deteriorated papers and silks and then remount the paintings without ever making them look new. We decided to cover three aspects of the process — shifting a painting from a hanging scroll to a solid back, shifting one from a solid back to a roller, remounting a big double six-panel screen. It was not," Chase adds, with feeling, "an easy movie to make."

The filmmakers first held a script conference with Sugiura and his two assistants. "It was a disaster," Chase recalls, "and very funny. We asked them: 'What's the first thing you do? You take the painting off the old mount? Yes? Good. Then the next thing. You wash it?'

" 'We wash it. Maybe we wash it.'

" 'Maybe you wash it ?'

" 'Yes. Maybe we don't wash it.'

" 'Maybe you don't wash it ?'

"Well, we went on like that for about ten minutes. I was very sympathetic with their approach, because you really can't tell what you'll have to do till you get into it. We said: 'Forget the script, we'll shoot this as it goes.' " Chase adds, "But you know it is very difficult to make a movie on that basis."

The filmmakers first had to learn what the men were doing and why. They spent days reading. They spent more days watching—always, Chase says, with a deep respect for what they saw. While the restorers went on about their work, sitting cross-legged or kneeling at long, low tables on straw mats, the filmmakers absorbed the pantomine of movement. They asked questions. They asked about the *shaku* as the unit of measure—one-sixteenth of an inch shorter than a foot— about the knives, the great pounding brushes which are expected to last a lifetime, the pans and paddles and sieves hanging from pegs.

They became familiar with the papers made from different plant fibers, each paper with special strengths and working qualities, and with the fine silks, some of them costing $50 a square foot. They learned the recipe for the all-purpose wheat starch, how it is cooked, how strained through a horsehair sieve. They found out that a glue made from sheets of yellow seaweed is good for patching and that cow, whale, or deer glue, once it is melted down from stick form to a gelatin, has to be stored in the refrigerator along with the *hyogushi*'s lunch.

It all took close to a year but in the end the film recorded what it was intended to record. It caught all the swift, sure movement, which comes across like a kind of dance— the men washing the paintings at the sink under shampoo nozzles, stripping off the silks, measuring, cutting, pasting, patching. And it caught the sound of the brushes pounding together the fibers of layers of paper, the sound of Buddhist beads being rubbed, hard, across the back of newly mounted paintings to improve their flexibility.

Years later Chase still enjoys looking into the Japanese restoration lab. It's a treat to the eye to see the work in progress — to see sunlight picking up glints of gold in the scraps of silk out on the tables and in the background of the double six-panel screen with its "Hundred Black Crows." He's glad, though, he isn't making another film.

 ## REGINALD (BUD) SAYRE
Model Maker

Nimble-fingered Bud Sayre, 62, is a model maker in the "magic shop" of Exhibits Central. A diminutive fellow, with glittery eyeglasses, sandy mustache, gravelly voice, and a dry wit, he looks — tapping away at his workbench — more like a shoemaker than a magician. There's magic, though, in what he does. For he and his colleagues turn out amazingly fresh-looking fruit and fish and fish eggs and crickets — either in miniature or 25 times life-size — as well as cactus and sea-weeds which they hang on lines to dry.

On any given day in that sunny workroom smelling of kindergarten clay and glue, half a dozen model makers in long black rubber aprons tinker away at their projects, snipping and whittling and stirring up messes in cottage cheese cartons. They work at benches equipped with air hoses curling down from the ceiling, gooseneck lamps, magnifiers, and a high-density clutter of paints and powders. They use, for reference, leaves and pods and propped-open picture books and specimens in bottles. They move about a lot between supply cupboard and sink, trading quips as they go, mumbling congratulations to themselves, grumbling over things that go amiss.

Sayre is credited with making some of the worst jokes in the shop and some of the best trees. Along with the other jacks-of-all-trades he has had a hand in most of the shop's products—in lightweight boulders and fieldstone walls (stones in 32 sizes, shapes, colors) that save the museums' floors from sagging, in the First Lady mannequins (also assorted sizes and unnaturally lightweight), in fake bird droppings, and in ears of plastic corn that discourage mice from nibbling. For the Zoo the models shop turns out, in spare moments, dozens of natural-looking bark-textured duck feeders—to hide unsightly buckets. It also makes plastic ham and cheese sandwiches on rye and bulgy apple pies running over with juices, and such glossy chocolates that guards on duty at the candy-shop exhibit in History and Technology have been known on slow days to bite into them.

Like just about everyone else in Exhibits Central, Sayre was unaware until he started museum work that jobs like this existed, Even the chief, James Mahoney, says. "It's a surprise to me every day to be here and I've been here 17 years." Of some 50 people on the staff, only two planned a museum career. The rest came to it by chance. Mahoney reached the Smithsonian through industrial design—products like cars, salt shakers, and bobby pins. The others came by way of theater work or electronics or carpentry or department-store display. Sayre was a sign painter in Brooklyn and the Bronx, specializing in fish, roosters, cows, and fine let-

tering. He painted signs on glass for the most part, for grocery and butcher shops, or he painted on the sides of trucks.

During the Depression he did this kind of work along with other odd jobs. From the time he was a seventh-grader, Sayre recalls, he lettered diplomas for his schools. In World War II he was a cartoonist for the Third Armored Division newspaper. "I did sketches of Jerk Osgood — me," he explains, "in the comic situations that occur on the front lines. It didn't excuse me from combat. I just kept my brush and ink with me, and a dispatcher from headquarters came by motorcycle to pick up my work."

When a friend after the war took him behind the scenes at New York's American Museum of Natural History, Sayre liked the variety of jobs he saw, and applied. "My first assignment was by way of a test. It was to paint a plaster sea bass. Luckily I'd done bass many times before on various signs." Sayre worked a dozen years at the museum, mostly on trees and foregrounds, and studied mold work and design at night. At the Smithsonian, where he came in 1959, he began by greening up the glass cases for the African mammals exhibit (in Natural History) with big leaves and breadfruit and papyrus, bending wooden papyrus stems with steam.

A collecting trip took Sayre to British Guiana. He brought back quantities of roots, vines, and monkey pods to work with, quantities of notes and pictures, and the molds he made in the field of leaves, plants, even a termites' nest. Learning to look, says Sayre, seemed to come naturally to him. "I'd be going through the forest with somebody and later I'd wonder why he never noticed the formation of the trees — how they bent and branched, how the leaves were formed in units, how they hung. I'd get it all down in notebooks and watercolors."

When Hall 23, a South American hall, was being re-remodeled in the Smithsonian's Natural History Museum in 1975–76, Sayre's wealth of materials came into use. Sayre and Sylvan Sean, whose name is appropriate for the tree expert he is, took advantage of 40-foot ceilings to create an impressive rain forest. They constructed their giant trees of wire and wood, covered them over with papier-mâché, plaster, and glue, roughed up to simulate bark. They used pipes under the mâche to shape up the fluted trees, wads of burlap to form the spreading bases for the prop-root and buttressed trees. The thousands of cellulose acetate leaves, which they hung from wire branches, they slanted toward the light source. The easy-to-see leaves near the ground, they touched up with veins and wormholes and spots.

With Hall 23 in production, the magic shop—like a classroom at the approach of Halloween or George Washington's Birthday—took on as an overlay to its clutter the look of the current theme, the look of a South American market-place, a beach, a forest, a grassland. The *ranchero*'s horse, stuffed, stood to one side while sculptor Vernon Rickman, working from a tiny model on the windowsill, built a life-sized cowboy, in clay, onto a wire armature. Rickman added one blob of clay at a time from a wad in his left hand. His rider, when he finished the job, sat the horse nicely, straining forward, his right arm upraised to swing a bola-balls weapon by its cord.

A stuffed llama was in residence, too, one that came out of storage a bit the worse for wear. It needed magic-shop attention to some bald spots and a torn eyelid which had to be relaxed with damp cotton, pulled back together with glue injected by hypodermic needle, a bit of wax poured into the crack and painted. Walter Sorrel, at the bench beyond Sayre's, had his work surface littered with the big flat skates he was making for the beach scene. He turned out fish that were flexible enough to drape over the uneven ground.

Sayre meanwhile was sorting through his old British Guiana leaves, softening them up to use for ground cover under his trees, and soaking them in formaldehyde to protect them from insects and mice. His work was interrupted when a crate of fruit arrived by air freight from the tropics. Sayre had to document the colors of the 23 pieces while the samples were fresh. He then passed them on to Mike Friello, who made molds from which to cast quantities of the produce. On his sketchpad Sayre caught with watercolors the lemony-yellow of the little round lemons, the orange of the *mashwa,* purple for the *pepino,* green for the *calaboya.* He didn't document the pear on his bench; it was his lunch.

Sayre's forestry work was interrupted again when Susan Wallace, the mannequin expert, needed his arms for the old lady in the market scene. Sayre's arms were small enough to be suitable, she figured. She liked his muscular hands. The casts she made—by pouring plastic into molds she peeled from his arms—retained Sayre's arm hairs, just the way cactus models made from hollowed-out cactus can retain cactus spikes. Wallace was proud of the results. Sayre was glad enough to oblige.

Once Hall 23 was completed, Wallace got back to some First Ladies who needed to be whittled down to fit into their dresses. Sean turned his attention to a series of tiny barrels for the merchant ship *Brilliant,* and Sayre made a 15-inch-diameter cannonball, its surface texture exactly like that of the original which had taken four model makers in the shop to lift. Balancing his replica on the palm of his hand while he touches up the seam with paint, Sayre says, "I've never worked in an office," and adds, "I can't say I've missed it."

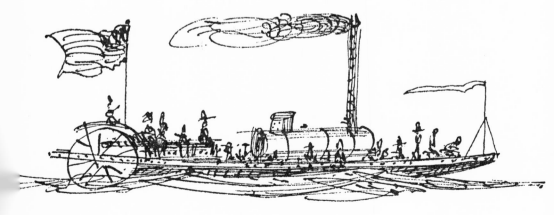

BOB MULCAHY
Designer

Bob Mulcahy, chief of the National Zoo's graphics and exhibits, came to the Smithsonian in 1974 and right away was put to work designing furniture for monkeys. "I saw batches of films. I read. There is just a fantastic amount of printed material on monkeys. I read a lot of it. Two days a week I spent just watching the monkeys move, and I sat up long nights talking to the curator." Mulcahy has daily proof that the new monkey furniture his office designed to its taste also appeals to the monkeys. He passes them every morning on the way to his desk and sees them giving the furniture joyful good use.

When the 1904 monkey house was remodeled in 1974, the decision was to furnish all the enclosures with the kind of timbers developed for children's playground equipment. Real trees the monkeys shredded in a matter of weeks. These extra-durable timbers could be put together, tinkertoy fashion, in patterns to suit different activities — with swinging limbs and two-inch manila ropes for the spider monkeys and jumping platforms for the colobus monkeys, who like to bounce. The plans were worked out between the designer, who knew his materials, and the curator, who knew his monkeys, but both parties were a bit nervous until the monkeys showed their approval.

The remodeling also cut back the number of cages from 24 to 12. It was decided to have fewer species of monkeys and to show them in more natural groupings — a change that would make for more normal interaction among the monkeys and more successful breeding. At the same time the cages were raised several feet for better visibility, and they were enclosed in glass for temperature control, though a nice side effect, Mulcahy claims, is that the monkeys no longer have to smell the people or catch colds from them, either.

Mulcahy was experienced in design when he came to the Zoo, aged 38, with a Master's degree in visual communication. He'd had his own exhibits studio in Chicago. He found the monkeys agreeable subjects to design for and to communicate with. "Our first decisions were which species to have. And which materials to use for the cages. We couldn't have a rain forest. People would probably never see the monkeys through the foliage if we did. But we could use timbers to simulate the basic environments.

"For indoors we planned to use gumbo. It's a swamp wood that cracks and checks during the day in the high heat and then closes up again as it regains moisture from all the hosing of the enclosures. Outdoors we'd have redwood, farm-grown redwood. We built some prototype structures — poles joined to poles by pipes — and tried them out on the monkeys. Then we made models, in miniature, for all the cages. We'd be throwing up our arms saying, 'They'll go from here to here to here. They'll brachiate across the top.' We'd allow for variations in arm spans and for the fact the South American woolly moves very very carefully through the trees with all five limbs while the black and white colobus moves at high speeds up to 40 miles an hour. We had a lot of stress-on-structure problems from that speed.

"One advantage of the system is we can vary the horizontals and verticals easily. Everything is usually so permanent in zoos. This isn't. The keeper sees where a new platform is needed or more ropes, and we put them in. We go in and change things frequently. A cage can be completely changed in eight hours. Our furniture has done away with neurotic pacing. You don't find sluggish monkeys here, zapped out from having nothing to do."

Of course the Barbary apes took apart the structure in their cage. They undid the monkey-proof clips which the welders made, untied the knots in their ropes and pulled the ropes out through the eyelets. Mulcahy figures he should have predicted that.

From monkeys Mulcahy had to turn his attention abruptly to birds, and the pileup of bird books on his rolltop desk reflected the change. Though he says he makes it a

point never to learn a scientific name — "I'm not here to be a scientist" — he steeped himself in bird literature. And, an exuberant person, big, pink-faced, with cotton-blond fly-away hair, he was soon voluble on such subjects as bird courtship practices and territorial calls, like the South Carolina wren's, which he found remarkable for being produced 1,800 times in a day.

"Once we filtered out the mass of information," he says, "we settled on the basic concept of flight. How does a bird get up there and what does it take for a bird to stay there? We'd keep our labels simple — use them to teach people to see the birds better, teach them to birdwatch by distinguishing color, form, flight patterns. I believe deeply in my informational exhibits," he adds, "but that stuff shouldn't invade the birds' space. It should be contained on a wall somewhere. It shouldn't compete with the birds, which after all are the best show going."

A zoo is a designer's dream according to Mulcahy. "You're communicating and you're using design as a tool to simplify complex ideas about species difference, conservation, and related life styles. And the nicest thing is you have nothing to sell. A zoo's major mission is extension of animal species. You have to think what's the best environment for the animal and what's practical for servicing it, and after that, what makes the best viewing for the visitor."

Mulcahy at the same time has been helping to plan a beaver valley, with beavers and wolves, otters, seals, sea lions, and cheetahs in residence. And he's carrying out his master graphics plan for the zoo, which involves newly designed benches, new un-tippable trash cans, and a system of trails for presenting the Zoo to the public in short, consumable sections so people won't wear out. There are six basic trails — for viewing hoofed stock, bears, elephants, lions, birds and ducks. The trails are identified by symbols — head silhouettes — which appear on everything from totem-pole signposts down to paper cups. The bird trail, which has a crowned crane for its symbol, has crane claw prints, silk-screened onto the walkway, to guide the visitor. The bear trail has bear paw prints. The duck trail has prints of webbed feet, spaced pretty much as a duck would have left them. "I was watching ducks walk for weeks," says the designer.

"The object is to get people from point A to point B, while providing enjoyable education along the way. Communicating without ornament. I'm against too many words. Nice clean, swift statements are what I like. Precise. No flowers. Our signs have to be clear and durable. And they have to be positioned well out of reach. People love to run off with zoo signs — especially ones that say BONGO or DIKDIK."

Mulcahy says he starts his Zoo days right — with a swing through the monkey house. "Even before I get to the door I see the one piece of redwood I put higher and farther from the central core in the howlers' yard. And there's one monkey on it. In the jungle he'd pick the farthest, highest branch for his territorial howling. He's howling here all right. Indoors, I see the spider monkeys using my high circular feeding platform for a bed. They're like a big spider-monkey ice cream cone, just a blob of black fur, all piled on top

of each other. And the elegant little colobus are going ber-
serk, whipping through their platforms so fast they're a blur
with a fluffy tail for a parachute. A fellow can't stay dejec-
ted," he says.

 ## RALPH RINZLER

Folklorist — and Others in the Performing Arts

The Smithsonian has a division of Performing Arts that puts
on concerts, cuts records, runs a popcorn concession, and every summer since 1967, offers the outdoor Festival of American Folklife on the Mall. People say the Folk Festival is one
of the nicest events in Washington. The Washington *Post*
calls it "a joy." The Washington *Star* calls it a "museum
without walls," and even though the Smithsonian has been
nicknamed the Nation's Attic until the joke has worn thin,
the *Star* follows through and calls the Festival the "open-air
attic of our origins."

From the start the director of this popular event has
been Ralph Rinzler, who has performed across the country on
mandolin, banjo, and guitar with the Greenbriar Boys and
Joan Baez, and who still charms audiences with his playing.

Rinzler works out of a homey office. His "conference"
setup is a circle of mule-ear rocking chairs, some of them
seated with split oak, some with hickory bark. The photographs on his walls are of singers, puppeteers, and banjo-pick-
ers who are his friends and his "finds." "I've always been
into finding," he says. He finds people who are "strong living
practitioners of the folk arts" — the creative musicians and
craftspeople, who keep alive hundreds of different traditions.
He invites them to come and be themselves on the Mall.

For his first Festival in 1967, two days in a tent camp,
he invited 40 performers. Ten years later, when the Festival
was running for 12 weeks, he brought to the Mall 5,000 performers — from 116 native-American Indian tribes, from 50
labor unions, every region of America, and from 38 other

countries. The numbers aren't important — his biggest production was for the summer of the Bicentennial — but the approach is, according to Rinzler, who sees the annual Festival as a way to celebrate "tradition bearers."

Tradition bearers are people like the Sacred Harp Singers of Ozark, Alabama, or the German-American brass band from Freistadt, Wisconsin. They're makers of sorghum molasses, dugout canoes, or three-legged milking stools. And they're people like Pappa Mateo, a Brooklyn electrician three generations removed from Sicily, who still constructs the four-foot-high puppets his grandfather taught him to make and who leads his family in rousing performances — in Italian — of *Orlando Furioso*.

"We give up our traditions too easily because we don't have access to them," says Rinzler. "Here in the Festival we're making them accessible. Radio and TV are always offering us mediocre replacements for creativity — music that's processed and packaged for us. It's baloney. Literally. Why should we listen to phony cowboys and torch singers in gingham dresses with sequins? My reaction is to find something I know is beautiful. I'd rather go out in the woods or down a street and find people creating music for their own needs."

Two of Rinzler's finds have been Doc Watson and Charlie Sayles, Doc in eastern Tennessee, where he was living on money-in-the-hat for playing at Saturday night dances on an electric guitar. "It was only when we got to know each other that Doc began to play the folk music of his childhood for me. And there he was — one of the best folk guitar players anywhere. It pleases Rinzler that Doc has become a star. Rinzler came upon Sayles in New York City, a street-corner harmonica player, performing for coins. "I was just walking down the street and I heard him. We got into a long discussion and became close friends. I was very impressed. Not only with his musicianship but with his quick wit and his sense of self — personally and artistically."

Sayles came to the 1975 Festival. He played for the crowds. And he played late, when the crowds were gone, for himself and the cleanup crews. "He was amazed people were that interested in his music and in him. Of course hundreds of people had heard him every day in New York. Some offered to help him but not on his terms. They wanted to put him in a band, change his name, make him into a junior Muddy Waters. He feels he has a long way to go musically. He's working very hard at getting sounds he has in his mind out of his instrument. He plugs into a very deep vein in himself and gets it out in his music. That's very different from putting on a show. As a performer he's quite new." Sayles went back to playing on street corners after the Festival.

Rinzler hears from his finds long after the Festivals are ended. They call him quite a lot and come to see him. Beyond their skills he savors their talk and often tapes it. He likes the answer a Georgia potter gave him when asked if he'd ever made an eight-gallon churn. "Well, I only made an eight-gallon churn once. I labeled it ten gallons and it probably held 12." He likes what a Clinch Mountain Boys singer said to him: "I've just let it come out exactly as I felt, and I never tried to copy anyone singing tenor. Just like I'm talking right now, the way it comes out is the way it's coming."

When Rinzler was six years old an uncle gave him a record of Anglo-American ballads. It featured two musicians who made an impression so deep it remained with him. He met both of them, years later, when he was on the road as a performer. By that time he was a Swarthmore graduate with studies behind him at the Sorbonne in Paris and work experience with folklorists. He had convinced his father, uncles, cousins he was not to be a doctor like them, and reluctantly concluded he was not cut out to be a conductor of Italian opera. For 18 months he had traveled the world as an airlines employee and listened to music at each stop.

After seven years of performing in the music world, Rinzler became a booking agent for some of the talent he found. "The thing I learned was: if you like cultural material that isn't accepted you can figure out a way to make it

acceptable. I did it, with bookings and articles and records."
He criss-crossed the country some more to gather performers
for the Newport Folk Festival. He taped Cajun music in
Louisiana, Gaelic music in Nova Scotia, prison songs in east
Texas.

From there it was a logical step to the Mall, where the
Smithsonian's Secretary Ripley decided the museum's musical
instruments should be taken out of their exhibit cases and
made to sing. Ripley said he thought museum-going should
be an "open experience," with people flowing in and out of
buildings, sensing a connection between their own lives and
the history of their culture.

The Festival helps people make that connection. "Every
American has his feet in at least two cultural camps," says
Rinzler. "We're all Americans. We all know the Anthem.
But we also have identity with other groups that derive from
where we grew up or what our jobs are or where our parents
come from."

A lean man, bearded, wearing a well-tailored, rough
tweed suit, Rinzler is restless. Talking all the while, he
springs from his rocker—to wind his clock, to straighten a
picture, to shift piles of papers. The year before the 1976

summer he was rushing, traveling the world over. He was off to the Far East. Or he was just back from a 12-country tour in Europe, with tales of "some joyous and surprising sound" he had taped — in Italy a little band playing on friction blocks, drums, and flutes, and in Belgium a group of Flemish bagpipers. The bagpipe, Rinzler was discovering, is, next to the drum, the most ubiquitous instrument. In one form and another, it's to be found all over.

The travels became tiring. The official functions too frequent, with the constant need to explain: "No, we can't invite your national ballet or your university choir. What we're interested in is the raw material they draw from. We're looking for vital, living traditions, not a costumed retrospective. We want what takes place around your town square, in your local church." Rinzler already was looking forward to demoting himself, once the big 1976 summer was over, and returning to the field to "find" performers on a more modest scale. That year, though, a large staff was doing the field work of "finding" with him — folklorists, anthropologists, ethno-musicians. They were busy scheduling with colored pins on maps the week by week comings and goings of performers. Washington's Festival requires schedules for the different mixes of groups with their different sausages and dumplings and games and embroideries.

Some field workers were involved in bringing together in Washington the sons and daughters of immigrants who settled in the New World and their cultural cousins who stayed at home in the Old — bringing together Greek-Americans with Greeks, Portuguese-Americans with Portuguese. Other field workers were scouting for loggers in Pennsylvania whose style of working timber was different from that of the Great Lakes loggers and the lumbermen of Oregon.

Folklorist Bernice Reagon made numerous trips to Africa and the Caribbean "looking for the tie-in between African expression and Black-American culture — the north Ghana dance that is like the Bump, the praise-singing that is like the Blues, looking for links in their wood-carving and ours, their cooking, the way they 'cornrow' their hair."

Like Rinzler, Reagon found she had to keep explaining: "It's not a slick performance we put on. We don't have a big stage. Church choirs that have to perform every week, to create the art their communities need — you send them! They make the strong statement that will be understood and accepted.

"I told them," says Reagon, "we don't have any stage that's more than six feet from the ground. The contact is close. We have an open-sided structure the shape of a church for our sacred music. And a little porch stage for *a cappella* singing and storytelling. We have a market area for our street performers and nightlife Blues and Calypso singers — the music you hear after the sun goes down."

It worked out as she hoped. In lulls between performing, members of a merengue band from Haiti and a high-life group from Ghana started up some music together and fiddlers from a Creole group from Louisiana joined in. There were spontaneous jam sessions. Drummers from different areas were fascinated to see the differences in their music, which basically was very much alike.

Reagon, a young, vibrant-looking woman with a lot of presence, found her job exciting. A dramatic-looking figure, in the black and orange robes she makes herself, she has a doctor's degree in oral history from Howard University. She grew up in Albany, Georgia, sang in the Baptist Church, and was a voice major studying classical music when she was caught up in the civil rights movement of the 1960s. "The movement clarified something for me," she says. "While I was in jail what sustained me was the music I'd heard at home, at church, not the music I was learning in school. So I began to collect civil rights songs. I developed a feeling for their roots, though I realized soon enough the need to know more history. I went back to school and did my dissertation on civil rights songs, tracing their origins in terms of the whole American protest movement."

Shirley Askew had worked in the trade union movement. Now her job was finding workers to appear at the Festival and to demonstrate the skills of their trades. She and her field team were looking for people able to relate to crowds, to share the jokes and customs and work styles relating to their occupations. She went to see hatters, furriers, canners, and glass-bottle blowers to extend her invitations. She went through automobile factories and paper-making plants, watched coopers and bricklayers and pipefitters, barbers and butchers as they worked. And she planned ahead with them what equipment they would need on the Mall, what electricity, what water. It was no surprise that transportation workers were a big hit. Everybody seemed to like the airline stewardesses she brought to the Festival, the New York cab drivers, the truckers with their big rigs, and the railroad tie-setters and engineers. There were always lines of people wanting to climb up into the diesel locomotive, into the engineer's seat so they could peer out of his window and fantasize.

Lucille Dawson did the finding among the Indian tribes. She's hearty and direct, herself a Narragansett Indian from Rhode Island, who dresses in slacks, shirt, vest, wears her black hair in two thick braids, and introduces herself as a registered nurse. "I've been a nurse for 20 years but I'm an Indian before I'm a nurse. I've always worked with my tribe and the Festival gave me a chance to work on the national level. Many Indians said to me, 'What do I have to celebrate?' I said, 'The fact you're still here. You come and say what you want to say. Never mind about the Bicentennial. It's *our* Tricentennial at least.' "

In 1975 she concentrated on northeastern tribes—the Passamaquoddy from Maine with their quillwork and the Six Nations of the Iroquois whose Grand Council was a model for the American Constitution and the Articles of Confederation. They made lacrosse sticks and demonstrated the game, as well as the rabbit dance and the stomp.

In 1976 she traveled the country. In Oregon she met with Indians of the Northwest and Plains Indians. She met Kate Pretty-wessel, a Crow, from Montana. She met Hupas who showed her how to make their basket hats, and Lummis whose hide dresses were covered with shells and strips of dried bark that swished as the wearers danced. "It was all

new to me, and yet so similar. We use buckskin where they use hides. Our fish is herring where theirs is salmon. Our large game is deer where theirs is elk. I love our New England seafood but I've never had oysters so huge as the ones the Lummis cultivate. Their fry bread and chili is so hot it brought tears to my eyes to smell it and I never could get it past the tip of my tongue."

Steve Zeitlin's job was family folklore. In 1974, aged 26, and a graduate student in folklore at the University of Pennsylvania, he was asked for his ideas on the Festival. He wound up with a job. He said he thought many visitors to the Festival might not identify their own middle-class lives with what they saw and that they should be invited to tell stories of their own families. That summer he set up a tent on the Festival grounds and taped interviews with people.

"I kept the questions in the interviews open-ended so I didn't wind up with yes and no answers, just a collection of facts. I tried to focus on the stories people tell over and over again—the stuff around which a family celebrates." He wound up with "history, fantasy, comedy, tragedy." Zeitlin liked what he got so much that he put out a booklet with a lot of the family lore under story headings such as the Civil War, the depression, Ellis Island (how immigrant family names were changed), family rogues and anti-heroes, family pets and cars and iceboxes, and all the family sayings that don't make sense to anybody else.

The next year Zeitlin put an ad in the paper for "families' home movies." Hundreds of letters streamed in to him from all across the country, all describing movies of picnics, beach holidays, bar mitzvahs, weddings, and baby's first bubble bath, first tooth, first haircut. Using some of the footage, Zeitlin made his own documentary — to be shown at the next Festival — on how the home movie became an American folk art, with its own rules and conventions.

For the 1976 Festival he filmed five of the 1,000 families he had interviewed and then made a movie of the folklore in their lives. One of the five was the Janney family, of Bethesda, Maryland, who celebrate St. Grunes Day. The tradition began at the supper table one evening as father Janney and his daughters sing-songed "Oranges and lemons say the bells of Saint Clemens." Mother Janney, deadpan, added her own last line: "Raisins and prunes, say the bells of St. Grunes." The next night she served a surprise feast, including bowls of raisins and prunes, and announced it was St. Grunes Day. Ever after, on a particularly nasty winter's day — "when we just can't stand winter any longer" — the Janneys get out their best dishes and celebrate St. Grunes.

When the 1976 Festival closed, Zeitlin went back to complete his PhD at the University of Pennsylvania. He said he thought it a funny quirk in his life that something he'd always been interested in should have become a job.

On the day the Festival ended, staff and participants and visitors sang together "Will the Circle Be Unbroken?" and "Amazing Grace." Director Rinzler joined some Cajun musicians on his mandolin, then told the crowd about a discovery he made that summer — that American banjo players, black and white, young and old, from seaside villages and mountain hollows, all use the same flailing stroke that African musicians have always used. It's a brush down with the fingers and a thumb pluck. He made the discovery, he said, while he was watching some musicians from Senegal. He was pleased. He didn't think anybody had noticed before. He expected other discoveries to follow as students went through the thousands of videotapes from the summer's performances.

 ## KAREN LOVELAND
Filmmaker

Producer-director Karen Loveland appears for five seconds in her own film called *Celebrating a Century.* She's Cleopatra on a couch, wears film-star Elizabeth Taylor's gold Cleopatra costume, and balances a green parrot on her outstretched hand. Loveland is willowy, and, when she isn't scowling over a camera angle or squinting into a view-finder, a natural beauty — though she had some difficulty on this occasion to keep from laughing. There are 250 other Smithsonian employees performing in the film, too, all in nineteenth-century dress, from gardeners, clerks, carpenters, and curators to the Smithsonian's current Secretary, Ripley, who flashes briefly across the screen in a speaking part demonstrating an ice cream machine.

The film is about the 1876 Philadelphia exposition, and uses as background the Smithsonian's own "1876" exhibit. Loveland knew from the start, she says, she didn't want her film to be a half hour of all "flat" material — maps, plans, still photographs. She wanted her film to come alive, through the use of live people in it. "I knew in my mind it had to be a spectacular — a Hollywood spectacular but with superb historical quality." She grins. "That's what you like to think you're making." Loveland was clearly successful in what she was attempting, for the film began to win awards almost as soon as it was completed.

"Our theme was the race against time to open the fair in 1876. It was easy for us to get in the mood. *We* were racing. Time was running out for us. The trouble was, time was running out for the exhibits people, too. They were clearing out the whole Arts and Industries building, making it one huge 65,000-square-foot period room to represent the fair. We spelled trouble for everyone there, bringing in actors and equipment as we did. But it was important. They understood, especially since this exhibition was to have no labels and panels of text. Our film was to tell what this collection of old things was about—what it was like when Philadelphia laid everything out, the great inventions and the bizarre, and said, hey, we really are a nation, let's let our celebration rip!"

Loveland and her film unit began work when Arts and Industries was still a shell, just before the mounting of "1876" began. The first scene shot was the hardest of all and the most dangerous—in it, "workmen" were sliding down ropes from the rafters into a room of intense activity below, where others were uncrating exhibits, filling medicine jars, hanging bunting, stenciling patterns on the walls, planting

trees. The mountain climbers she hired came down the ropes so fast they set the chandeliers swinging.

The film unit photographed dozens of quick vignettes which would later be interspersed with pictures of ticking clocks—all to illustrate the narrator's opening lines: "Time was running out on the builders of the Philadelphia Centennial. . . ." They were building the biggest fair that ever was. One hall of Arts and Industries had to serve as Loveland's set, and she hoped to suggest the size of the completed fair and its army of visitors by crowding all 200 actors into it.

"The whole production was just so huge. It was overwhelming. The numbers were frightening. I'd never directed hundreds of people before. I'd directed animals, objects, and some people. But not on that scale. Of course I had advisers on the nineteenth century right here in the building, and make-up and costume consultants helped us get the effect we needed—the hairstyles, the dark rich palette of browns, purples, orange in the clothes. A composer found music of the period for us and wrote a theme with a sense of urgency, full of ticks and tocks. And I had my constant collaborator John Hiller as photographer.

"But on the day of the crowd scene I was dying inside. I had technical problems on my mind. I worried about the logistics—how to have all our lights and power cables and equipment and all the machines going in the hall at once, how to have the actors on the floor and up on the balcony, all looking right. I worried about the people who were costing us so much money. And I worried about the people who were giving their time. I had to force myself to stop, to forget all this and think instead about what it was we were doing, and what action we were trying to get across."

Once Loveland held up work on the set for three hours to wait for a special high-speed motor. She wanted to film in slow motion "the brigade of broom wielders, the fast-stepping legion of messenger boys, the platoons of artists painting rows of eagles" (these lines were from the script). No one else thought it was important or even a very good idea. "You have to fight for what you want," says Loveland, "and the worst part is you're not sure that what you want will work anyway. You just know it's your responsibility in the end." It did work. The slow-motion scenes in some peculiar way added a zany, frantic air.

For the crowd scene Loveland made sure she had machinist William Henson on the set, in costume, to keep all the machines operating. She photographed him riding the Otis elevator. No one else would have known how to run it, or dared. She set the scene for the opening-day ceremonies on the balcony of History and Technology, with blue sky for a background and the 55-piece U.S. Marine Corps band, on loan to the Smithsonian, playing the Centennial March. Her dignitaries, standing on bleachers, looked properly impressed, and bored with the too-long speeches. And her 50 singers (to represent 1,000 voices) belted out the Hallelujah Chorus while she bombarded them with a recording of it, at top volume.

"It was fun, the most fun thing I've done in a decade. What kept it that way, even through disasters, was that all our actors were people we'd known for years. They were doing this because they wanted to. And they had fun — meeting people from other buildings they'd never known, talking to people they hadn't talked to in years. Things just happen when you put people in costume. Good things. It has an electric effect. They perform for you. Half the people around here live in the nineteenth century, heart and mind, anyway. They knew how to respond. They knew the machinery already."

One of the crowd attractors at Philadelphia's fair had been the "Mohawk Dutchman," a fanatic band sawyer who turned out wood objects like spoons, stools, rocking chairs. He wore a wooden hat with a windmill on top, a wood collar, tie, buckle, shoes. Benjamin Lawless, exhibits director for History and Technology and writer of the "1876" script, made a wood costume for Edwin Battison, a reserved New Englander, who was playing the role. Long ago a machine-tool maker, Battison has been for years curator for light machinery, clocks, and watches. When he was posed as the Mohawk Dutchman next to the bandsaw he amazed everyone. He not only played the part, he began turning out spoons and scrollwork, attracting a crowd himself.

"We didn't just pick people at random," Loveland explains. "We looked for the proper mustaches and beards. We looked for faces that could be nineteenth century and then asked the people the faces belonged to, to be in the film." Five actors were hired for the lead roles. The sixth lead went to an exhibits-crew laborer with an Irish face; he played the Irish mayor of Philadelphia.

Peter Marzio in a derby hat was considered just right for a fair visitor. "We needed some action, but before we could direct him, he was already in a marvelous argument with a machinery salesman, and talking with his hands. We got the musical instruments conservator working on a tiny steam engine, registrar Virginia Beets sipping tea, transportation curators Don Berkebile wielding a wrench and Melvin Jackson as a Supreme Court Justice. Paul Garber, Mr. Air and Space, we cast as a Smithsonian official in a top hat. We shot the liberty bells Collins collected — huge ones made of Kansas wheat, of wood, soap, stone, and we wanted to include Herbert Collins, too. But his face isn't nineteenth century."

Director-producer Loveland came to the Smithsonian, aged 24, to work as a secretary, with nothing more definite in mind than wanting to work somewhere surrounded by the arts. She had been a pianist who gave up the idea of becoming a concert performer when she found she "couldn't practice eight hours a day and still love it." New to filming, she found she could use her musical training and talent in an art form she didn't know anything about. "I was told if you have a sense of rhythm and pace it makes all the difference. You have the beat in you and you know when something's wrong. I've found it's true."

Loveland did her first film on shells — playing with their

variety. Her next, *Ode to the Pinniped*, complemented a Natural History exhibit on seals, sea lions, and walruses — all members of the family of *pinnipeds*. She used existing film footage and keyed it to verse, a take-off on "The Walrus and the Carpenter" ("The time has come/the walrus said/to speak of many things/of shoes and ships and sealing wax/or *pinipeds* and kings . . ."). British actor Cyril Ritchard narrated it for her in a snooty accent. "I just asked him and he agreed." Today the film plays continuously beside a large stuffed walrus with nose in air. And Loveland has been head of the film unit since 1968, responsible for turning out television spots, slide shows, and short films to introduce and enhance exhibits.

In 1975, she set up the film coverage for the Folk Festival on the Mall. She's pleased with the film of the Festival, especially with the ending where the street-corner harmonica player is making music for himself, all alone after the Festival is closed. "The sun is setting. Papers are blowing. You get the loneliness and the beauty in his music. He's playing there with the big shapes of the tents in the background and the Lincoln Memorial in the distance. We didn't have that in the script. It just happened. And the director and photographer Hiller had the creative sense to capture it. They had to make an immediate decision."

She has learned over the years, Loveland says. "You start out with a concept, a visual image and a script, but you don't have to follow it in a rigid formal way. Things have a way of changing, for better or for worse. The pace of images can change. Or the order. That all grows with you. When I started making films I thought it was all straightforward. But you follow your instincts a lot. The final editing and mixing can be the most important thing. You aren't just cutting images. You're blending the narration, too, and the music and the sound effects."

In the years Loveland was learning she also learned that "museums basically don't think much of films. They believe films are frivolous and inappropriate, a substitute for the first-hand museum experience." Loveland hopes this will change. She'd like to see museums committed to film-making—"spiritually and financially. I think our '1876' film gave people a different idea of what film can do—to complement an exhibit. They realize what it takes to make one. They like it more, trust it." All the museum-people actors came to a preview to see themselves in the final product and also in the "out-takes"—a half hour of the blunders and repetitions—all the parts that had to be cut.

Loveland is still a bit apologetic for appearing in her own film. The rest of the crew talked her into it. "There was an automated wax figure at the fair, billed as 'Cleopatra and Her Electric Attachments.' They told me I was the only person with a long enough neck in all the Smithsonian."

PART THREE

The Work

Collecting

Keeping Track

Conserving

Exhibiting

5. Collecting

Museum people collect. It's the work they do, and they're good at it. They go at their collecting deliberately, aggressively, with persistence and glee and style. They know what to collect — what is special and important in their fields, what will fill in the gaps. They know where to collect and how. Smithsonian collectors have networks of friends and resources. They have the backing of a national institution to give them clout. From time to time they have a supply of cash as well, as Herbert Collins [image] did when he bought George Washington's military camp stool at auction, handing over a check for $12,500.

Museum people know what to accept when it's offered and what to reject. The Smithsonian turned down some Thai pottery because proof was lacking that it was imported legally. It recently turned down the San Francisco Mint, the St. Louis Post Office, the liner SS *United States* — as handsome gifts but unwieldy.

Secretary Ripley [image] says such restraint is necessary and right. "Museums must have priority lists" of what they want most, what they want least, what they don't want at all. Ripley recognizes, too, that museums must pounce, on occasion, and never mind the priorities. "At such a moment a proper curator throws caution to the winds and acts as decisively as James Bond with one minute to solve the fate of the world. The curator knows as surely as 007 that in the business of acquiring certain things, from time to time there is no priority. There is only the urgent necessity. Equipped

197

with such powers of discretion, sureness, and authority, curators may act as coolly as any great intelligence operative,
knowing that what they are after may represent one of the
world's precious legacies for the future."

Something like that happened when the National Collection of Fine Arts saved from certain destruction the
Throne of the Third Heaven, abandoned in a Washington garage. Recognized masterpieces aren't the only works which art
curators at the National Collection collect. They are interested in contemporary folk art. They are interested as well in
works that have now fallen from grace but were taken seriously in another century and may even have stood at a piv-
otal point in taste-making. And they are interested in the
lesser works of an artist, which may be important for documenting his early period, or may have played a significant
role in his development.

"To collect well," says Peter Marzio   ▓▌ , "you can't
be a mouse." The collector's attitude is: "There's no harm in
asking." Smithsonian people all up and down the line ask for
what they want. Though Margaret Klapthor   ▓▌ scarcely
has to ask these days for First Lady gowns — First Ladies
know they're supposed to send them around — she asks for
other Presidential accessories, such as White House china,
toys, jewelry, musical instruments, furniture — anything that
shows a First Lady's interests for the time she is in office.
"People are flattered to know you prize their things and want
them for the national museum. Whether they choose to give
or not, they're pleased by your interest and respect. They can
only say no."

From his position at the top, Ripley asks — openly,
cheerfully, brazenly. He asked Joseph Hirshhorn for his im-
mensely valuable art collection. When he won out over a lot
of competition to get it, Congress put up $15 million to
house it. And as icing on the cake, Hirshhorn donated a
further $1 million. In a report to the public in the Janu-
ary, 1976, issue of the *Smithsonian* magazine, Ripley let it
be known that the railroading collection had a serious gap — a

"donkey"—the type of small shunting locomotive long since discontinued. He would dearly love to have one, and only hoped that one might yet be found, rusting away in some Southern pine forest logging camp. A year later Ripley made it known that the donkey of his dreams was on its way to the Smithsonian. It had not been rusting or abandoned anywhere. A Mr. G. M. Best, of Beverly Hills, California, had preserved and lavished years of attention on "Olomana" (vintage 1883).

The one way Smithsonian collectors are hampered is in not being able to swap freely and fast. Collins did make some fast swaps at the Republican and Democratic national conventions in 1976—shrewd swaps, he felt, of a duplicate hat for a noisemaker, of one button for another—but that was only while he was still on the convention floor, picking things up in the aisles, "talking them off" delegates. "Once the objects were accessioned into the museum's collection, my trading had to stop." Trading even then is still possible, at least on some things. But it is more complicated and requires the approval of committees of higher-ups.

Zoo people tend to swap more frequently than the rest. It makes sense, because zoos are trying to specialize in animals they can best show and care for and have a good chance of breeding. National Zoo director Theodore Reed says in trading animals he has to know their value. "A giraffe is worth $10,000 and a clouded leopard $4,000, so when trading a giraffe for a clouded leopard I want more than one clouded leopard in exchange." The Zoo's trade of its rhinoceros, Tony, for an African black male rhinoceros from the Columbus, Ohio, zoo, didn't turn out very well. The rhino on arrival proved to be 26 years old, not six years, as expected. "The record longevity for a black rhino in captivity is 27 years, 10 months and 15 days. So we sent the old boy back to Columbus."

Air and Space people swap, too. "We have to be sure we get the best deal," says Don Lopez, assistant director . He has helped trade a Hawker Typhoon to the British for a

Hurricane, and a spare engine for some very much needed Spitfire and Messerschmitt parts, and one Bear Cat for another. "The Bear Cat we had was plain vanilla. When we swapped it, we got one that was butter pecan: it set a world speed record."

One of the Smithsonian's expert collectors is postal history curator Carl Scheele 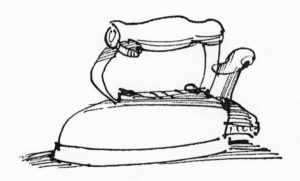 of History and Technology. He collects on several different levels. He collects at home, on a rather modest scale, for himself, he says: beer bottles (he has 50), popular and jazz records (78 rpm), commercial pin-back buttons (Red Goose Shoes), and buttons relating to local politics or trade unions (Bricklayers Picnic 1928). He collects regularly, and on a far grander scale, for the Smithsonian's postal history division, by adding to its approximately 14 million stamps. And as the person in charge of the *Nation of Nations* exhibit, he spent three years gathering—in fields beyond postal history—some 8,000 items, of which 7,000 in the end were used.

Like Herbert Collins, Scheele was pretty much born to collecting, growing up in a household, in Cleveland, Ohio, where his finds of arrowheads and matchbooks were appreciated. "Our home was the kind of place where a lot of familiar things had been for a long time. My family didn't throw things away. Nothing ever quite wore out. My grandfather and father were accumulators—of old eggbeaters and carbon-filament lightbulbs and iron banks—back when those things had no monetary value—and artifacts from the fields around our house. They spent their weekends in the attic, building showcases and organizing and classifying what they had, to make some visual and intellectual sense of it."

As a teenager, serving as telegraph operator for the B&O Railroad, Scheele worked in old stations and used nineteenth-century instruments and equipment. "I enjoyed those things and felt comfortable in the environment." Later as a cowboy on a ranch he lived with a family that fixed its worn saddles and kept its aged trucks running.

Once he became postal history curator at the Smithsonian, having earned a college degree at age 26 and a Master's in history at 29, Scheele set about enlarging the scope of the museum's collection. It was essentially stamps at that time—plus Owney, a stuffed dog which in life had hitched 143,000 miles of rides in mail cars. Scheele's aim was to collect more and more three-dimensional objects. He went after the canceling devices, starting with 1876 models. He obtained the pouches, letter boxes, and locks which represented security and were visible evidence of the American belief in privacy. After that he wanted, whole, for the museum, a rural post office.

He was looking for a typical crossroads post office combined with a store, the kind of post office that for thousands of communities served as a social center, where people came together to gossip and sit around playing checkers, the kind of post office that was being phased out of existence with the spread of rural delivery. Scheele knew he'd come to the end of his 10,000-mile search for it when he parted the weeds and put his nose to the dirty window of the former post office in Headsville, West Virginia. In it was the original sorting box—a panel of pigeonholes, solid, with no glass, so that people had to put their heads around the corner to check if they had mail. The post office even had names on its shutters, traceable to Civil War soldiers passing through. They must have leaned against the front wall and signed. It was just what Scheele wanted, and Chuck Rowell uprooted it and moved it into the museum.

Scheele's collecting shifted gears when he was put in charge of the 1976 *Nation of Nations* exhibit. As head of a team of curators he had to comb the Smithsonian's exhibits and storerooms for objects to tell the story — of the immigrants' role in America — and search out, borrow, or buy the rest.

"In house" he found important historical items like Washington's Revolutionary War uniform and his mess chest and Jefferson's lap desk on which he drafted the Declaration of Independence. In house also, he had vehicles that served immigrants in the new land — a mudwagon (stagecoach), New England tin peddler's cart, Model T roadster, and plans for the "immigrants' sleeping car" (convertible day coachsleeper) built by the railroads for East-to-West immigrant traffic. He had his choice of Spanish grain sifters and Chinese carrying baskets and, perfect for his purpose, a button-making machine (for mother-of-pearl buttons) brought in steerage across the ocean by a Czech immigrant. The division of musical instruments had on hand, ready to show, Irving Berlin's piano.

The Natural History Museum next door sent along its Great Plains Indian bull boat made of buffalo hides (the Indians were immigrants, too). From across the Atlantic the British Museum sent, in a first-class airplane seat, its Akan drum, made by a Virginia slave. The Park Service on Ellis Island lent a bench where immigrants sat while their papers were processed. Scheele went by launch to collect it. Some Texans sent a 31-foot windmill. Other sources lent a looking glass that came over on the *Mayflower,* a silver christening cup made by Paul Revere, and baseball bats used by Babe Ruth, Stan Musial, and Joe DiMaggio. Muhammad Ali donated in person his boxing gloves, saying as he presented them, "My gloves will be the most famous things in this building." And the curator of costume managed to locate a Russian tailor's equipment — his tables, sewing machine, shears, and shop sign and the patterns he cut from Yiddish-language newspapers.

A lot of objects were bought, such as the American Gypsy wedding dress and Peter Marzio's neon signs and foreign-language comic books. Some of the finds were free for the taking, such as political posters on telephone poles, featuring Polish, Irish, and Spanish names. Some items Scheele took from his family — sheet music from his mother, sports cards from his 15-year-old son. Some came in response to Scheele's ad in the Smithsonian's newspaper asking for World War I and II dogtags. One of the best sets of tags came from a Smithsonian guard whom Scheele already knew as a stamp collector. His name: Rochambeau Herosian. Born on shipboard as his Armenian parents immigrated to America, he was named Rochambeau for the boat. "Rocky" Herosian also gave documents to go with his dogtags, including the telegram to his parents which said he was wounded. He gave his elementary school report card.

Scheele went into the field after big items for the exhibit's section on "shared experience" — public education, the Army, sports, the American dream home. He hunted for the public school classroom in Cleveland. "I went there knowing large industrial centers attracted immigrant populations, and also because I knew my way around in Cleveland and felt historically comfortable there." Scheele didn't attend the Dunham School from which he took the classroom, but he went to another Cleveland school very much like it. And for a time he taught in one like it, too.

"I wanted a school where children of different origins had streamed through — getting a common education, singing 'My Country 'Tis of Thee,' sitting alphabetically, getting along with each other, or not." Checking the Dunham records he saw that the population of the classrooms changed over the generations and the changes reflected the waves of immigrants to America. Early on, the pupils were from English, German, Irish, French families. Then they were of Middle and Southern European stock. When the school closed recently, the children were Spanish, Puerto Rican, American black, Appalachian white.

"There are certain things you think will be available and you make an effort to get them. When I heard Yankee Stadium was being torn down and rebuilt, I went to the New

York Yankees' head office and asked for things. The ticket booth we were given was just fine, because everyone going there would have dealt with it. It was a touchstone of common interest. So were the stadium seats."

The American dream house of the early twentieth century with its mass-produced furniture could have been Czech-American or Polish-American. Scheele decided on Italian-American because that group was heavily represented and because a large number of household effects was available from a single source, an Italian-American doctor, Arcangelo D'Amori, who had recently inherited them from his parents. Included were religious pictures from the walls, with a portrait of the patron saint of the family's home town among them, as well as the sausage crock, the icebox, the iron for making Italian waffles, the doilies made by the mother, and a guest towel embroidered "Felicita."

"If you've collected, you have practice in going out and asking questions and you have confidence," says Scheele. "It's easy to learn *what* to collect. *How* to collect is harder. It depends on a variety of experiences." All the jobs he has ever had, he says, are useful to him in museum collecting, including his railroad work. When the track car arrived in the building from the Atchison, Topeka & Santa Fe — to illustrate the place of immigrants in the work force — he helped to lay the track. "In fact, I don't know what this exhibit would look like if the people putting it together didn't understand tools and the ways people work and know the look of the workingman's home."

Scheele worked on the *A Nation of Nations* exhibit all through the preparations, a short, rumpled-looking figure with a fluff of flax hair and mustache, a briar clenched in his teeth, and a pair of suspenders holding up his pants. He was a willing wielder of paintbrush and hammer when they were needed. In Karen Loveland's "1876" film he performed as a rigger, roping a totem pole into position. Wearing a costume of derby hat, baggy pants, long-sleeved underwear shirt, and a vest that didn't manage to button across the middle, he looked right at home at the work.

"You use all your contacts, personal and professional, and you use hearsay before you're through," says Scheele, "especially to collect things that have no particular market value. There are places to buy stamps. You know where to go for Ali's gloves or Hank Aaron's uniform or Billie Jean King's tennis dress. You ask and it's either yes or no. Other things can be really obscure, like the items for the Italian-American home — common tablewear, really common, door-knobs, bathroom fixtures. There's no single place you can find electric lighting fixtures of a particular decade." He got the right brass lighting fixtures without too much difficulty. He would have been stuck for the glass globes to fit in them, but a friend of the curator of glass and ceramics gave him six.

Scheele and an assistant, Ellen Roney Hughes 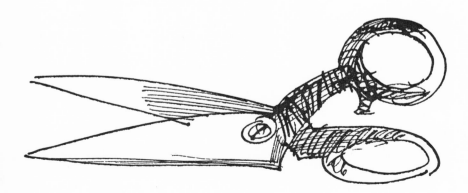 , checked old Sears catalogs for period clothespins, curtains and curtain rods, a bathtub on feet. They combed antique shops and junk stores, telephoned dealers, gave lists to friends. And two items eluded them. The first, inkwells for the classroom. They were delighted when a plumber from Dunham school gave them one he'd carried home, years back, in a pocket. (The others had to be copied from it.) Second was the ice card, to hang in the kitchen window of the 1920s home, indicating to the iceman an order for 25 pounds of ice, or 50, or 100, its numbers written large enough for him to read from his wagon. A friend brought the card in on the day before *A Nation of Nations* opened.

Scheele, who was not able to buy a suitable 1920s-type button mattress for the bedstead, hauled one away, free, from a curbside. He fumigated it and put it on the bed. "Part of the how of collecting is to be historically correct. You make an effort to obtain the real thing, even though a bedspread covers the mattress anyhow. That's the classic attitude. It ought to be a mattress rather than a box built to look like a mattress. You feel much better if the article is original, documented, and can be authenticated. Some people feel that's going too far. But for a museum of history and technology it's important. At the other extreme you have wax museums or stage sets. If we deal with the past there is no substitute for the real thing."

Sometimes collecting real things for an exhibition leads to an entirely new category of museum collectible—as it did when Marzio collected neon signs for *A Nation of Nations*. Sometimes it leads to a specialty on the part of the collector, as it did for Edith Mayo ▉▌▎ , who was assigned to find protest materials for *We the People*—among them, signs and banners to be held by protestors (who appear as life-sized photographic blow-ups) standing on steps before a painted backdrop of the Capitol. In the course of her search Mayo came to be expert on protest materials. She knew the people and the organizations. When her work on *We the People* was over, she found she had carved out a full-time occupation for herself. She was named the Smithsonian's curator for political reform movements and also for women's history, with a territory including women, blacks, Indians, farmworkers, youth, the poor.

Mayo's first telephone calls for materials were a flop, she recalls. "It took me some time to establish rapport. The first reaction of the social action groups I talked to was shock. They didn't think I was serious. They thought the Smithsonian was too elitist, that political history here was confined to Presidents, First Ladies, and statesmen. They just couldn't see themselves represented in the museums. I kept calling till I found someone who began to respond. After that I was on the grapevine."

To portray the blacks' struggle for political equality, Mayo especially wanted material from the Voting Rights March from Selma to Montgomery, Alabama, in 1965, which was led by Martin Luther King, Jr., other churchmen, and civic leaders. First she put in a call to the headquarters of the Southern Christian Leadership Conference in Atlanta. SCLC didn't have anything for her. Then she reached Hosea Williams, who had been in charge of march logistics. He told her to call his wife, Juanita. "I talked for an hour with her, wanting her to understand why we were asking for the things she had. Pictures are fine, I told her, but there's something about objects that evokes the spirit. What we were trying to evoke was the spirit of the marchers.

"Mrs. Williams understood that. She said she still had things from the march, like her shoes with the heels worn off from the marching. I told her we'd like those. She had her husband's coat, torn when he was beaten. We wanted that, too. She said they were in her attic, along with some of the hats that were given to marchers who completed all 53 miles and the little flags with the slogan "One Man One Vote" that were run up—in haste—on the march itself at each of the stops. I was excited about everything. And she was glad to send it."

In line of her collecting duties Mayo attended rallies. She found for her storage drawers homemade peace posters done in marking pens, paints, and crayons, and some of the mass-produced posters as well put out by major peace organizations like Women Strike for Peace, SANE, and groups of Quakers. Outside the Bureau of Indian Affairs, in 1972 when the American Indian Movement took over the building, she was given the list of demands.

Mayo collected materials from the drive to lower the voting age to 18, which wound up successfully when Congress passed the 26th Amendment in 1971. She obtained youth-vote posters ("If You Let Them Register, Next Thing You Know They'll Be Voting"), clothing with VOTE lettered on it — T-shirts and kneesocks, and also voter registration materials on the theme of Old Enough to Fight, Old Enough to Vote.

The rundown shoes from Selma, the posters, the youth-vote clothing all went into *We the People* and were put on view together with pinback buttons that say "Boycott Lettuce" and "Don't Eat Grapes" (part of the effort of the United Farm Workers to be recognized as bargaining agents for farm workers) and also a plywood hut from the Poor People's Campaign, which camped on the Mall in Washington in the muddy spring of 1968 to demonstrate for jobs. A Smithsonian truck picked up the hut as police closed down the Resurrection City encampment when its permit ran out.

Though she collects in what is very much a new field, Mayo feels she started almost too late. "These things die. A year after an event and they're gone." Like other collectors she has to decide now, at the moment, what things will be important in another ten years. She is collecting heavily on the women's movement — on the progress of the Equal Rights Amendment (ERA) and on women in politics. She received as a gift to the museum one of Bella Abzug's hats, as a symbol of that New York Congresswoman's colorful stint in the House of Representatives, and one of Abzug's campaign posters ("This Woman's Place Is in the House").

She's still filling in the gaps on the suffragists. The Smithsonian already had Susan B. Anthony's red shawl, worn when she lobbied for women in Congress, the table on which the Declaration of Sentiments was written at the first women's rights convention in 1848, the key to the Washington jail where women were imprisoned in 1917 for picketing the White House. Recently on a visit to Radcliffe College she was offered ten woman's suffrage banners—"a stroke of good fortune." It was an important acquisition for the museum, which had plenty of banners from national groups but none, such as these, of local groups with grass-roots origins.

Robert Vogel   , whose field is power machinery and civil engineering, carved out a collecting specialty for himself in History and Technology—industrial archaeology. He seeks out bridges, mills, factories and other physical survivals of engineering's and industry's past, things which were built to last. Though eventually they may disappear, they don't disappear fast. But he's hampered in his collecting by their size.

The "1876" show welcomed his finds of big machinery. But he can't really go out and collect factories for the museum, even though certain of them go right to his heart, the way the wooden wheel factory did, in Westchester, Pennsylvania. "That factory took in raw logs at one end and turned out wheels at the other, using entirely one-purpose machinery unchanged from a century before, producing an obsolete product by an obsolete method." That pleased him. But he had to be satisfied with documenting it descriptively and graphically through measured drawings, photographs, and films. Vogel had to settle for that kind of documentation, too, for the water-powered sawmill he stumbled on during a holiday and for a factory in Connecticut making water turbines.

Scientists at the Natural History Museum spend part of each year in the field—observing and collecting. They go out with nets and buckets and picks to collect insects, algae, coral, volcanic rock, fish. They collect birds and mammals too, though in far fewer numbers than they once did. Many are already well represented in the collections by genus, species, and subspecies, so that collecting more really isn't necessary. Others have so dwindled in number in the wild that they are not attainable however much the scientists want or need them.

Mammals curator, Richard Thorington, Jr.   , "collects" howler monkeys with an anesthesia dart gun. He shoots at a howler and catches it in a net when it wobbles and falls from the tree. He takes its measurements, tooth casts, fingerprints, blood and tissue samples. He marks it, by freeze-branding rings on its tail (which turns the hair white). And he releases it.

Thorington's short-term collecting of the monkey is part of his study of a troop of howlers on Barro Colorado Island in the tropics of Panama. He is studying their population dynamics—lifespans, death rates, the frequency of births to different-aged females. Since howlers live for some 20 years, it's a long-term project.

Following the howlers' movements through the forest isn't all that difficult, Thorington says. Even though the "lugubrious-looking fellows," as he refers to them, tend to be 60 feet up in the treetops, they move relatively slowly. They make a considerable racket, roaring and engaging in territorial howling battles. And the white rings branded on the tails help him to distinguish one from another.

The problem with observation and data collecting is that one avenue of study always leads to another and then to another. To learn about the monkeys, he found he really had to learn about the trees which the monkeys lived in and moved through and fed on. He had to map his 500-by-500-meter forest plot and consider how many trees there were and of how many different kinds, how they were distributed, whether randomly or clumped, how their distribution related to the monkeys' search path for food, how a season's poor fruit yield related to a monkey die-off.

"I hammer a tag on a fig tree or a hog plum tree where I see howlers eating," Thorington explains. "Then I have to study the fruiting and leafing cycles of that tree, which may fruit, say, in February, April, and September. The monkeys forced me into it. It's the kind of thing *I* need to know because the monkeys know it." The monkeys also forced him into conservation. "Nearby forests are being cut for farming, cattleland and wood. I'm afraid if I don't do something about saving at least part of the forest, in another 20 or 30 years I won't have monkeys to study at all."

Still another problem, basic to his research, is how to get specimens he can use for anatomical studies. Thorington's howlers, which are the mantled howler monkeys of Central America, are an endangered species and protected by strict government regulations. He can't bring specimens back to the Smithsonian. "If I find a dead monkey, I can't bring it back. If I find a legbone, I can't bring it either. I can't import a monkey or any part thereof. The regulations are made that way to prevent the making of monkey-fur pocketbooks or wastebaskets from elephant feet to sell to tourists. There are reasons for the regulations and for not excluding anyone, but it means I have to want the material enough to go through a lot of governmental red tape to get permits."

The mammals division in the museum has a "moderately good collection" of howler monkeys already, he says. It's just that there are not enough specimens on which he, or other researchers,.can do studies of anatomy. "I wouldn't collect more skins, because we have them, but we need more cadavers and more skeletal materials for dissections." Thorington gets what cadavers he can from drug companies, which use the monkeys for medical research. He gets them from zoos.

"It's the same with other mammals. There are anguishing aspects to collecting. Species are going to be extinct and we won't have the opportunity to do further anatomical studies. It's because we have collections — because we have mammals here from all over the world and from many different periods — that research can be done. Were there armadillos in Florida in 1900? What was the heavy metal concentration in a particular animal in a particular area at a particular time? If we have the feathers, the bones, the hair, then someone can possibly find out. These are questions we'll never be able to answer if we don't save the animals.

A telephone call, interrupting Thorington as he talks, is right to his point. His eyes light up with pleasure. He practically sings his response. "Why, I'd be *delighted* to get a frozen baby camel. Yes, yes, dry ice. And use a lot of newspaper around him and be sure not to send him here on a Friday. Let me know what flight."

At his home in the Washington area, off-hours, Thorington collects squirrels on the same capture-and-release basis as he collects his howlers. He bags gray squirrels in his backyard and snaps little bead necklaces on them for a study he's making on the survival tactics and life-styles of suburban squirrels.

Mammals curator James Mead 🐾 , who specializes in whales, uses a truck as his collecting tool. Though he has been known in the past to carry a nine-foot whale carcass in the back of a Volkswagen, he now has a four-wheel-drive truck equipped with a hydraulic bed and a winch. He is alerted to his whale finds by telephone.

Mead depends on sources outside the Smithsonian to let him know when there's a specimen to pick up. Thousands of posters with a mug shot of a whale have been posted in public places all up and down the Atlantic Coast alerting people to his Marine Mammal Salvage Program. WANTED, say the posters. *Information Concerning Stranded or Beached Whales, Dolphins and Seals. Call the Smithsonian Institution* 202 381-4174.

Through 1975, on the average of once a week (now somewhat less often) Mead or his assistant, Charlie Potter, would be out in the truck making a pickup. Most of the 40- to 70-foot whale specimens they work up on the beach, often with help from passers-by. A smaller one they bring in to the museum — even though, as it happened with a 22-foot infant finback, the tail fluke may drag on the pavement all the way — and they put it either into a walk-in freezer or on the floor in the preparation room where, Mead says, "We make a large mess and hose it up after."

Mead's interest is to find out from a whales census what species inhabit the Atlantic, how many exist of each, and where. He figures it will take him years of studying the strandings and of flying over schools of whales, counting them. He has already learned a lot. One of the extraordinary finds through the programs was a Blainville's beaked whale that washed ashore in New Jersey, still alive, though just barely so. "It had never been studied live by a biologist. We were able to see how its blowhole worked. The breath is directed forward over the snout instead of straight up into the air. There may be more of this species out there in the ocean than we suspected, because the way it blows it is virtually impossible to see it at sea unless you're up close."

In the first two years of the salvage program Mead examined several hundred whales. With about 20 strandings a year of the pygmy sperm whale he had an idea of how relatively common a species it is. He had an idea of its seasonal distribution, food habits, reproduction. At a mass stranding of 35 pilot whales off South Carolina, Mead noticed that all the victims had parasite roundworms in their middle ears and sinuses. Potter had seen the same in beached dolphins. The men became pretty sure that the worms must have cancelled out the animals' natural sonar devices; with their navigation thus thrown off, they had blundered onto the beach and died. Mead says that scientists don't yet know whether healthy whales might also have such parasites in their ears.

With funds a bit shorter in 1976 Mead was more selective about his pickups. He settled for information and parts of the animals if the find happened to be a common bottle-nosed dolphin or a fin whale. He continued to drive out after the rarer whales, especially after the beaked whales, of which some of the 15 to 20 species are known only from single specimens. He went to the massive whale kill in Florida in 1977 where close to 200 whales died, most of them females carrying fetuses.

Word of the whale sightings reaches Mead through the Scientific Events Alert Network in the basement of the Natural History building where he works. The Coast Guard may call in that a 40-foot whale was seen stranded off the southeast tip of No Man's Land, Massachusetts. Or the Fish and Wildlife Service may call that it has a man up in a Navy helicopter following a drifting whale that seems to be in trouble. Or individuals call to report a whale they came across on a beach walk.

Mead has prepared a whale spotter's handbook to help untrained observers identify species and take measurements. Shirley Maina   in the Scientific Events office helps, too, on identifications, asking those who telephone in the size, color, shape of head of their find, asking whether it has teeth or baleen. She asks whether the whale is still alive, in which case it may need to be covered with blankets and hosed down, or whether it is dead, in which case she wants to know if it's fresh or rotten. She asks if the whale is reachable by four-wheel-drive vehicle or by boat. If a crew doesn't go to the site immediately she gives advice on how to secure the specimen or get it to a commercial freezing plant and what photographs to take.

For scientifically minded and hardy people who are willing to work up the animal on the spot she has a checklist of measurements and observations that will be needed — how the stomach contents are to be saved, the parasites, the glands, the blood samples, the skeletal material. And she gives the whereabouts of a California graduate student who would like to have the eyes forwarded to her in a plastic bag packed around with ice.

Mead sometimes goes on collecting trips for specific animals that are poorly represented in the Smithsonian's collections—such as Weddell seals or Southern sea lions. What often happens, though, is that he finds a specimen that he isn't looking for. Mead is convinced there is a lot of luck to his collecting. It's practically spooky, he says, the way his trips to meetings seem to coincide with unusual strandings, and not infrequently, he comes home from these conferences reeking of dead whale. Once on a trip he walked on a Patagonian beach on the southern tip of South America and came upon his most extraordinary find of all—a freshly beached beaked whale, probably the rarest and least known of all marine animals. He was able to do a thorough job on it on the spot and send the whole skeleton home to Washington.

Museum people agree there's luck in collecting. There's luck in a whale's washing ashore, luck in a tattoo kit's being offered out of the blue just when marine-man Jackson was giving up his search, luck in a Knox tractor's coming to the museum just when cars-man Berkebile needed one. Collectors accept their luck with pleasure. They try to encourage it by being available and imaginative, by being knowledgeable in their fields, and persistent.

Silvio A. Bedini   , deputy director in charge of research at History and Technology, and one of its best collectors, is known for having a good share of luck and an extra measure of persistence.

It was Bedini who recently obtained for the Smithsonian an entire rare books library, including manuscripts by Einstein, Faraday, and Newton, one manuscript page of Darwin's *Origin of Species,* a letter by Galileo, and a book containing the first account of Copernicus's then new view of the universe.

Bedini got Helen Keller's watch for the Smithsonian through a long search that at first led him down many false trails. He knew that the gold pocket touch-watch had been the blind woman's prized possession from the time she received it on her fourteenth birthday, and that she had lost it at least once, inside her green crocodile purse left in a New York taxi. It was restored to her on that occasion by a pawnbroker. And Bedini felt sure it survived her death. By the time he tracked down the watch through a web of people to Helen Keller's niece and nephew (who gave it to the Smithsonian), the search had taken him 15 years.

Bedini received on loan, in time for Bicentennial display, the gold pocket watch which Washington gave to his friend Lafayette commemorating the victory at Yorktown. The watch had been stolen from the French general and was rediscovered more than half a century later, along with a written confession, in the secret compartment of a desk. Bedini, with the watch in hand, researched his find still further.

He searched through Washington's papers, Lafayette's papers, newspapers, hoping to find a reference to the gift. He made a horological search, by which he learned that the watch had Dutch movements. The English name on the face, J. Halifax, was a fake. The watch was made in Holland, probably sneaked across the channel, and sold out of England—a common practice at the time. Bedini also did lab work on the watch, by which he determined that the inscription on it from Washington to his friend was consistent with the period both in the way it was engraved and in the style of the writing. One point worried Bedini from the start: the watch was not in Washington's style of spare elegance. "I knew every watch Washington had from the time he was born and this one was more ornate, by far.

"When you trace something back into a family, like this watch or like Washington's false teeth—which the Smithsonian has on display—you rely on the documentation that goes with it. You accept the family's account. But you verify it in all these other ways to make sure you have the real thing."

Bedini has collected for the museum along with the timepieces many items of machinery, many tools and instruments, including the instruments used in surveying the District of Columbia. "There are a lot of things you collect which are not popular," he says. "Tools don't interest everyone. The components of the first radio compass are not charming to see. Nor is the seven-ton generator from Niagara Falls. But they're important historically and technologically. They're significant milestones and important to keep."

Some objects the Smithsonian has are baffling as to their identity and purpose. Lacking all documentation they baffle even such a tools-and-contraptions expert as Bedini. They have been put on display in a History and Technology showcase with a plea to the public for enlightenment. A sign in the *Whatsit?* case, containing several dozen mystery things, explained that guesses were welcome and documentation appreciated. Visitors wrote in: Your Whatsit (4) looks like a primitive lemon squeezer. Or, I think your Whatsit (7) is an instrument of torture. Couldn't you bunch asparagus with the

tall-standing apparatus (9)? Occasionally a visitor had the definitive answer: Your Whatsit (7) is a crab shank laster used in shoemaking to grip the leather and pull it around the last. A picture of it appears in an 1880 catalog and price list printed in St. Louis.

Documents are sought out by museum people with the same exhaustive techniques they use for objects. Bedini has dozens of letters of inquiry in the mail at all times. For papers he hopes may exist and thinks ought to exist he writes to town officials and librarians all over the world. "I say, 'I assume you have these documents' or 'Surely the following papers are in your care.' It's a positive approach and nine times out of ten it works."

A Vatican librarian, Cardinal Mercati, after many letters back and forth, once wrote to Bedini begging him to cease his inquiries for some Vatican patent documents. "He told me, 'I'm old, weary, ill, I can no longer carry the burden of your correspondence.' He told me once again that the papers I wanted simply did not exist." Bedini admits he was almost ready to give up, when, the following week, a fat packet arrived, covered with Vatican seals. The papers existed after all and had been found. Bedini has since had a letter signed by the Pope, inviting him to search in person behind the scenes in the Vatican library and into the tunnels and the clockworks of the basilica of St. Peter. "I sent the Pope my book on the moon," says Bedini, "knowing he's a space nut."

Bedini's early collecting, before he came to the Smithsonian, consisted mostly of guns, which he bought and repaired. His rule then was a $1 limit on a purchase. The one time he exceeded his limit and bought a dirty old clock, mouse nests included, for $20, he opened up a new field for himself. The clock, he found, was signed by a clockmaker to the Vatican.

Since that time Bedini has written widely on timekeeping, and on clockmakers and other scientists, whom he refers to as thinkers and tinkers. When he wrote on black scientist Benjamin Banneker, who helped to survey the site for the District of Columbia and who built a striking clock without ever having seen one, he was told that Banneker's papers had been lost in a fire. It took a dogged search but Bedini found Banneker's astronomical journals in an outbuilding on a farm in upper New York State. And he found Banneker's "commonplace book," a pocket notebook bound in shoe leather, which contained jottings of expenses and calculations, in an attic in Baltimore. The finds were strokes of luck. Bedini in the meantime had taught himself the same math and astronomy known to Banneker by reading the texts available to that unschooled son of slaves. Just recently Bedini discovered the whereabouts of Jefferson's collection of 200 fossils, wrapped, labeled, just as they had been left by their collector. It was luck, here too, for no one knew the fossils were anywhere to be seen.

"The point is," says Bedini, "everything survives. Or almost everything. Things survive, though they may not be in the place you expect them to be."

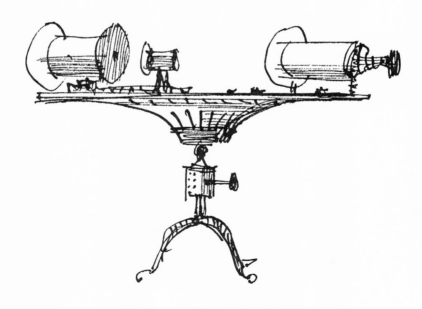

6. Keeping Track

Keeping track of collections involves good recordkeeping and good housekeeping and just about never throwing anything away. To do the job every museum and gallery has its registrar, as History and Technology has Virginia Beets. ▓▓ It has its way of numbering, its way of taking things in, lending them out, handling them, packing them. Keeping track is tremendously complex. It's complex because most objects don't file away as easily as books. They're awkward. They're either fragile or odd in shape or just plain big, or, like some dinosaurs and airplanes, they are all three. Keeping track is complex, too, because the collections, which are huge, are growing all the time, spilling out of their cupboards, filling up the corridors, overloading the buildings.

National collections pretty much have to grow and they have to be kept together. They can't very well be divided up and dispersed around the country. The value of collections for study is in being complete. It's possible of course to keep a lid on acquiring things. Museums try to be selective in their collecting. Curators try to limit themselves to things that are significant and special, even though what's special about them may be how ordinary they are, how typical of a period. They try to discipline their intake of Piper Cubs and chests-on-chests and election billboards. Still, healthy collections grow.

Museum people say it's not possible to stop them. It's not possible to stop collecting manmade things as long as they last because the art of their making is vanishing. It's not possible to stop collecting natural history specimens when the Smithsonian's purpose is to tabulate "all the species of plants and animal forms on the face of the earth and under the seas and in the skies." It's a task that everyone expects to take generations to complete. Yet there's a special urgency about it as the face of the earth is now changing rapidly, destroying environments that nurture birds, beasts, grasses, insects, fish. Species are becoming extinct before they are known to exist.

If collections continue growing at a rate between one and two percent a year the people who keep track of them have to make the best of it. So they welcome the 800,000 insects that come to them in one year. They don't complain when rocks arrive for the paleobiologists in five-ton lots. They still have to be sure that all the collections are in order and are accessible, that they themselves know what they have and can get at what they want. It ought to be possible for them to put a finger on any one of the 100 million things, or at least to know that it's in the fumigation tank or under study in the conservation lab or on exhibit or out on loan or laid up in the Zoo infirmary.

Much recordkeeping is done by computers that take in information and spit out cards. Numbers are one part of the recordkeeping. Basically they come in two kinds—accession numbers and catalog numbers. The accession number is assigned by the registrar. It's one permanent number that applies to one transaction from one source no matter how many things are involved. A quilt, a clock, a cap, a car from donor X on date Y is given one accession number for the lot—the quilt the same as the clock, the cap, the car. As the items arrive at the textiles division, or the clocks division, or clothing or transportation, each item is given a catalog number and storage space according to the systems used there, which may be very different one from another. If quilt, clock, cap, car were all possessions of a U.S. President they'd all go to one place—to political history. They'd still receive individual catalog numbers but the numbers would be consecutive.

Natural history specimens have field numbers as well as

the accession and catalog numbers. A scientist carries a field catalog with him which is his personal collecting record. He may choose to number in sequence, assigning number One to the first bird he skinned at age eight. Or he may start a new number series with each expedition. The Smithsonian's Secretary Ripley , who goes out by yak in search of high-altitude birds, has a new number One for each expedition.

As Ripley prepares a bird skin in the field he writes its field number on the back of the tag, the locality, date, his initials, the bird's sex, measurements, and any notes, possibly on soft-part color which might fade before he sees the bird again in his lab. Back in Washington the bird skins are entered into the Smithsonian's birds catalog one by one, the catalog numbers go on the front of each tag, and the registrar assigns an accession number to the lot.

As special top-man treatment Ripley was given one whole catalog volume to keep in his lab, a fat book labeled on its spine 517901–522900. All those numbers are his, given to him when he came in 1964. They're almost used up, and the book is almost filled—handwritten, column by column, in a fine hand. The birds division has 110 such volumes, starting back with bird number One in 1858, which was a whip-poor-will collected by the Smithsonian's second Secretary, Spencer F. Baird, 19 years earlier in Carlisle, Pennsylvania. When the birds division reached Ripley's block of numbers it just picked up again beyond him, with

522901. It was reaching 600,000 by 1977. That's 600,000 for the skins and skeletons collection only. There are other volumes and another numbering system for eggs and nests.

Beyond the numbers and paperwork there's the actual storage—the stowing away of objects in some order so they can be found when needed. Congress is appropriating money for the Smithsonian to build a big modern storage facility away from downtown Washington. In the meantime most of the storage space is overstuffed. There's a sense of never enough space or time or hands to do all the filing away that needs to be done, or packing, or the maintenance—whether dusting or oiling or mothproofing. And while some of the collections look manageable, some look as though chaos were taking over.

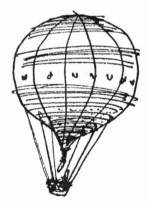

Throughout all the museum buildings people on various levels of jobs are involved in keeping track. In a few cases the collectors themselves do it, the finders being also the keepers. In others, there are special people to do it. They must cope with a whole range of problems.

Air and Space has 265 planes. Its recordkeeping isn't anything like entomology's, which has 23 million insects. Still, it has been something of a triumph, just to get all but two of the 265 airplanes under cover (the *Sacred Cow*, assigned to Presidents Roosevelt and Truman, and President Kennedy's *Caroline* are still out in wind and weather). And

the Air and Space people look on their Charlie Parm-
ley   🛡   as something of a wizard for having devised
racks for stacking wings and for having custom-fit every airplane with its own stand. Planes were getting damaged, just
in their indoor moves to and from the restoration shop.
Planes, especially when they're partly dismantled, don't move
easily on the ground—certainly not a "Betsy" bomber that's
only half there; nor a fragile old Blériot, which looks like a
baby buggy from the airshow days; not even a Waterman
Aerobile, part-plane, part-car, but which the air mechanics
say combines the worst features of both.

At History and Technology, a look-in at just about any
of the storage rooms, on the windowless side of the corridors
from the offices, gives a glimpse of curators and their assistants "curating"—tending, managing—their collections.

Elliot Sivowitch   ▦|| , specialist in electricity and elec-
tronics, looks like a boy with baseball cards from bubblegum
packs, as he sorts his QSL cards. He is surrounded by a batch
of equipment which he calls his "electronics fairyland." Ham
radio operators (he's one himself) send the cards to each other
to acknowledge conversations they've had. QSL is part of the
Q code, used in early radio communications, QSL being the
symbol for acknowledging radio contact. ("Do you QSL?" "I
QSL.") Many of the cards have a nice bit of colorful artwork
on them, but the value is in the place they came from—the
more remote the better. Sivowitch has about 100 in hand, the
best from places like the Galapagos Islands and Burma and
Russia. "It's a subhobby within a hobby," he says of the
cards, "and it's become kind of a big operation."

There's always work to be done on the other materials
stored on shelves up and down the aisles—research on the
patents, a tracing of pedigrees—but day-to-day jobs put most
of that work in the future. Sivowitch had more than 100
telephones to select from the storage collection for a telecom-
munications exhibit called *Person to Person*. He culled the
ones that represent periods of technology, and some sections
of cable as well, and some fire-alarm telegraphs. The exhibits

people had to go elsewhere for a telephone pole. He didn't have one.

There are altogether more electric appliances than space to put them. That was the fault of a too-enthusiastic response, Sivowitch says, to the museum's request for them. "It took one person a full year to answer all the offers of toasters and waffle irons that came in from the public, and to put into reasonable order the ones that were accepted *plus* the electric heater which one donor simply dropped in a mailbox with a tag, 'To the Smithsonian.'" He plans to do some more work on them when he can and on the collection of 155 electric razors made between 1930 and 1965.

Audrey Davis　　, a medical history curator, has completed a research project on some papier-mâché body organs, made in France, for use by medical students. As she sits in the armchair in her office she seems to be engaged in conversation with someone in the chair across from her, but it is only one of the objects of her study—a large, curvy, palely colored, 200-times-lifesized ear. The ear comes apart in various sections by undoing little hooks. It has 30 labeled parts, some of them, like the eardrum, removable. On her desk she has a larynx and a brain by the same maker. Her paper on them completed, she is returning them to her storage room across the hall to rejoin the lung, of similar scale and construction.

Davis must then get to the job of integrating new items to her "bleeding" collection, from the days when patients were bled by their doctors as a "cure-all" treatment. She already holds bleeding bowls, leech jars, lancets and scarificators, which shoot out 16 blades at once. The new (that is, newly acquired) items have to be dated and verified and have cards made out for them. On the cards medical objects are filed alphabetically: braille writers before bronchoscopes, cardiac pacers or heart pumps before surgical saws before thermometers. On the shelves, however, they are filed by usage: pill-making machines in one place, Civil War ether cans and acupuncture needles (to "anesthetize") in another, bandages, bedpans, baby bottles, and pap boats for invalids in still others. Dental items, both in the card file and on the shelves, are arranged by usage. All the extractors are together—the forceps and the keys—and all the tools, like Paul Revere's tooth-measuring calipers, and all the toothmaking devices and the teeth.

It's kind of an old-time pharmacy, this storage room, an old-time pharmacy and medical appliances store combined, its shelves stacked high and its aisles narrow. Although three people work in the room, no one can be seen right off. They're hidden away behind cabinets in little clearings where they've managed to find work surfaces.

One of them, a volunteer, is arranging spectacles by date. Two others, museum technicians, are sorting objects to go into the "1876" exhibit. Everett Jackson 🎐 is pulling out surgical instruments, checking the contents of a surgical kit to see what pieces might be missing. Michael Harris 🎐 , having washed the glass jars from a 100-year-old collection of Chinese crude drugs, unrefined, is replacing their contents. In piles on his table he has many of them: cuttlefish bones, fowl gizzards, mulberry bark, snakeskin, and little nuggets labeled dragon's teeth, which he thinks came from cows. Harris is eager to finish that chore and get back to the patent medicines collection. He's studying them—the blood purifiers, the hair growers, the rheumatism remedies—for their content and for their labels. He has seen that many of the labels picture either Indians or women or members of the religious sect of Quakers, as symbols of integrity, and he wants to find out more about them for the catalog.

In the same building is Edwin Battison ▦▍ , a watch and clock collector by hobby, who came to the Smithsonian years back, he says, "to see how they catalogued their watches and I stayed on to do the job instead." A lean and leathery-looking Vermonter, ex-tool designer (and the Mohawk Dutchman band sawyer in Loveland's 1876 film), Battison was hired because he knew the sort of things about clocks and watches that isn't in the books and he could improve the quality of the collections and broaden their scope. The cataloguing chore became his, too. "I'll never finish it," he says, "because there's such a lot of research you have to do in order to catalog these things properly. You must determine a great deal about the history of a piece, for example. It's not like cataloguing a keg of nails." All he'll say about the system he devised for bringing order is "Now I know the problems."

It takes him a trip or two between his card catalog and specimen drawers to put his hand on Helen Keller's touch-watch. He has it, safely stored in a drawer, between the watch that came to the museum just before it and the one that came just after. Except for outsize pieces, that's how things are put away, numerically, as they are in the card file, by the order in which they arrived, though the card file also organizes the pieces by countries of origin and by different engineering features.

Battison has a Swiss music box to return to its drawer. With the turn of a key he sets off its tinkling tune, sung, it would seem, by the fluttering bird up top, which ducks back into its nest on the final note of the song. He just got the music box back from Switzerland, where he had sent it for a repair job on its mouse-skin bellows. Most of his items he packs himself. Any expert packer could do the outside packing for him, the outer case; but it takes someone who knows the inner workings to support the delicate parts properly. He uses inert, resilient material, something that won't shred and won't cause corrosion.

Rosemary DeRosa ▦ knows a lot about the art of

packing art objects. It's something she does in the course of her job in the registrar's office in the Hirshhorn Museum. She learned the art more or less backwards, by unpacking. In the year before the museum opened she was hired as an art handler to unpack Joseph Hirshhorn's collections as they arrived at the new bagel-shaped building on the Mall. There were more than 6,000 pieces, and DeRosa, 26, a painter, was one of six art handlers, all of whom had college degrees and all of whom were practicing artists.

"It was Christmas every day," she says now of that recent exciting time, "a glorious experience" — keeping up with the flood of crates, some of them crates-within-crates, unscrewing the wood panels, unwrapping pictures and mysterious shapes from layers of padding, unlocking portrait busts from boxes which had pull-out sections shaped to the contours of the face. Paintings were moved in padded carts into exhibit halls. The overflow went to a rank of panels on the fourth floor which, compared to the rest of the Smithsonian behind the scenes, looks like a setting from the year 2001. Overflow pieces of sculpture were filed by the dates of the sculptors' birth in racks arranged around the room.

"It was muscle-building, backbreaking work," she remembers, even though she had dollies and pedal lifts to help. "I'd be wiped out at the end of the day. A mind-stretching time, too," she adds, to work with crane operators and curators, learning from the designers why they placed things as they did, how they hung things to look right on curving walls, how they drilled into walls with special hardware, learning from artist Kenneth Samuelson how to reassemble his sculpture titled "Needle Tower" from the jumble of metal tubing and cables in which it arrived. "It was all very mathematical, with wires needing to be pulled in certain ways for proper tension."

Art handling can be scary. DeRosa and fellow art handler Lee Aks   , a sculptor, agree on that. They're thinking of the crate they had to cut into to release a plexiglass sphere which was badly packed by the artist. And they're thinking of the 11-by-20-foot painting by Ad Reinhardt that had to be bent to fit into the freight elevator. A man was brought down from New York to bend it—someone who knew how to adjust the tension so as not to get a wrinkle. DeRosa and Aks are proud that nothing was thrown out in the mountains of packing materials. And nothing was damaged.

Both young people have moved on to jobs of greater prestige. Aks does conservation. DeRosa does registrar work—like wrapping 27 pieces of sculpture to go on loan to Richmond and doing the paperwork to go with them, including instructions for opening the crates and unpacking and for displaying small pieces so as to protect them from theft.

Both, looking back, can sound crabby about the low estate of the art handler—ranked way below other jobs. "It's a tremendous responsibility," says Aks. "You're not just moving things. You're in charge from the minute things leave the truck. You have to be sensitive. You have to know how works of art are constructed, what stresses they can take, how to handle complex crates without damaging anything or killing anybody. It's tremendous work." They agree, though, that they can't complain. "The PhDs upstairs were involved in the planning and paperwork. But all day long we were involved with the art."

Packing and shipping is an art at the National Zoo, too. "The animal shipping crates," says Rick Croson , one of the carpenters who makes them, "are not junk. They're real cabinets." Croson made kitchen cabinets before coming to work at the Zoo but nothing, he says, to approach in quality the tiger crates he worked on, for shipping the Smithsonian's white tigers to Cincinnati and Chicago and back again, or the crate he made for a juvenile giraffe's recent truck ride to Connecticut.

The gray-painted wood tiger boxes were completely metal-lined, and mounted on skids. They had close-set bars at one end and a sliding door at the other and handrails on either side for lifting. They cost $500 each to build.

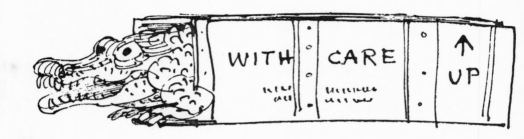

The giraffe crate, which was a $1,000 job, had to be six feet high by eight feet long by five feet wide—big enough to prevent the young giraffe from panicking but not so big that he could injure himself by crashing about in it and not so tall as to be a problem with tunnels and overhead bridges. Giraffes, he was told, need to face forward and be protected from flying particles. That meant hinging ten-foot wing-boards on the bottom of the crate on either side, which could be folded up to serve as wind and side-vision breakers. Mattress bumpers were installed around the chest area and rubber padding on the floor. By the time the giraffe was trained to the box, though—by being lured into it for his meals—and by the time several unsuccessful attempts had been made to load him, the youngster had grown five inches, and the box was really a bit short. Croson improvised a railing as an extension.

In each case, Croson says, whether he's building for a monkey or a rhinoceros or a wildebeest, the cratemaker has to think of the animal's privacy, his food, his sanitation, as well as his safety and security. Smaller animals get boxes with strong mesh screens instead of bars. Venomous snakes are put in a cloth bag surrounded by packing material inside a box well labeled with warnings. Croson sometimes works on as many as 40 bird-shipping crates at a time, making them from tomato boxes he picks up from the commissary.

Keeping track of the Zoo's birds is a birds registrar (there is a second registrar, for mammals) who, as the cratemakers know, arranges quite a lot of bird shipments in exchanges with other zoos. The curator makes the decision. The vet examines the bird. The keeper advises on the kind of box—which should be dark so the bird isn't "spooked" on its introduction to mechanical flight—and the registrar draws up the health papers, checks the airlines schedules, and waves the traveler off. She has done that for a lesser Magellan goose, a St. Vincents Amazon parrot, and an Eastern crowned crane among many others.

In an office where voices have to be raised to carry over the honking of a shelduck down the hall, the registrar logs in every bird as it arrives. She tries to catch misidentifications right at the start. "The donor may think she is giving us a purple rail, but it turns out to be a common gallinule." The registrar bands the bird, unless it's a parrot. Parrots aren't banded because they pinch the metal bands with their beaks until they're too tight. She enters a card for the bird in the file, which is arranged by order and family, starting with the primitive ostrich through the pelicans, geese, eagles, peafowl, cranes, gulls, owls, and on to the songbirds, ending with New World sparrows.

Onto the card goes the bird's history: where it was hatched (the black-crowned night heron was hatched in the rookery, a mallard in the incubator); who its parents are and its siblings (important when it comes to breeding); its location, including moves (from the tortoise yard to the Komodo yard); its development, vaccinations, worming, illnesses. (The infirmary roll at any one time may include a black swan with a broken wing, a cassowary with frostbitten feet, a redtail hawk with a bad leg, some canaries with malaria, and a pair of lovebirds off their feed.) The file card also records deaths and death numbers.

In the end the registrar makes a head count and a paper count, and the two have to come out even. Left out of the records are the freeloading pigeons and sparrows that get into the Zoo buildings and can't always be trapped and evicted. Counted in are thefts, and the Zoo, unique among the Smithsonian's museums, has a category for "escapees."

Sheryl Gilbert   , birds bio-technician, has an active job compared to the registrar's — out and about a lot in the cages and by the ponds — but, like lizards keeper Demeter, she has her share of recordkeeping, too. A small figure, wind-blown, wearing high rubber boots, she stops briefly by the registrar's office and is off again, holding up a large nene goose egg. She has just brought it in from the nest, having exchanged a dummy egg for it. "It's a first for the red pair," she calls over her shoulder to the registrar. The Hawaiian nene geese, a severely endangered species, receive when they choose their mates plastic bands of red or blue or yellow so the pairs are distinguishable. Then when the young are sent to zoos in Chicago or San Francisco to start new flocks, care is taken to send unrelated males and females.

On the shell Gilbert pencils the species, cage number, identification number and date, then dips the egg in surgical scrub, and places it in the incubator where it rotates automatically. Three days before hatch she transfers it to a higher-humidity incubator. After it hatches she feeds the gosling nothing for 24 hours, then chopped greens and mashed hard-boiled egg.

Every egg is recorded in her egg book, which has columns across the page to show whether the egg was fertile or infertile, whether the embryo was dead in the shell (early, middle, or late), the date of hatch, accession number, death date and death number. There's also space to write down anything unusual which she notices about the egg's color or size or weight.

During the most active months in the incubation room, "things happen quickly," says Gilbert. "It's a race to keep up with the hatchings, to set up ever more pens, to see to the diets, to make the moves to outdoor pens. There's time to keep only the most basic records."

In less hectic periods she tabulates and she writes her reports. There may be just one hatchling in the pen by her desk, one five-day-old ostrich chick, stamping about, taking lessons in how to peck for worms and grains from the two young chickens she provided as companions. On that same afternoon there may be just one force-feeding for the ailing adult emu whose beak she holds shut on the feeding tube as the green brew of alfalfa, trout chow, and vitamins empties from the pitcher—"Come on, hon, good bird, no throwing up!"

Between attentions to the patients, Gilbert reviews the year. She has a total of 1,124 eggs, most of them from ducks and geese, 34 of them from the nenes, of which 22 hatched and 19 birds survived. She adds to her count parent-incubated birds like the owls. She adds five buffleheads that hatched without anyone's having noticed the eggs and two baby guans, also missed, that hatched in a nesting platform in their cage, flew down and slipped through the wires. They were found running up and down the birdhouse halls.

Red Kilby 🐦 keeps a different kind of bird record. Above the table in the preparation room where he spreads out his pans he has some 100 different menus printed out on cards tacked onto the bulletin board. He uses them in his job—starting at two o'clock in the morning—of filling the individual bird feeding trays. The menus remind him that the crested green wood partridge gets trout chow, diced kale, mixed seeds, and a trace of oystershell flour and that the parrot gets a side order of peanut butter sandwiches.

Recordkeeping snowballs in modern zoos. Diets are computed precisely. So are health records. In the infirmary the vet has a stand of clipboards to refer to, with daily reports on the patients, just like the setup in a hospital's nursing station. The days of the vet with the little black bag are over. The infirmary technician Thomas Schneider makes regular inventories of the drugs. He keeps the equipment in order—the capture guns, the poke sticks, the contents of the veterinary kits, the sterile packs that are used in surgery.

Moles Benson 🐦 , commissary chief, came to the Zoo with experience as a butcher. The orders he makes out are for tons of hay and grain, for meat and potatoes, for earthworms and dried flies, for the 40 pounds of bamboo required daily by the pandas, for rabbit chow and monkey chow and running-bird meal and all the sacks of sunflower seeds and the stacks of sugar cane and the freezersful of fruits, vegetables, butterfish, rats, mice, and bread. He also keeps track of the tons of hydroponic grass that he raises in trays of water — thick mats of seeds, roots, and sprouts which make a nutritious salad. The maintenance of zoo collections takes, along with loving care, a lot of highly technical support and good records all around.

The predicament of James Mead , in the Natural History Museum, is an example of how research is hampered by neglected housekeeping. A collection just isn't useful to scientists if it's not easily referred to. As whales curator, Mead has had an easier time of finding new whales than of keeping the ones he has. The problem with whales, which begins and ends with their size, has always been where to put the collection — how to get it all laid out to see what's in it, to see how many kinds of whales there are and how they compare.

"There are 70 species of cetaceans (whales, porpoises, dolphins). Twelve of them are large whales and very difficult to tell apart. We had a large Bryde's whale, supposed to be very rare. But I'm finding that many of the other whales we have are really Bryde's; only they've been misidentified." Whale-sized material is just awkward. Where to put the series of sperm whales, which he describes as "just huge, preposterous creatures like boxcars with fins"? Where to put the single blue whale that takes, he says, more space than Natural History's entire insects collection? "To fit in my office", Mead says, "its skull would have to be broken up. And the blue whale we have is not an awfully large one at that. We have its skeleton in 20 desk-sized crates in a barn."

Half of the world's marine mammals are represented at the Smithsonian and two-thirds of the North American marine animals — in all about 7,000 specimens, the best collection in the world. "People here have always been interested in mammals but not in curation. It's chaos," he says. "They didn't keep their closets clean. No one has felt the compulsion to go through them for 60 years. Things have been moved a lot, broken, displaced. As a collection, it has been scattered through the building and around the city—some specimens embalmed, some in freezers. Skeletal stuff was even kept for a time in a torpedo factory. Then it was moved to our storage facility in Maryland where an entire whale got lost in the woodwork! Well, it was stacked under some dead helicopters. We have leaks in the basement and disarray in the attic and I get calls from the freezer people in Georgia who say 'Get your pygmy sperm whale out of here!' I just want to get everything in order so it's usable, so people can do a lot of research on it as quickly as they wish."

Mead has special storage problems. More and more, though, as natural history collections grow, museum scientists are turning over their recordkeeping and storage to people with the titles of museum specialist or collections manager. The mammals division has two museum specialists, Frank Greenwell   , whose background is taxidermy, and John Miles, Jr.   , whose background is library work, and there are five technicians to help them. They do what they call the museological chores, so that the highly specialized scientists are free to devote themselves to research.

Specimens come in to the mammals division either frozen or putrefied or in skeleton form or as "study skins" (stuffed) or even sometimes alive. Most of them come from Smithsonian people, who knew how to prepare them for the trip and what data to send along with them. "The tag," says Greenwell, "is the all-important part of the game, even more important than the specimen. The specimen is only as good as its tag."

The museum specialists prepare the study skin if it wasn't done in the field. They stuff rodent-size animals with cotton, larger ones with excelsior, and most of the fox-to-elephant-sized animals they skin, salt, and tan like shoeleather. They do the cataloguing, matching up the numbers for the skins with the numbers for the skulls.

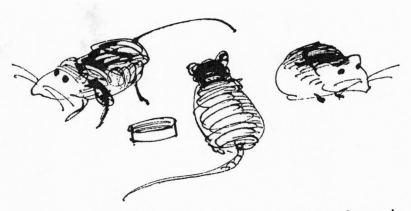

They put the specimens away—in the ranks of cases in the huge mammals range. Miles and Greenwell pretty well have the Simpson's classification list by heart, which is how the maze of stacked white storage units is arranged—by 18 living orders of mammals, which break down to 118 families. When it gets down to genera, species, and subspecies they may have to sneak a look at the list. Bats come before monkeys, which come before rabbits before pocket gophers, beavers, rats, tapirs, buffaloes.

Within the individual drawers they arrange a whole series of gray squirrels in flat-out position, the stiff little forms in order by locality, from the front of the drawer to the back, from left to right, with the boxes of skulls up front. They fill in measurements on the tags. Measurements are all in metric system—length from nose to tail, length of ear, length of hind foot. Some museums count to the tip of the toe; some, like the Smithsonian, count to the tip of the toenail.

Greenwell and Miles fumigate twice a year, filling a container inside each case with a liquid insecticide. Also, strips around the edge of each case contain arsenic. They update the collections, moving cases around to fit in new specimens. They mail out specimens on loan. They do maintenance when an ear is damaged or a leg broken or when a skin needs further de-greasing.

One of these days, the big elephant in the museum's rotunda will need its skin rewaxed, Greenwell says. He was around, newly arrived, in 1959, when that elephant was mounted. As the newest, and last, taxidermist to be hired, he even got to do some menial chores on the mannequin, before the elephant skin was stretched across it. Waxing was the last step in the year-long process. Hot brown wax, sprayed on, brought back an alive look to the skin and helped to bring out the "beading," the overall pattern of bumps. Experts will be called in for the rewaxing job, Greenwell figures.

As it is, there is always a backlog of work for the staff in the freezers. "We have one freezer that's 20 feet long, but most of the animals are rat-size, since two-thirds of mammals are rodents anyway."

Miles complains that a lot of collections management is donkey work. Stocky and strong, he figures he has moved just about every storage unit in the mammals range on his own back. It takes a lot of planning as well as strength, though. And it takes a lot of practical technical knowledge and skills to handle all the skins and skeletal materials, the pelts, the pickled items in this vast collection of half a million specimens. Like a mis-shelved book, a mis-filed wombat can be lost forever. Miles has a reputation through the building for being able to put his hand on any specimen, for knowing what locker holds any given goat, bongo or giraffe.

In addition to donkey work there is paperwork, dealing mainly with bone identification. "Dear Mr. Seymour," Miles writes, "The tooth you found is a left upper molar from a not very young domestic bull or cow." Or, "You have sent a tail vertebra of a whale." Or, "Your skull is of a young adult coyote."

A Japanese or French biologist, speaking no English, can give the scientific name for an animal and be led to the drawer. Miles relishes the tongue-twisters and bafflers — the fact that a walrus, like a dog, is in the Carnivora, but a seacow is Sirenia, the fact that pigs and peccaries are Artiodactyla. He can't allow himself to be tripped up by the fact that a tree shrew is a Primate but an elephant shrew is an Insectivore and so is a hedgehog, though another prickly animal, the porcupine, is a Rodentia and the spiny anteater is a Monotreme.

In the course of any work week Miles travels many miles through the collections. He's a speeder, rushing along at a rolling gait, past swamp rabbits, marsh rabbits, mountain rabbits, prairie rabbits, cottontails, out through the marine mammals room where blades of whale baleen are piled up on trolleys and where river dolphin and pothead skulls with long snouts are lined up on racks. He bounds down stairs and flings open doors.

Chamois skins, mailed in from the tanner, he takes to the fur vault, a chilled area in the basement where skins hang on hooks side by side. The vault contains rows on rows of thick pelts, some shiny, some rough-furred — black bear, grizzly, polar, Himalayan bear, fur seal, hair seal, river and sea otter, caribou, puma, mountain lion and jaguar. And lots and lots of wolves that had been turned in to the government for bounty.

Overhead, seen through the grillwork ceiling, are hundreds of hoofs, dangling down from the sheepskins in the second story. Skins are arranged in order of genus and then locality, Alaska before Alberta. Most of them are headless, though there's a pile of lion and bear heads in one corner and the head of a Texas longhorn steer on top of the filing cabinet.

Mounted animals which are lent out to schools are kept

in a bit of dead space behind the mammals exhibits. The animals are no longer of display quality, but they're good for teaching purposes and for petting. Miles has a lineup ready to go out — porcupines and beavers — all standing with paper blankets over their backs to protect them from dust. While he's in the vicinity, he lets himself into the American buffalo diorama from the back, removing a panel of the showcase with his screwdriver to get in. He picks his way through the Western plains scene to verify a museum number from a tag in a buffalo's ear.

Errands on Miles's list also send him to the bug chamber — a pair of lockers where the larvae from colonies of dermestid beetles work for the museum, for free, cleaning flesh off skeletons. Museum people call the chamber the bughouse. Miles brings in large marine animals for the dermestids to clean when there's no particular hurry about the work. More often he brings in reptiles and small rodents that require the beetles' meticulous and delicate attentions. They do a perfect job on a shrew's head, for example, which may be the size of a pencil eraser. Miles has learned to put small materials in egg cartons, so that the pieces of one animal aren't carried about and mixed with those of another. Humidity in the tank is kept high, though not so high that the beetles are attacked by a fungus. And if the workload isn't heavy enough, the beetles are fed fish or bacon or dog biscuits — to discourage them from eating each other up.

An errand regarding a bear skull that is being cleaned by hand takes Miles to the prep lab, a moist place with sinks and hoses and puddles on the floor, where preparators in rubber gloves and rubber aprons wield their knives. There is apt to be, salted down, an aardvark pelt on a table, and a macaque skin soaking in gasoline to get rid of some of its oils, and some porpoise heads having their flesh cooked off in a cauldron from which steam billows about the room.

The other prep lab, used for stuffing animals, is as dry as this one is moist. It has supplies of cotton and wire and pinning boards and a sandbox for working in. It has a big screen-cage drying chamber from which Miles picks up a pair of finished whitefoot mice and a bushbaby.

When the "1876" exhibits people sent around a list of mounted heads and antlers they wanted, Miles went to the east-attic storage room to get them, picking his way along the catwalk that surrounds the skylight over the museum's whale hall. Blue lights in the attic play across glass trays of water to create the deep-sea look for the whales exhibit down below. The lights add an eerie touch to an already eerie scene, where the walls are lined with hundreds of mounted animals. The not-in-service animals stand in herds of a very unlikely makeup—glassy-eyed musk oxen side by side with a Netherlands dog and yaks and a baby camel and Marco Polo sheep. Tied to a railing is the skeleton of a sperm whale fetus.

Some of the specimens are very old and no longer in good condition. Blind children are sometimes brought to the attic, though, to feel them—to feel their way through the forest of antlers Miles has there. The children feel the difference between the fan-shaped antlers of the moose, the crescent ones of the water buffalo, the shovel-like ones of the caribou, covered in velvet, and the corkscrew horns of the greater kudu.

The west attic has a lot of oversize bone material. It's put there, out of the regular order, because it needs the space—skeletons and partial skeletons of elephants, rhinos, giraffes. The west attic also houses a collection with one example each of the animals of the Washington area. "When someone brings me a bear scapula," says Miles, "I like to take him up here to a full skeleton and leave it to him to figure out what he's got."

Specimens in the alcohol room, where animals are kept in wet storage, are filed in the same manner as skins and skeletons—by their order in the classifications list. A card file gives the stack number, the shelf number, the jar number. The whole room is a library of glass jars—a jar with a duck-billed platypus floating in an amber liquid, jars of bats, jars of brains, jars of eyeballs. Around the walls bigger specimens float in opaque trunk-size lockers. A sea lion shares a locker with a chimpanzee; a porpoise with a spotted hyena.

Entomologists are willing to concede that the mammals people have their storage problems, but they are not much impressed by the mammals statistics of 500,000 specimens. The insects collections manager Gary Hevel and the half-dozen technicians on his staff have more than 23 million insects to manage. In 1976 alone 800,000 insects came in to the Smithsonian. There are years in the world of insects when 10,000 new specimens are being named and described for the first time.

Some collectors mount their insects in the field, but most send them directly to the Smithsonian to be mounted there. They send the "hardy critters," Hevel says, in alcohol, the small, delicate ones in pill boxes packed with tissue, and moths and butterflies in folded paper triangles inside stout boxes. "We could really start our own collection of boxes," he says. "We get cigar boxes, cigarette tins, even oil cans, from a collector in Brazil. We call him Oil Can Harry."

What entomologist Hevel describes as "huge" specimens aren't huge by anyone else's standards, though he has six-inch rhinoceros beetles with horns that he says can break a car window. The beetles come in all sizes, the smallest probably the feather-wings, mere specks, which have to be mounted on paper points at the head of a pin. Butterflies and moths, arriv-

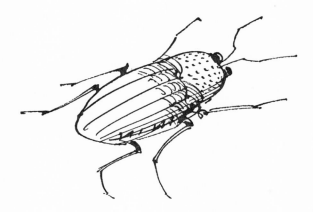

ing in paper triangles, go first into relaxing chambers. Then, opened out, they're dried for two weeks, pinned to spreading boards, and transferred into storage drawers. The very tiny butterflies — microlepidoptera — are the specialty of a number of Smithsonian scientists. A thousand of them will fit in a drawer, in an elegant formation of wings, each yellow, salmon, gray specimen with its individual label. All of the drawers are regularly mothproofed against attack by live members of the insect families.

Mailing isn't as troublesome as it is for some divisions. Hevel has 400,000 mites and ticks out on loan to a laboratory in Montana, and shipping was a small matter. It's the volume that's overwhelming — the numbers of little specimens to be impaled on the long thin, insect pins. It's the sheets and sheets of fine-print labels to be cut apart with long-bladed haircutting scissors. It's the stacks of new trays, filled, waiting to be integrated into the great lepidoptera bank.

The collections manager for paleobiology, Fred Collier, who has a Master's degree in geology, thinks his fossil animals are even more unmanageable. There are more of them — 30 to 40 million in all — and they come in all sizes and states of preservation "from things you could kill someone with to things you could break by breathing on them." And the preparation is far more difficult.

Pinning insects or skinning or pickling rodents is pretty straightforward work. At least the preparators can see what they're doing. Extracting a fossil animal from rock is painstaking and slow. It may take months, a year, three years. A lot of highly skilled work has to be done before there *is* a specimen for a curator to study or for Collier to keep track of.

Doing that work are a handful of highly trained preparators such as those in the vertebrate paleontology laboratory who bend over their lumpy projects in a room sometimes hazy with rock dust and buzzing with their machinery. Tools include saws, drills, chisels, dental picks for tearing away the rock around the bones. They even include a huge sandblaster, the kind for cutting inscriptions onto tombstones. When the bones are freed, the preparators assemble them into a skeleton on the sand table or on plaster supports made especially for each specimen. Some they strengthen with an infusion of beeswax.

The preparators are versatile people who know their anatomy and their rocks. Given a rock with a corner of bone protruding from it, they can predict the direction in which the bone will lie, how long it will be, what other bones may be with it. They know how the rocks will break. They have a stonemason's skill in their fingers and a mechanic's ability — to build up and brace a skeleton for display.

It's slow-motion work, filled with suspense, as Arnold Lewis "reliefs" the bones of a seal — exposing them to a point where the skeletal pieces stand out from the rock like a relief map — or as Leroy Glenn extracts the jaws of little deerlike animals from a crumbly red rock. The jaws are fractured. The rock is fractured. Glenn picks along, intently, evenly, even serenely, at a task that would make most people cry. When there's something very special in preparation, like a complete sea otter skull, of a species described in the past only on the basis of one fragment of a skull, then the suspense is extra-keen. The research scientist from upstairs will keep popping in day after day to peer over the preparator's shoulder, scarcely able to wait for the next quarter inch of tooth to show out.

Collier and his staff don't really have to keep track of work in progress in the prep lab. They do. But it's more out of curiosity than duty. Their job is keeping track of the rocks that go in and the specimens that come out. Quite a lot of the massive fossil-bearing rocks for one project are sent by a skilled collector in Oregon, who finds them along the coast where they weather out from the soft-sediment bluffs after storms. His success in finding them he says has something to do with wearing magnets in his hat. "He just lets us know that he's shipping us a new five-ton lot."

Other fossils arrive embedded in limestone blocks. The limestone is dissolved in acid baths in the museum's acid room, leaving behind fossil snails and clams and the skeletons of other sea animals. When truckers once lost one of the blocks, they asked Collier how much it was worth. "By the time I figured for them how much it would cost to equip and send a scientist to the Glass Mountains in West Texas to look for a replacement, they looked more carefully and found our piece of limestone."

And then there's the mud. Collier knows he has a new shipment when the guards at the loading dock call to say, "Come and get your smelly boxes. They're leaking all over the place." A number of U.S. Government ships take sea-bottom samples for the Smithsonian, and send them along in ten- to 100-sack lots. They are stored at sea-bottom temperature in a walk-in refrigerator that holds 30,000 sacks at a time. It's a full-time job for one person to dry the mud in an oven — which prevents further biological change — and to store it.

Mud in even greater quantities is shipped back by Smithsonian scientists doing their collecting at sea. Their eight-foot-long cores of sediment are stacked on racks and still more racks, and where racks run out the cores are lined up three-deep across tabletops. Mud collections are kept in a basement area fondly called The Pit by those working on the collections. They share the space with heavy apparatus like dredgers and scoops and coring devices and with petrified logs that are ten feet long and weigh several tons and might cause some sagging of museum floors. They also share Pit space with a pile-up of bundles sent in from the field. Some of the bundles are done up in newspaper, some in plaster casts, with labels taped on, such as "rhino skull" or "pothead." The bundles stay there until preparators can "mine" them.

Specimens also arrive as gifts. A collector of brachiopods (clam-size invertebrates which beachcombers call lamp shells) recently sent 200 footlocker-size boxes. Collier was hard-pressed to find space to unpack and arrange the lot systematically. It meant moving a series of cases. "I always have to ask myself, 'Is it a wise move?' There's X amount of space and Y number of cases. And the cases each cost $300. I need to have a good idea of the rate at which collections grow.

The active ones have to be in the most accessible cases. Others can be stacked in crates."

Ideally everything is under cover. In practice there's always the odd woolly mammoth part or a triceratops that doesn't fit anywhere. And one whale has been spread out across some mattresses for years. The big, bulky materials just don't stack, Collier complains. Some of the dinosaurs, poorly mineralized, are fragile. They're hard to move. Pieces have to be reachable without jostling others. It takes nearly two whole floors to store the 10,000 big specimens.

A collection of more than 200,000 foraminifera, on the other hand, fits nicely into one small room, a compact library of little drawers, each one of which holds 50 trays of 13 slides. The forams, which come in an immense variety of shapes (some straight tubes, some highly convoluted coils), are so small they have to be placed under a microscope to be picked out individually with a brush and mounted on slides for storage. "We always called them microfossils," says Collier. "Now we call them macro-microfossils (the big among the small) because now we're dealing with much smaller things—things you couldn't see without using optical microscopes. You isolate them with a red circle on a smear slide or mount them on special holders. They're measured in hundredths of microns and studied by electron microscopy."

Cataloguing the fossil collections was done until 1970 in handwritten ledgers that looked as though Bob Cratchit had made the entries with a quill pen. Now it's computerized. Seven people on the collections staff work full-time putting numbers on specimens and feeding information into the computer.

Two other people on the staff do the packing for mailing. "A scientist in Germany may want to compare a crab finger he has with the type specimen in our collection—the specimen that was described and illustrated in the literature. We have thousands of type specimens out on loan at any one time. For packing, every specimen is individual. One crab finger is so strong you could stand on it. Another is fragile and you pack it with a layer of cotton under it and tissue on top. You avoid putting cotton over it as well as under it. The two cotton pieces mesh together and you can crush a specimen pulling them apart." Skulls to be mailed are fitted with fiberglass jackets. A ten-foot sloth goes out well braced and boxed.

In spite of all the traffic through it, Collier's office is immaculate. When he leaves at the end of the day, the surfaces are cleared. There are no papers in sight, nothing. "I hate clutter," he says. "I try to apply that to 30 and 40 million objects." And he has to do it without throwing anything away.

"There's the occasional specimen that has no scientific value, because there's no information with it. You don't know where it came from in time or geographically. It couldn't be used in a scientific paper. But it can still be used for demonstration. There's the occasional specimen that's broken beyond repair. Well, you really have to show it—not just to any paleobiologist—but to the one who's working on that particular organism. And he may say it's irreplaceable. He may say the half that's left shows something very crucial. So you can't throw that out either."

There's a condemnation procedure by which a committee decides to get rid of something. A batch of sea-bottom mud samples was almost condemned in the 1960s. It took up a lot of space, filling a whole rank of drawers, floor to ceiling, with tens of thousands of dusty little bottles collected on nineteenth-century oceanographic expeditions. Fine script on the yellowed labels gives latitudes, longitudes: SS *Tuscarara* (July 29, 1874) 812 fathoms. Or, SS *Albatross*.

"We thought we could throw the collection out but then came the mercury scare, the scare about levels of mercury and lead and other heavy metals in fish. People wanted to do studies. Congress was asking if the oceans had changed. Did we know the level of mercury 100 years ago? Well, century-old fish would have been preserved in formaldehyde in jars with metal caps that distort the findings. Here we had all these sediment samples, in bottles, corked, that could be ana-

of dope would shrink up the fabric to the point of crushing the structure inside).

Roderick as a former Air Force mechanic had all the old skills of stitching and of applying dope, of woodworking and welding and rigging a plane's parts. And with years of museum work—he came to the Smithsonian in 1959—he acquired the approach of a conservator. Working on the plane he took care to document every step of his work. He replaced only what had to be replaced. He labeled his repairs for what they were. His goal wasn't to make the *Chicago* fly again, but to prepare it for exhibit and to put it in a state—as close to flying condition as possible—that would save it from further deterioration.

Roderick was influenced in his choice of techniques and materials and in his attitudes by Robert Organ ⫟⫟ , who is the Smithsonian's conservation chief. Serving all the museums, Organ is prepared to advise on a rust inhibitor for engines or a benign solution in which to store bats or on crystals for mothproofing the insect collections or on the possibility of sandwiching the brittle wings of a World War I French Spad in a mesh which worked nicely in preserving paper money. His lab will analyze moon rock or the metal tube of cosmonaut food or the glass from medieval stained glass windows. Most of his jobs, though, come from people in History and Technology. Organ figures that's because of the location. They pass his conservation lab on their way to the cafeteria.

From his desk in the glass cube which is his office, Organ looks out, alert and birdlike, over the ranks of spic-and-span workbenches in the lab. He's a man who is combating mold, mildew, dust, excessive heat and light, and such pests as insects and rodents and people who handle museum objects without wearing white cotton gloves. He doesn't appear gloomy or suspicious. Rather he has the sharp look of someone who does not intend to be caught by surprise and will give as good as he gets in protecting 100 million museum objects.

The comfort of visitors to the museums is nothing to him, Organ says cheerfully. It's not his concern. He implies that visitors are a bother, coming in as they do, breathing out vapors, shedding dust, wanting prime light to see by, wanting to touch. The comfort of the objects, on the other hand, is everything. Any conservator worth his salt would really rather the objects didn't have to be on display at all.

Strong light fades colors quickly. Dust abrades. In air that's too hot and dry, leather saddles get stiff and crumbly, maps and baskets go brittle, wagons and wooden statues shrink and check (crack). In air that's too wet they grow mold and fungus. Automobiles and sewing machines rust and coins corrode. Over the years oil paintings darken.

That's why Organ keeps the air and light filtered and keeps the temperature and humidity in just the proper range, day in and day out, nights and holidays. At least he tries to. Ten too-wet days in a year did in a bronze goddess at the Freer, activating her bronze disease. Good housekeeping is the most important thing he can do for the objects, Organ says. Beyond that he favors proceeding with extreme caution, since practically anything that's done to objects alters them. Cleaning can be very damaging if wrongly done. Overcleaning is a conservator's nightmare.

"The curator brings us an object, a chair, for example. We examine it. We let him know what results to expect from a whole range of procedures which we test on dummy objects. He decides which to use. It's for him to say what state we should bring the chair to. Some curators expect it to be as bright and shiny as when it was new." Organ's voice registers disapproval. "Others have a deep sense of historical value and prefer to retain every scrap of evidence—not just in notes and photographs—in the object itself."

That means retaining signs of wear and use in chairs and battle flags and flutes, in old photographs and baby cups, in tools and cars. That means not altering things—as Peter Marzio said, ▥|| he would not alter the colors in his neon signs—any more than an art curator would alter a Van Gogh

or a Greek antiquity. "Just suppose you had a vase which George III had smashed in a drunken rage. Even if you put it back together you'd want the breaks to show."

Conservators don't like their work to be called "restoration." Restoration is a red-flag word to them. It implies a too enthusiastic, disrespectful approach, they say. It implies stripping off finishes, scouring, repainting to make things new. Organ calls restoration "a stagy art. On museum objects it's forgery." He admits there are cases where it can't be helped. Old zinc carburetors are one. "They fall to powder in ten years and you've no choice but to replace them with carburetors of purer metal. There you have to restore."

Conservation involves one prickly decision after another and a lot of compromises. Conservators may decide to smooth one dent because they figure it was caused by an archaeologist's spade while he was digging or by a storage accident. But they leave other dents. They leave the dent on the nose of the Northrop 2-B Gamma *Polar Star* and even call visitors' attention to it in the label which describes the airplane's hard landing in the Antarctic. They clean the smoke from one Indian basket, to reveal the color and decoration beneath it, but they leave a film of smoke on another as a clue for future scholars who might want to know what firewood the Indians used.

Conservators have a code of ethics. They try the gentlest procedure first and work up to the fiercer ones. They make their work reversible, so that glues they use can be unstuck and paints, used to touch up or patch, can be dissolved without affecting the original paint. They keep their work visible instead of hiding their traces. When the gouged-out midriff of Miss Liberty, a plaster statue by Hiram Powers had to be replaced, the new portion was made to look slightly different in color and texture. It was not different enough to jar, just different enough to be noticed on close inspection.

No one looking at the Smithsonian's original of the Star-Spangled Banner is misled into thinking the flag survived the battle intact—or the snippeting of early souvenir-seekers. The missing portions appear on a backing cloth of slightly off-colors, which indicates the full size of the original flag.

Organ is pleased with the lab he designed. The scientist-conservators are in one space together with sophisticated equipment with which they identify paints and fibers or distinguish between the stain which is rust and the one which is coffee or tell whether a nose-ring has been pounded into shape or cast in a mold or whether a corrosion crust is malachite or cuprite. (It makes a difference, in terms of getting rid of it.)

The conservators who work on objects are in a separate place. Each has a workbench equipped with a fume hood, light table, a sink with distilled water. Organ is proud of the setup but he does not welcome visitors into the lab to see it. His conservators need to concentrate. They need to hear a small item if it drops. Organ is not about to have them jostled or distracted by comings and goings or by the advice of passers-by peering over their shoulders.

Besides, he clams up on the subject of projects in the works. He doesn't talk about them any more than a doctor talks about patients. It's not the conservator's place, he feels, to noise it about that he is testing inks on a map which may prove to be a forgery. It is not up to him to say a goddess has wood rot on her foot or an amphora has come down with bronze disease. It isn't done. The curator can say these things, but not he.

Eleanor McMillan ▓║ , the conservator seated at the lab's first workbench — a binocular headband high on her forehead — has several jobs going at once. They may be a torn and glue-stained can label, a creased chewing tobacco billboard, a lithograph with a spider egg sac to be removed strand by strand. She'd rather talk about jobs completed than the ones under way — and in the library, away from the objects. Most of what she knows about conservation, she says, she has learned since college, on the job. She has learned by doing — little things like telling from its translucence when rice paste has been cooked the right length of time. Some things she learned by course work. At one course in Florence, Italy, she was shown, among other things, how to deal with stains that resulted from using salami as a bookmark.

The technical files in the library are open. Anyone can read the reports there on how McMillan removed ink from the left-hind felt paw of Roosevelt's Teddy bear and how she tackled the complex job of separating three paper dials, glued one on top of each other, on a compass from the Lewis and Clark expedition. She had to separate them without damaging the water-soluble ink on one dial and the red paint on the other.

Other files tell how Henry Clay's hat was blocked and how the handle of the first nylon-bristle toothbrush was firmed up again where the celluloid was turning to crystals. And how the image which was completely lost on a century-old photograph was recovered. The fattest report in the li-

brary is on Martha Washington's knife box, which required 1,000 hours of work. The box had a long list of ailments: warped wood had to be reglued; the black coating on its sharkskin cover had to. be removed with needles. Poultices didn't work though seven different ones — hot and cold — were tried on dummy bits of sharkskin.

The library also has a card file and a specimen case on the pests that have made their way into the collections. It contains a packet of mouse droppings and a house-borer carcass, labeled "G Washington's tent, 1974." It contains spiders from the First Ladies Hall, 1973, vials of carpet beetles, carpenter ants, German cockroaches, one book-louse, one sowbug, from various sources, and a centipede that was found in Lincoln's coat in 1970. To combat such pests, fumigation is required as objects are brought into the museum collections. An aide, pigtailed Eleni Martin   , with two years of art school, runs the fumigation chamber. She loads a week's accumulation of items onto her trolley — uniforms, flags, a piano bench — rolls the trolley into the tank, which was originally a sterilizer for hospital mattresses, and she turns the wheels and dials that bombard the tank with gas. She takes care not to include hollow objects that might collapse under the vacuum or wax ones that might melt.

Part of her job is to order lab supplies as they run low. She has lists and catalogs to go by for the tools and the chemicals, and the rolls of papers, plastics, felts. There's a six-page list for brushes alone, including test-tube brushes, stippling brushes, dusters and tips (for gold leafing), dobbers, scourers, and hogbristle fitches.

The whole staff helps to answer the more than 600 queries a year that come in to the lab from the public. What should be done about new wood sculpture that is cracking? Either store it in an airtight plastic bag in a cool place for two years to let it adapt or let it crack as much as it will and get it mended. What should be sprayed on old newspapers to preserve them? Nothing. Newspapers self-destruct from the acids in them, especially papers after 1870, wood-pulp rather than rag.

Some of the queries can be answered with form letters or recipes — for making wheat starch paste or leather dressing. Many can't because almost every answer has to begin with "it depends." How do you save a fading autograph? It depends whether it was written in India ink or with a ballpoint pen, whether it was written on a baseball, on cardboard, or on a ballet slipper. When people ask, "Isn't anything in conservation simple?" Organ says, "Yes. Baking soda powder applied with a moist fingertip does nicely to remove tea stains from crockery."

For conservators Organ gives a series of 80 lectures every year covering the chemistry and practical procedures of their work. The lectures are packed with information — comparing in detail six kinds of plastic envelopes and many times as many glues. Conservators consider the lectures a goldmine, but they are nobody's idea of entertainment. They are dry, the only drama in them the occasional stern warning — to beware of packing marble in newspaper or wood shavings or straw and not to clean armor with cleaning rouge.

For people who handle museum objects but are not conservators there is also a series of how-to-do-it slide shows. One show pictures two people in hospital coats lining a drawer in which to store clothing. Step by step — the show runs for half an hour — they insert the paper and muslin linings that will trap acids escaping from the wood and keep them from reaching the clothing. They use not just any paper but buffered paper, not just muslin but unbleached muslin with its sizing washed out.

Another slide show, one hour long, covers the washing of a cotton hanky, a linen coverlet, a wool baby bonnet. Fibers are identified under a microscope: cotton appears flat and twisted; linen seems like bamboo; and wool is scaly. A glass rod is used to stir the suds, and the acidity of the water is tested even on the seventh rinse. The object is supported in the water between plastic screens. It is blotted with napless white cotton towels and, instead of being ironed, it has its wrinkles worked out with the fingertips.

Several shows cover the cleaning and treating of paper. A severe schoolmarmy voice reminds that the hand, if it is ungloved, steadies paper with its knuckles, *not* with perspiring fingertips and that "no lumps will be tolerated in the paste." Urging caution, it says, "Avoid overenthusiastic attitudes."

For the average person the shows are mesmerizing. The conservator moves so deliberately. No haste. No sloppiness. No impulsive action. There's a mental orientation that comes with dealing with museum things, Organ says, which may take two or three years to acquire. Organ has years of experience, at the British Museum before the Smithsonian. He lists as his qualifications knowledge of chemistry, respect for objects, manual dexterity. In England he once worked on an ancient musical instrument, a corroded lyre, that had to be reconstituted, back into its solid silver state, without losing the marks of long-ago rotted-away lyre strings. At home he fixes his wife's pocketbooks.

At 31, Katherine Eirk   has the mental attitude of the conservator. "Scientists come to conservation who have a leaning toward art. Artists, like me," she says, "come to it with a leaning toward science. I skipped chemistry in college because I hated it. I've taken a lot since because I need it in my work. Now I even like it."

Everything in paper conservation appeals to her. She likes the orderliness of it. Her work surface in the conservation lab at the National Collection of Fine Arts is clear as she works on a print—her tool caddy in reach, her rings, which might snag, put to one side. She's a neat person anyway, an inveterate tidier. "I'm always putting a lens cover back on a camera before someone has finished taking pictures with it."

She likes "the boiling of things for hours, the stirring, the pottering about with beakers and pipettes—the kitchen chemistry side of the work," though she adds she'd like to have a "wife" at home to take care of kitchen chores there.

She likes the tools—her surgical microspatula, for example, bought in a medical supply store, which will separate layers of paper and is handy for applying a tiny bit of paste on a tear. Also the weights. She has leather-covered weights to hold papers flat and fishing weights to hang from strings for stretching things. When she took over as paper conservator for the National Collection of Fine Arts, she found it a treat to make up the checklist of equipment she'd need. She ordered a large sink, a new camera, microscope, lights, more Japanese brushes, a still, and a de-ionizer column. She already had on hand a pH meter, for measuring acidity, a light box on which to put torn paper for rejoining its fibers. And she had an oven for artificial aging, in which to test out materials and procedures on scraps to see how the work will last.

What Eirk likes especially about conservation is the very aspect which would put many people off. "I like the fiddliness," she says, "the almost yoga-ness of it, the precision and control. Your brain is controlling your hands. You're joining up fibers underneath a microscope or you're taking cardboard from the back of paper. Your hands feel the difference in the fibers you want to keep and the others even when you can't see them."

Eirk even feels that way about removing pieces of transparent sticky tape—a pesky job that may take her three days for one small strip "and sometimes I can't get it off at all." To almost anyone but a conservator sticky tape seems ideal for mending a paper tear. But it's damaging and it's devilishly hard to remove. Eirk stars in a film called *Marked for Life,* which shows why conservators hate the stuff.

The tape stains paper; it causes paper to curl and shrink. As she demonstrates in the film it has to be lifted away, a fraction of an inch at a time with tweezers. She's shown working it diagonally away from the paper fiber of a poster, brushing on a drop of solvent to loosen the tape's grip. The solvent was the one among many she tested which did not also dissolve the ink on the poster. Then she had to draw out the stain with poultices. And she had to rehydrate the paper and relax it with blotters and weights from the "stress" it suffered in shrinking.

Eirk has reached the point in her work where, she says, it doesn't matter to her if her next assignment is a matchbook cover or a Rembrandt. "I'm attracted now to the problem rather than the artist or the subject matter. At first

there's a tendency to feel you're working on junk. Then you come to see it as part of a collection. And you pass on to a phase where you just want to get your teeth into a juicy problem."

She usually works along at several paper problems at a time, picking up one while another soaks or dries. Recently she worked on a 1755 engraving— a camp scene from the French and Indian wars—which had gone quite brown from being mounted on cardboard. She scraped the cardboard away, washed the print in de-ionized water to which she added marble chips. She flattened it, patched it, backed it because it was brittle, and she "in-painted" across her patches in a way that pleases her. "It's not un-detectable, but it *is* subtle." The "before" and "after" photographs she took show that the ink was "feathered" to begin with. She didn't cause the blurriness of the line with her washing. It was there.

Her "juicy problem" with an Audubon print of a cardinal was that it needed washing and the paint was watercolor. She had to float it on a screen rather than dunk it. Her problem with a woodcut was that it was printed on tissue-thin paper that was "torn, stretched and wrinkled like something in a shoebox." She kept it stored between large white blotters with a note on top that said OBJECT—"so that no one coming in would think it was just a pile of blotters and throw them out or cut into them."

"You never have the same set of procedures from one project to the next," says Eirk. "Each project pushes you a little further. You're always hanging over this cliff." Tom Carter 🐾 , paintings conservator, works in the same lab with Eirk. He says; "We are doing scary things every day. There's some gambling involved"—certainly, in putting new backing on paintings. When Carter went to an international conference in London on the subject, "We were 25 people from 25 countries," he says, "and every one of us had a different system." His own system involves work with a warm iron and a vacuum hot-table. He irons a wax and resin adhesive across the back. The wax infuses into the surface and pulls flaking paint back onto the surface of the painting. Then he fortifies the back with two new layers — of linen and fiberglass. The three layers all come together with about 45 minutes of treatment, sandwiched by vacuum pressure between the hot-table and its covering sheet.

Carter's techniques were put to a severe test when he worked on a collection of paintings by contemporary black artist William Johnson, who often painted with cheap materials. He painted on surfaces like cardboard and loose-weave burlap, and on plywood, whose layers pulled apart. And Johnson used oil paint and water-base paint in the same painting.

Cleaning paintings has its element of risk. It's done with little cotton swabs, a tiny patch at a time, and different solvents are used on different colors, since the one that is right for a white collar might wipe out a black tie. "We're all perfectionists here," says Carter, "and when it comes to the objects we're professional worriers." There's risk, too, in cleaning marble statues. Calcium carbonate has to be mixed in the bath water to discourage the marble from dissolving. The sculpture conservation room has a way of sometimes looking like a sick bay. It's not just the white coats of the conservators. There's apt to be Ben Franklin, with a damaged foot, laid out on quilts on a sawhorse table. And a plaster Miss Liberty at the same time, awaiting attention to her midriff. Hinting at accidents, the label on an open cupboard drawer reads "Noses."

Bethune Gibson , who runs the conservation lab of half a dozen people in the Natural History Museum, seems to live with all the risks of her work cheerfully. She's a jolly, expansive, can-do sort of woman who skids her swivel chair from her desk with its paperwork to her work table with its rows of eyedropper bottles and beakers. "It's the actual work I like," she says, "rather than running the lab. Ten years ago I *was* the lab. I learned pretty much by doing, and taking training where it was available."

Gibson, with a degree in anthropology, was clerking in a department store when the museum hired her to begin conservation work on a loom and an African woven mat, then a

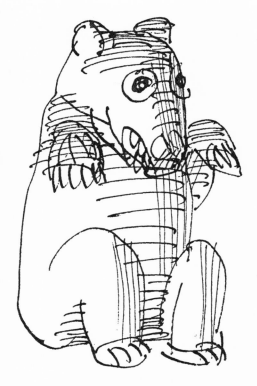

rusting sword from the Philippines. She took to the projects with pleasure and settled in to be a conservator of ethnographic materials, working on baskets, kayaks, snowshoes, buckskin dresses, masks, items of feather, grass, fur, ivory, metal, fiber, leather.

A chemist is teamed up with Gibson, who has extra hands from batches of conservators she trains from small museums around the country or students working toward a museum studies degree. She has apparatus and glassware enough to stock a chemistry lab, objects enough at any one time to stock a little museum.

The volume of things under her care — and the variety — is enormous. She can't pick her way daintily, especially since these things, most of them organic, are vulnerable to moth damage and molds and fungi and bacterial decay. She just keeps going and treats some 1,500 items a year.

The proof of her success is in the before-and-after look of the items that have gone through that great, high-ceilinged, airy, light room. It's there in the work in progress all up and down the long tables where men and women are bent over, nose to object, working hard, with great concentration and attention to detail, but talking to themselves, to each other, groaning over difficulties, laughing. "You want to avoid tension," says Gibson. "A stress situation isn't good for the objects."

Pictures in her files record where grime has been removed from a series of objects to reveal design and color. Gibson has cleaned dirt from baskets. She has removed fish oil from wood objects where it was turned into a black sticky mess from being stored without air conditioning. She has replaced the rancid butter of Herero-tribe clothing with a leather dressing. Otherwise she tries not to tamper with finishes. She leaves the resin, which was waterproofing, in Indian baskets. She leaves fire-black where she thinks it's important as evidence. In cleaning a basket she leaves the corn flour or acorn flour in the bottom. She leaves a berry stain on a buckskin dress. Using a needle, she fills in the cracks of a Georgia clay vessel, without up-ending the urn or disturbing its contents — an infant's remains (the curator believed these were too fragile to remove from the burial urn).

One of the devices Gibson likes to use best is an air-abrasive machine which cleans by blowing grit — particles of powder or tiny glass beads — across an object and into an exhaust chamber. It's the same principle as sandblasting, but highly refined and more delicate. Her air-abrasive unit saves her from using a lot of chemicals which might be corrosive. It saves her in some cases from scraping at surfaces. It saves her from washing things that might harden with water and go brittle. It is spectacularly successful with cleaning stained leather clothing, or clothing that has shells or feathers attached to it. It's good on rusted metals where wet cleaning might cause further rusting. It's good on tarnished metal threads, on baskets and on pots.

Cleaning a Plains Indian buckskin dress, she directs the nozzle of the blower around painted areas which might flake. She picks her way carefully around a painted war scene, avoiding every splash of painted-on blood. As she works she watches the dramatic contrast appear — between the smoke-blacked portion and the cleaned portion, which comes out a pearly cream color.

Kept on high tables are the items her crew must get to next. At one recent time they included a bear-claw necklace, a rope llama collar with bells, Siberian skis lined with caribou fur, a pair of Eskimo pants of fish skin which was going brittle—all waiting their turn while current work continued on items already set out along the tables.

One was a huge pot from the mouth of the Amazon which was needed for the South American Hall. It was being washed, cautiously, because of the fragile glaze. Its encrusted crystals were removed with a hot chemical on tissue poultices. Its fine cracks were filled with glue applied by a needle, its big cracks with plaster of Paris, then painted.

Another item was a big cone-shaped Pomo Indian basket of willow, which had insect cocoons to be removed, insect holes to be filled with tiny mulberry-paper "pills" or pellets, and an Indian mend to be admired and left just as it was found.

A third object among many was a wad of cloth from Spiro Mound, Oklahoma, which had been folded, then buried. With Gibson's encouragement the various layers were separated out by floating them apart and drying them on screens. Vegetable fibers were found in the warp—pawpaw and sugar cane; animal hair in the weft, from buffalo, rabbit, muskrat, beaver, with some goose and turkey feathers as well.

In the attic at the same time Gibson had a crew of school-age volunteers working with boxes of pot shards from broken Southwestern bowls. They were solving 2,000 three-dimensional jigsaw puzzles, the pieces of which were covered with 50 to 100 years' deposit of dust. It was satisfying work, especially in such an eerie setting with its rows of cabinets labeled Cayuga leggings, Iroquois cradles, Cree greenstone carvings—and with its big, unpackable shapes of drums and canoes up above the lockers and its log-jam of totem poles in the aisles.

When one of the girls built up, on her sand tray, a jug out of jagged pieces, she said it was so exciting to see a shape emerge she wanted to jump up and down. That sounded reasonable to Gibson, who said, "Why don't you go ahead and do it — out in the hall."

Conservation isn't all painstaking "fiddly" work, at least not for conservator Lee Aks 🔳 , who spends much of his work-time outdoors in the Hirshhorn Museum's sculpture garden. He takes care of emergencies there — when a visitor rakes a statue's surface with a ring or when wind dislodges a moving part or when Henry Moore's massive bronze *King and Queen* has to be moved indoors for tests, including X-ray by a machine designed to X-ray horses. And every six months he gives baths to the 50 pieces of outdoor sculpture as a bit of routine maintenance.

With a cleaning solution, conservator Aks removes dust, grime, fingerprints, and bird droppings from the outdoor statues. He rinses with a long hose, sloshes off statues in the corners of the garden with buckets, reaches the oversize ones with balancing acts and fancy footwork from ladders. Following the bath most of the pieces are painted with a beeswax solution applied with a narrow brush. Then they're buffed to protect them from the elements and give them a luster.

Many mornings Aks is out early in the first sun, washing, waxing, buffing, while chains across the stairway still close off the garden to visitors. It takes him two mornings to do a massive piece like Rodin's *Burghers of Calais* with its six oversize figures. Passers-by stop to peer down from the wall around the sunken garden. They watch him, buffing hard, his hair blowing in the breeze. Aks leans into his work, his feet, in loafers, planted on the statue's base among the bare feet of the heroic-sized men, his head, though he's tall, reaching just to their shoulders.

From past experience he moves warily, avoiding the outstretched bronze hands which he knows can pack a wallop. He puts a lot of power into his broad rub-a-dub strokes across the chests, gouging hard into eyes and ears, slap-slapping across the arms, shoeshine style, with his cotton diaper. "Hey," a passer-by called down to him one morning, "that's some job you've got — giving the Burghers a bath."

8. Exhibiting

Exhibits are the show side of museums, inviting the public to come and see things from the collections — to look, learn, be pleased, stimulated, amused. Exhibits take years of planning and the work of many people. Carpenter Chuck Rowell ▓||, animal freeze-drier Rolland Hower 🐗, film-maker Karen Loveland ▓||, model maker Bud Sayre 🐾, mannequin maker Susan Wallace 🐾, bracket maker John Wink ▓||, all contribute to putting on exhibits. So do the writers, the craftsmen who work with silkscreen and gold leaf, the people who hang airplanes, paintings, and pterodactyls, and those who knock holes in the floor in order to install the engine room of a ship. Exhibiting requires designers like Bob Mulcahy 🐒, with his furniture for the new monkey enclosures at the Zoo. Above all exhibiting requires people trained in the art of communicating ideas and information through a show of objects.

"Our job is showmanship," says Benjamin Lawless ▓||, exhibits chief for the Museum of History and Technology. "It's theater. We bring the public in, take them up to the trough, and count on the curators — the historians and scientists — to give them something to drink. In fact," he adds, "we don't even leave all that to the curators. In the past curators would say, 'Here's the show.' Now they submit their show ideas to a committee — people in all kinds of jobs all through the museum — other curators, exhibits people plus people who have nothing to do with exhibits. They submit their specimens, too. And we say 'Show us, get it all out on the table, let us see what you've got.' "

Heated talk, arguments, and fights are all part of the planning process for exhibits. "The curators tone me down," says Lawless, a large and expansive man with a shock of white hair, explosive black eyebrows, and big hands which he flies through the air as he speaks. "They get me to give up some of my extravagances." (Lawless longed to have a full-size replica of the Statue of Liberty's arm and torch out in front of Arts and Industries as a come-on for the "1876" exhibit, but "never mind," he says, of the scheme that was flatly turned down.) "I, on the other hand, liven the curators up," he adds, "so they're not so dull. The mission, mind you, is fully understood on both sides. It all works nicely for the exhibits, which end up not so theatrical as I would have made them, nor so dull as they would have been without me. We're like a close family here," he says, to explain the fights. "Many of us have been together for years. I'm one who came down from the Philadelphia Centennial with the original 40 box-carloads of stuff in 1876."

In reality, Lawless came to the Smithsonian in 1954. At that time exhibiting still consisted pretty much of "storing" things for the public to see. Designers refer to "visual storage" — an arrangement of objects more or less as they would have been in a closet but substituting glass for solid doors. Practically everything the museums possessed was out to be seen. Lined up in mahogany and glass cases were thousands of birds, animals shoulder to shoulder, ranks of antlers, rows of skulls, rows on rows of arrowheads, butterflies as far as the eye could see. People came to look at the collections which were set out almost as they were collected. Almost no attempt was made to communicate anything about them to people who might not already know.

A new concept of exhibiting began in the 1950s, when Cliff Evans ⬛ , an archaeologist, and the late John Anglim, ⬛ a science illustrator, revamped the Latin America hall of the Natural History Museum. From one eight-by-six-foot glass case containing 45 Mexican funerary urns and other cases similarly crammed with mortars and grinders and

Peruvian pots, Evans winnowed out a few especially fine specimens, and put the rest away—into real, invisible storage. He divided up his space to show his selection in a sequence that made sense to him, that had some meaning. For one case of stone carvings Anglim made a false back and painted it red.

The red, which was intended to show up the carvings, did so nicely. It also sent a shock wave through the institution. Evans and Anglim, a Welshman and an Irishman accustomed to battling with each other, did good battle on behalf of their exhibits concept all the way up to the Secretary. They won. The Smithsonian hired its first exhibits staff. The red wall remained (at least it remained until, 20 years later, Hall 23 was revamped again, this time to use the model shop's three-dimensional marketplace scene and its walk-through rain forest).

Lawless in the same period was looking at the First Ladies in the Arts and Industries building, where they stood in a row of bare glass cases, in amongst postage stamps, Lincoln's death mask, and the last of the carrier pigeons. "I saw those First Ladies standing there in the sun, just like the antelopes in Natural History—and in the same cases as the antelopes—and I said, 'This is terrible. They need my help.'" With Klapthor, ▒▌▌ he created period environments for the Presidential wives, so people could understand why they dressed as they did.

"Suddenly we had two good things—the new Latin America hall, the new First Ladies. Money began to pour in for more innovations. Natural History redid its displays of birds and gems. We modernized power, textiles, health. By 1959 we had 140 people working in exhibits. All types. We needed a lot more people, fast. I wanted first-rate artists. And I got them. But with the money there was, I had to hire lunatics—skilled people, creative, but crazy. The very nice thing is that there's a great understanding of eccentricity around here. After all, the curators are eccentrics themselves, and this saved us. We were also hiring people who were highly skilled at writing about specimens. Altogether, it was a period of tremendous excitement and growth.

"Suddenly, we were doing eight brand-new huge exhibits in a year. We did them fast when we had to. I have a theory: if it takes 3,500 man-hours to do a job, you ought to be able to get 3,500 men and do it in an hour. Sometimes we've almost done it that way. We learned a lot in those years. And though we've slowed down since then, the Smithsonian became the fountainhead of the exhibits business.

"We learned about silk-screening our labels (early labels were often typewritten or made up from lick-and-stick kits) and applying photographs and doing panels. We learned about writing labels for people who don't want to read a book while they're walking by at three miles an hour. We learned how to lay out a progression of things and ideas to be followed without a floor plan in hand."

Those were years in which exhibits people were using sound to unlock the secrets in objects — the cough of the 1903 Cadillac as it started up; the stack and track noises of the Southern Railway's steam locomotive #1401. They were setting machinery and waterwheels in motion. One lively innovation led to another. Live people were put at looms and printing presses, to work them, and at a ham radio station and a pencil-making machine. Visitors were urged to "Please Touch" — a Brontosaurus bone, a mastodon tooth, swatches of tiger fur and elephant hide and now, even a rock that came from the moon. The public was invited to walk into a ship's radio shack and onto the bridge of an aircraft carrier. Outside the buildings, on the Mall, live craftspeople and musicians were shown, making quilts and playing bagpipes like the ones in the collections.

Experiments in exhibits technique were exciting but some of them didn't work out. For example, the smells introduced into a number of exhibits had to be given up — for fear that the oils which carry scents of chocolate and apple pie and lavender might damage museum objects. Also abandoned was the use of live Dominique chickens, even though they performed well, giving an old-time homey look to Early America halls, and laying Grade A eggs. But the Dominiques were messy, and when one attacked a visitor they were fired from History and Technology.

"We're learning what techniques *not* to use," says Lawless, "the ones that dominate the objects, overwhelm them. People will watch a movie at the drop of a hat. Movies can wipe out the point of an exhibit unless you keep them subordinate to the objects. Movies should show the processes — how a pot is made and not the history of pottery; how a coverlet is woven. Processes are a dog to try to show in museums. We used movies in *Nation of Nations* for an express purpose — to show music and sports events that were part of the immigrants' lives in America. The story of immigration was told in other ways.

"We're finding out you need to have a lot of stuff for a good exhibit. The exhibits we do here in History and Technology are sort of hearts-on-our-sleeve. We romanticize, fantasize, let our imaginations go. We make up stories and research them — like the story of *Suiting Everyone* — how clothing went from homemade to store-bought and how the plumber now dresses like the banker. We have to remind ourselves: people come here to see things. It's neat to have story lines. Sometimes it's also neat just to put out everything we own and see if people can stand it. We did that with *We the People* and "1876." The story line is there but we're piling everything onto it. We're learning to use humor. We can be a little frivolous, not so up-tight."

Lawless is enormously pleased with the new panel he mounted on the wall near the Foucault Pendulum. Visitors watch that big "old faithful" pendulum, semi-hypnotized. They know its swinging there, suspended from the fourth-floor ceiling, knocking down one at a time, in turn, the markers arranged in a circle on the floor, somehow proves that the earth rotates daily on its axis. Most are reduced to gibberish, though, if asked by a child or an auntie: How? The new panel has a title, written large: EVERYTHING YOU

ALWAYS WANTED TO KNOW ABOUT PENDULUMS BUT WERE
AFRAID TO ASK. The curator, Faye Cannon ▓▓|| —he's curator
of classical physics ('I stop where Einstein starts,' he says of
himself) — knew enough to have fun with the subject. "So
we built something intriguing. We put it together like pages of
a scientist's notebook — with equations, stray thoughts in
the margin, doodles. Is the Mystic Formula

$$T = 2\pi \sqrt{\frac{L}{g}}$$

Really True? No, the Mystic Formula Is Not Really True,
but it would be if the string were weightless and the support
were frictionless and all the mass were in a little ball at the
end. . . .' That kind of thing. We have buttons to push with
answers to 20 questions, some simple, some cosmic."

A member of the museum staff complained to Lawless
that he was making fun of scientists. "I said, 'I'm not mak-

ing fun of scientists.' He told me, 'You're teasing people.' I said, 'Of course I am.' I'm teasing them into reading the panel. I've put it together so they're dying to read it. It's like looking into a secret notebook. It's hard to read. Some of the type is so small you practically need a magnifying glass."

Lawless thinks it takes a certain maturity to spoof. New curators are hardest to work with, he says, because they still want to do a long text, sound scholarly to impress their friends. Scholars who have been around a long time are better at describing objects to people who don't ·know anything about them. On the other hand he's thinking maybe museums should "go way out sometimes, too" to put on exhibits for people with highly specialized knowledge.

With years of experience at badgering curators to understand that exhibits are for the public and not just for fellow scientists, Lawless recently lit into one curator about his script on atom smashers. "Practically the first word in the script was 'phantasmagoria.' I said, Who's going to know what that means? You never explain it. You never explain anything. You go right into comparing this atom smasher with that atom smasher. Aren't you going to tell what an atom is? No, he said, he wasn't. Aren't you at least going to tell what an atom smasher is? No. Who, I asked, would understand what he was talking about? Well, he could think of nine people, he said, and they would probably be very much interested. I said, That's fine. We spend a quarter of a million dollars to build an exhibit for your nine friends.

"Well, you know," Lawless adds, in a quick about-face from outrage to a baffled sort of pleasure, "it might just be the thing for us to do. We might just do this exhibit, at that. We're loosening up a bit. It's a sign of maturity."

When the National Air and Space Museum opened, its audiovisual shows outdid all the others on the Mall. Melvin Zisfein ⬦ , an engineer, did a large part of the writing. "I found I like to do it," says Zisfein, who among other things is in charge of the Air and Space exhibits. "I'm good at it. It almost has to be one person and not a committee. Thinking up a show and writing its script is a personal thing. But once it's written, we're great believers around here in review. We show our concèpt scripts to outside experts in the field. We show them to people who don't know the field at all. The more people who see it the better. The designers go through the same process. They produce a design concept. They make models and drawings and play around with them; we even make full-scale mock-ups, so we can see if an exhibit 'works off the wall' — see if it looks good, makes its point, comes alive.

"We really try to communicate," Zisfein says. "Making it easy for people to understand difficult things — that's what this is all about." Flight technology was a particularly difficult thing. He decided to communicate part of it through puppets, not just moving, talking puppets, but puppets whose thoughts appear in balloons flashed above their heads and who manipulate slide projectors themselves to make their point. "We kept that technique secret till the museum opened." Zisfein laughs appreciatively. "We didn't want to see it copied in salami commercials."

The setting for one puppet show — on airplane design — is a 1933 conference of five men designing a racing plane. Propulsion engineer Bulldog Powers, a cigar hanging from his lower lip, growls out his opinion. He wants a giant engine, a giant radial engine. Slick Camber, the aerodynamicist, complains that a bulky radial engine will have too much drag. Speed's the thing, says Slick, who pictures, in the balloon above his head, a sleek, streamlined shape with paper-thin wings. Structures engineer Reginald Pick, as finicky as his name, wants superior strength for tight racing turns. He puts some thickness back in the wings to house the structures he wants but mollifies Slick with a promise to use all flush riveting. Ace, the pilot, just wants a plane that will handle like a sweet, old friend. While the others visualize their design in blue or gray or yellow, Ace sees his in lipstick red.

By the end everyone is picturing the same plane. The same design (resembling the full-size Hughes H-1 Racer, which is on exhibit) occurs in the balloon above each puppet. Above four heads it appears in brown; above Ace's head it still appears in red, with ACE spelled out on the fuselage. The puppet show, which lasts for two minutes, took six months to make. The preparation included dress rehearsals with members of the staff sitting in for the puppets. "The rehearsals broke us up," Zisfein recalls. "We had all the predictable cracks: the second dummy from the left looks wonderfully realistic — that sort of thing. But the rehearsals were essential to get the wording we wanted and the gestures and the timing."

To do the show on sea-air operations, Zisfein went out in the Atlantic on the aircraft carrier *America*. "We could just have got the NC-4 and put a label on it and said, This is a distinguished Navy plane. We tried instead to show what it's like to fly over big expanses of water and to operate off a carrier — what it's like factually and what it feels like, how thrilling and interesting it may have been," Zisfein adds, "for the photographer I can only guess, as the photographers had to perch on a narrow ledge over the flight deck, outside the carrier's island, in order to film the takeoffs of the planes."

Museum-goers today, if they stand on the Smithsonian's navigation bridge beside the mannequin Captain in his large swivel chair, have the sensation of watching the plane takeoffs from above. They look down at an angle to the catapult activity on the flight deck and to the ocean beyond. At another place they stand in the "pri-fly," the carrier's air-traffic control tower, crowded with telephones, radios, closed-circuit TV sets, sound boxes and gauges, as the "air-boss" monitors the landing approaches. When they descend the ship's ladder they see the ocean again, through a hatch. This time they see its waves at water level. They see a ship passing on the horizon and a helicopter flying above in the sky.

Zisfein speaks of using "Japanese garden techniques" — manipulating the museum space to suggest the vaster spaces on a carrier, using the hatches, using doors along solid walls, to suggest areas beyond. From the Navy, as it dismantled the

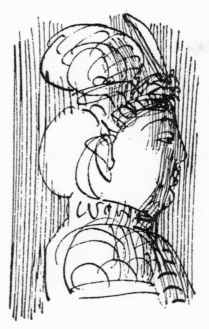

carrier *Hancock*, he got all the authentic "hardware" he wanted — the telephones and the instrument panels, the pipes and electrical fittings and fire equipment, the yellow wall cupboards labeled Abandon Ship Lockers. "They're the things that cover a carrier's walls," he says, "and convey a sense of place."

The audiovisual games, which seem right and appealing at Air and Space, would seem wrong, inappropriate, in many of the other museums. They would not be permitted through the door at the Freer Gallery of Art. Objects of oriental art on exhibit at the Freer are set out in airy rooms, given generous space, fine light, immaculate walls. Information about them is conveyed on spare and simple labels. There are *no* audiovisual contrivances, no sound and motion effects, no panels with maps, diagrams, photographs — nothing to distract the viewer. "The Freer philosophy," says Martin Amt , an assistant to the Freer's director, "is to attract people to the objects themselves, to charm them with the objects and not with theatrics." The tone of the museum is dignified and elegant. It is subdued, but not without an air of quiet excitement. Even Charles Lang Freer was known to turn a backwards somersault at the pleasure of seeing an object for the first time.

Pictures at the Freer are hung exactly as Charles Freer intended them to hang—at eye level, 62 inches from the floor. They hang from two copper wires that are cut one inch short and then tugged on, to bring them even. "Like this," Amt demonstrates, swinging his weight from two wires. "The world progresses around us. We do not."

Pieces of sculpture are mounted on substantial bases. The three-foot-high South Indian bronze goddess which conservator Thomas Chase treated for bronze disease has a walnut-veneered pedestal that is tall enough—three and a half feet—to bring her to eye level. The figure is bolted to the pedestal which in turn is anchored to the floor. A larger goddess, life-size and more (at five foot eight inches), the wooden Kuan Yin, which Chase treated for rot in her feet, stands on a low base, just 24 inches off the floor. Because this figure, standing on weakened feet and with one arm extended out from the body, is especially vulnerable should a visitor jostle it, the base was recently fitted with a railing. The railing is of walnut, Buddhist-style, with its carved lotus-shaped finials, like little tops, at the corners. The Goddess of Mercy received an extra "leg," too. A two-by-four piece of new wood is now fitted up into the base of the statue and down into the pedestal, as a stabilizer.

The fine old woods which Freer favored are used throughout the museum. The basements are still well stocked with the supply of walnut boards and cherry and mahogany which he provided. The woods are used to make frames, stands for objects, display cases, and recently to make a 24-hole umbrella rack for the museum.

Santi Diblasi   , a Freer carpenter, who is expert at creating the wooden latticework cores for standing Japanese screens, made the umbrella rack. He drew his plans first, put together a mock-up in scrap lumber, then crafted the whole thing, handsomely, of walnut. "Possibly once in ten years it rains hard on a Freer lecture night," says Amt. "We could stick the umbrellas in wastebaskets. It's just that we don't do things that way at the Freer. Mr. Diblasi will be making a 100-hole stand next."

Designers for the Hirshhorn Museum's Sculpture Garden had no precedent for doing a layout of the garden. They found it hard to visualize the pieces of sculpture in the setting, without testing them first in position and, what's more, without even having the pieces in front of them to look at. Though they fixed on a layout on the basis of small models, arranged in a model of the garden, they felt uneasy about it. Before its opening in 1974, they thought a dress rehearsal was needed in the real garden, using full-size styrofoam copies of the originals.

On the day of the rehearsal, workers carried the marsh-mallow-light copies out into the garden, some slung over shoulders, some tucked under arms. It had taken two sculptors six months to make the copies, hacking them out of crisp plastic with rasps and saws and finishing them with radiator paints to look bronze and steely and gold. Passers-by, stopping to watch the rehearsal from over the garden wall, were heard to say that the new collection of sculpture — or what they thought was the new collection — looked flimsy, ready to blow away on a breeze. So much for modern art, they said.

The designers were dissatisfied as well. There were too many pieces, too close together. Sculptures like Rodin's *Balzac* and his *Burghers of Calais* and Moore's *King and Queen*, even a skinny head by Giacometti, needed space to breathe, more space than anyone had calculated. The rehearsal saved the designers from blundering about on moving-in day with two-ton art works dangling from cranes. It saved them from offering an overstuffed garden as their exhibit.

A building that is itself an exhibit is James Goode's responsibility. As curator of the Castle, the Smithsonian's first home, he is charged with its appearance. He keeps it looking, inside and out, the way a nineteenth-century medieval castle should look. As a Washington landmark, with offices in it for the Smithsonian's top administrators, the building is more of an exhibit than anything it shows in museum cases nowadays.

Recently Goode furnished the Castle in a mixture of ornate Victorian styles. He fitted the offices with hatracks and hatrack-mirror combinations, rolltop desks, carved wood chairs, chandeliers, Canterburys (magazine racks). He found wallpapers, carpets, and fringed draperies for the period, bootscrapers and spittoons. He installed potted palms and proper iron crypt gates for the crypt containing the remains of James Smithson.

Goode is responsible for all the furnishings in the Castle's 93 rooms, and for repairs, including repairs to the windows which require tiny diamond-shaped panes and lead crisscross muntins, the strips between the panes of glass. He is responsible for the Castle's owls as well — their installation and feeding.

According to historian Goode, owls in the Castle towers were mentioned in an 1889 guidebook to Washington. Smithsonian people wanted them there again, especially former Secretary and birdman Wetmore, who had fond memories of studying tower-owl droppings in the past. Wetmore, in his 80s, reopened the tower trapdoor to admit a pair of barn owls, Alexander and Athena. And while they settled in and hatched a family Goode daily climbed the series of five ladders to feed them their mice and rats.

Alexander and Athena eventually left. But owls flying in and out of the Castle's windows were once again a part of the Smithsonian's image. Barn owls Increase and Diffusion were the next of the tower's named inhabitants.

Exhibits at the building shared by the Portrait Gallery and the National Collection of Fine Arts are exhibits-within-exhibits. That building (the old Patent Office Building), too, like the Castle, is one which people come to see for itself — and to walk through its marble corridors, its courtyard, the stately room where Lincoln held his second inaugural ball. Val Lewton   , designer for the National Collection, helped to convert the building from offices to galleries when the Smithsonian took it over. He remembers pitching out hundreds of chairs in the process, dismantling a room that was used for sterilizing cuspidors, removing layers of "government green" paint from the walls, even from the pillars — a job which had to be done with white gasoline and wet poultices.

"It was always a problem," says Lewton, "of whether the rooms were going to dominate, or the paintings, or whether they could be sympathetic and enhance each other — which is just what came about. It's a good old building and much more flexible than we ever imagined."

In designing exhibits, Lewton plays with the space over and over. He is not gutting it, he says, but "recannibalizing it" — which sounds almost as bad — throwing up new partitions, inventing new traffic patterns, creating the color and the atmosphere that seem right each time. For an exhibit called *Made in Chicago*, where much of the painting was derived from popular culture like comic books, he designed a motel-like pattern of rooms and let each artist pick the color for his walls. "It came out pretty wild and frenzied, a blast of color — orange, pink — all very bilious," he says, happily. With the show for Mark Tobey, an inward-looking painter,

Lewton wanted to isolate each work. He redesigned the space to give the effect of a circular room, with partitions leading viewers to see each painting separately, to see one at a time and to see it first from a distance, before being on top of it.

In some exhibits, Lewton says, chronology is important. Paintings are hung in the order in which they were done. It was important in the exhibit on black painter William Johnson. "Viewers were walked right through his life—from the early, primitive paintings to the work of the mature period and finally to the work showing the almost Van Gogh-like breakup of his mind.".

In other exhibits chronology doesn't matter. "It was design, not history, that was important in a show on saddles. I built all different levels for the saddles, to mimic a tackroom—getting the flavor through the levels, not through any props or representation of a tackroom." He wouldn't design the show in quite the same way if he had it to do again. The stairs he put into the passageways between cases were hard to maneuver. They distracted people, made them think about their footing.

Designers learn with every exhibit, says Lewton. They learn about objects and about design. That's *one* of the good things about being a designer. Another, he finds, is the moving about. A designer isn't always at a drawing board. He's going to the cabinetmakers in their shop or to the contractors. "History always interested me," he says, "but I tended to doze off in libraries. I still do," he adds. He gets an extra dose of the moving about he likes by running eight miles a day as a member of the museum's team, which competes in a league with the Pentagon.

At the small Renwick Gallery, which specializes in American design, exhibits come and go at a brisk pace. They are put together with eyes on the calendar and dismantled again with some regret. A designer like Mike Monroe immerses himself in a subject for months, then moves on to another.

When Monroe's exhibit, called *Craft Multiples,* was

closing, he took a last look at it. He went through its rooms, ruminating about his design decisions in setting it up, making notes to himself on pieces he could reuse — partitions, pedestals, cases — for the next show on his drawing board. "The designer has to have in mind from the start what an exhibit is trying to achieve," says Monroe, who spent three months on *Craft Multiples*. "Why are these objects together in these rooms? What point are you trying to make with them? The point here was not history. I didn't have to stick to chronology. The point was qualities of design. I just had to put things together in a very pleasing way."

Working from photographs, Monroe saw he had a lot of objects in wood and a wide range of other materials — silver, leather, glass. With such a diversity, he wanted the way they were all presented to be a uniform, constant factor. He decided to use gray-green panels, redwood slats, canvas, and plexiglass labels, and to repeat these materials throughout. He found woodcuts picturing craftspeople at work and put them together in a block to use as a motif on panels through the rooms and on posters and on a catalog — a visual sign of crafts and of multiples.

He had to think about permanent factors — the carpets, the draperies, the walls which in the Renwick have ornament and moldings. He had to think about security. Things in the show that were out in the open, like fabric cushions, were tied down. He had to think about the requirement of four-foot aisles, and about total space. The horse buggy, the hot-air balloon, even the balloon basket, had to be represented by photographs.

"As I worked, I kept playing around with the possibilities," says Monroe, "coming back to the gallery to measure and to reassess whether I had the right place, looking again at my photographs. It's only when you have the object in your hand that you're dealing with reality, and then it's often too late to make changes. It's kind of like a giant jigsaw puzzle. You can't end up with an object or two left over, because the catalog is already at the printer."

Monroe put a dinosaur pillow, shaped like triceratops,

next to a covered jar, because he liked the contrast of soft and hard. In another case he put a doll dressed in lace together with an ivory-handled knife and some letter paper and some ornaments made of dough. All the colors in the case "worked together," he thought. So did the textures. The dough ornaments, which fit in well, would have looked out of place in the case with silver and crystal things "which were kind of elegant."

In another area he grouped the full-size birchbark canoe with the baskets he had and the carved ducks. They seemed "naturally related." He used a batik dress with shell decorations to make the vertical accent he needed. The black and white of the dress fabric related to the black and white dishes on the wall. An iron kitchen rack shaped like an eagle related to the rest, because it was a bird and it was black.

"The traffic pattern is important. I think it works better if you walk through the rooms and have things gradually revealed to you. The wooden bathtub takes you nicely by surprise because you expect it in another material. The way I design, you *have* to wander around. You're involved in looking at one case and then you're led over to another. You don't see the whole room at once. You see only a few objects at a time. It's not as tedious that way."

"People don't think about exhibit design," says Monroe, who studied studio art in universities and art institutes. "They look at objects. And that's as it should be. In fact, when you realize you are seeing a beautiful installation, then it may be an overstatement. Yet someone made the decisions on how the objects are presented. Their presentation can detract from them or enhance them, and it's an important factor in how you remember them and in the total feeling you go away with."

As Monroe watched his *Craft Multiples* exhibit come down, Beth Miles 🐗 , 26, at the Natural History Museum, watched her *Insect Zoo* being mounted. It was in a new hall, and combined the educational approach of a museum with the live exhibits of a zoo, containing as it did, live insects. Like Monroe, she was concerned for the feeling people would take away with them. "I knew I wanted to win people over, make them see what's interesting in the lives of insects. Particularly I wanted to get them to set aside their first response to bugs in general, which is usually 'ick!' To do that I first had to learn enough to get enthusiastic and stop saying 'ick' myself."

It took her two months of study. In that time Miles learned enough to put the right questions to the scientists on the first outline they wrote for the zoo exhibit. "I would never contradict scientists about something in their field. My job as a designer is to communicate what they want to say. But if I can't understand it, there's no way I can communicate it. Perhaps it's not clearly put, or it may not be exhibitable, if there is no visual evidence in the collection to support the text. Then it's a question of rethinking the text. People have the right to see lots of real things — in this case, bugs, which speak a great deal for themselves. You want to have as much for them to look at as possible.

"Or, it may be that there is *just too much* information to put across in the space. You simply can't knock people over with a full introductory course of entomology. An exhibit isn't a book. People take up a book because they're already interested in a subject. They can read it at their own speed, put it down, come back to it. An exhibit is something you see. It's physical work. Even a bugs enthusiast or a scholar can look only so long before the eyes glaze over and the feet hurt.

"For some people coming in off the Mall, it may be their only visit. If they come in for only five minutes, what is it you hope they assimilate? Might they get a mistaken impression? It ought to be clear to them what the exhibit is about, how it's arranged, whether it's for specialists only or for them, too, how it will go for them if they stay. That's a first level of engagement which scientists are apt to skip. They're more likely to start right in with a barrage of words. For the *Insect Zoo* we had to put across immediately that we had *live* insects, and not just insects but a large family called arthropods. Once we did that successfully, we could go to the other levels and really convey much of what the scientists wanted to say."

Three months went to mulling, writing, rewriting. In that time Miles also made rough floor plans, dividing up the exhibits space. And she made some broad decisions. She would build a big free-flight cage as the focal point of the exhibit — 30 feet long, with three habitats in it to represent forest, grassland, and pond. She wanted to build it partly of screening, so people could hear cricket chirpings, and partly of glass so people could put their noses to the pane. In her design natural light from the museum's windows would give a lively atmosphere to the flight cage.

Miles decided not to use big photo blow-ups, showing insects many times magnified. "Bugs are great to see," she says. "But they're small. You have to take some time, and work to look for them. Big pictures make it look as though you're promising bugs on a silver platter. Without them, the focus is down, onto small things, the way they really are. It's not as though you're promising something you can't deliver." She planned to put freeze-dried specimens instead next to the cages to help in finding and identifying the live specimens, and use small and silent filmstrips as well.

When the scientists' rewriting produced a script she felt confident about Miles knew the crisis point had passed. She could lay out her cases and build. "Once you've cleared up your themes and subthemes," she says, "you can stay on course." Even so, *Insect Zoo* was the first exhibit she had designed all the way through by herself. She was "vaguely uneasy" because the scientist in charge of the exhibit was frequently away. This was beetles expert Terry Erwin 🐘 , who was studying ground beetles up in the treetops in Panama. Also, there were old beetle specimens too fragile for mailing which he had to examine in Europe. He was available to her only about one fifth of the time.

She was uneasy, too, in not knowing exactly what specimens to expect. Deborah Waller 🐘 , in charge of an insect rearing room, was experimenting with various species of insects, seeing which would perform satisfactorily, which

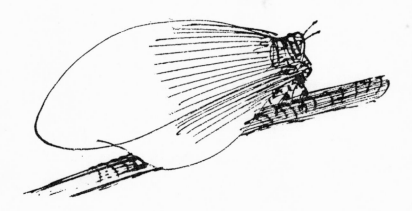

would hatch out, year-around, to suit the exhibit's schedule, which would accept substitutes for messy or hard-to-get foods. The rearing program was always a bit touch and go, and Miles found herself running frequently to the rearing room for bulletins. "I was always pumping Deborah for information on her critters, to know what conditions to build into their cages—did they hide from light, need a lot of moisture, need a big growing plant to eat?"

Lubber grasshoppers were early successes. By manipulating their dormant period—through trips into the refrigerator and out into warmth again—Waller could promise a steady supply of them at all stages of their development. They were ideal for display—big, brightly colored (green with yellow stripes), clean-looking, hardy. Presented with a head of lettuce, they gave a hearty and dramatic demonstration of insects chewing. They were naturals for the section on how arthropods eat.

Tobacco hornworms could be counted on, year-around, to demonstrate metamorphosis. Tarantulas were no trouble to rear, nor were roaches, 14 species of which were thriving in the nursery on dog food. Unicorn beetles were available in Washington even in winter, from holes in oak trees.

Butterflies (monarchs, for the mimicry case) proved chancy to raise. But more could be ordered, special delivery, from California. Mosquitoes were undependable. They died off. Dung beetles, though, did nicely, and the U.S. Department of Agriculture provided the *Insect Zoo* with special cow dung for them to eat. It was collected before it reached the ground and guaranteed to be unpolluted!

The introductory area, the first part of the exhibit that people would see on entering, turned out as Miles wanted it. It was a kind of table of contents. In it she used her biggest and hardiest specimens: first, a case of glistening patent leather beetles to support the opening statement: Insects Are Arthropods. For the next statement, All of These Animals Are Also Arthropods, she showed, like crown jewels in four high-standing glass cubes — one big, wriggling millipede, one centipede, one crustacean (a land crab), and three arachnids (a tarantula and two scorpions). A bar graph on the wall demonstrated that the creatures on show were the world's most successful animals, adapting themselves to fill every habitat on land, underground, in trees, and in oceans. Four main sections of the hall were blocked out to cover the subthemes on diversity — in habitat, in patterns of growth, in eating, in form, size, color.

As someone who came to the museum from design work in printing, Miles took special care with her text panels. "You put onto the big vertical panels what you want people to see first," she says. "General information, not details, not how many legs to a grasshopper. The big panels are never that specific. You don't want to change them every time your grasshoppers are out with flu and you're substituting crickets. More detailed information, on the individual insects, including their Latin names, is mounted down by the railings, where people stepping up for a close look will see it."

Months after *Insect Zoo* opened Miles was still building modifications into it — new labels, a new mosquito feeder, new cages. She had to redesign entirely for the leafcutter ants, who moved out of their see-through nest. They moved queen, workers, soldiers, their whole society, and resettled in the dirt under their chrysanthemum plant. The leafcutter colony from Louisiana had arrived late, close to *Insect Zoo*'s opening date. She had built the cage on too short an acquaintance. Mistakenly she planned to show how the ants crossed the ground to forage, how they carried petals back into their chamber, cut them, chewed them, glued them. When the ants resettled in the dirt, no one could see anything. She studied their habits, and her second design eliminated the dirt and offered the ants fresh cut-flowers on a bare floor. The ants liked this all right, and were visible to watchers as well.

Some plexiglass cases warped from the moisture, and had to be rebuilt. "That was embarrassing because our permits to import some of the insects required us to keep them in escape-proof cages." Some of the screening in the big free-flight cage had to be replaced with glass. The screen let in too much cold air from the museum's air-conditioning. "We noticed we were only getting good activity in the cage — a lot of chirping and fluttering and hopping about — on days when the air-conditioning broke down." There wasn't much she could do to keep the butterflies from drowning in the pond, but she put a stop to the tarantula's wanderings. It was supposed to live in the grassland and kept rushing off instead to hide in the forest. She built it a burrow and covered it with a glass jar until the tarantula established itself.

Miles still finds it something of a shock to see *Insect Zoo* filled with people. "For 18 months I had it almost to myself." Yet she likes to see people using the magnifying glass to peer at the mites. She likes to see them dragging along her thoughtfully provided camp stools so they can sit in front of the camouflage cage. She likes overhearing in the elevator: "I saw the most awful bugs! They were fascinating." It still surprises her that she herself found the bugs so fascinating.

Her next assignment for Natural History was to design for pottery from Cyprus, which she liked, too. "I got to handle the pieces and think about them for a long time. When you get to know things intimately, you begin to cut down on the words and decorating, and make the objects stand out for themselves. Bugs, pottery, I'd feel that way about rockets as well. Things are just so interesting."

Gene Behlen exhibits programmer at Natural History, who oversees a number of projects like *Insect Zoo*, is very sympathetic to the enthusiasm Miles has for objects. He says he is "hooked on objects, too." Handling a Ming vase after months of writing about Ming vases as an art history student was actually what led him to apply for museum work. *"Real objects,"* Behlen says, "are the strength of the museum. Having the real thing is what makes the difference between the Smithsonian and Disneyland. That's why it's important for us here, as museum designers, to avoid over-designing. Miles doesn't have to resort to writing out INSECTS in butterfly wings—gimmicky things like that. People will see the flight cage and it will say insects to them. Sure, there must be the right ambience to a show. You wouldn't put Louis XVI chairs in an *Insect Zoo* any more than you'd put them in a show on lasers. But you don't want to over-stress props either."

Behlen likes the fact that the whole *Insect Zoo* can be seen at a glance. He differs in that from designer Monroe at the Renwick, who likes an exhibit's contents to be revealed a little at a time. (But then, their subjects are very different, too.) Behlen thinks people are comfortable with exhibits that are laid out like a cafeteria line, where they see everything there is before picking a dessert. That's how the new South America Hall was laid out, with the rain forest, the cowboy scene, the marketplace—all visible from the doorway. "There's a kind of security in seeing everything from one end to the other," says Behlen, who likes that hall better than the hall of gems, laid out more like a maze, and which he believes gives people an "uneasy feeling."

There's security, too, he thinks, in the layout of the Natural History building, which has a central rotunda, four stories high, and halls radiating out from it. The trumpeting elephant in the center of the rotunda gives the building a focal point. People come back to the elephant and feel oriented and strike out from it again. "Museums aren't built like this any more. But it's got presence. You either have to abolish it or learn to live with it." Behlen likes living with it. He approves of the way Miles designed the big windows into *Insect Zoo,* bringing an interesting play of natural light into the flight cage. "For years we boarded up the windows in order to control the lighting for exhibits. It's very funny how styles go in cycles."

James Mahoney 🐾 , working out of an office in Arts and Industries, is head of the workshops called Exhibits Central. He is involved in setting exhibit styles, and also offers practical services to all the Smithsonian's museums, galleries and Zoo. Mahoney was in on making Natural History's 92-foot whale which marked a spectacular start for casting museum models in molds, using the newly discovered plastics of the 1950s. Now he's pondering design problems for a tank in which to show a whole coral reef, alive and growing — a new exhibit well along in the planning stage at Natural History. "It's going to require a tremendous amount of light and continuously agitated water. We've never tried anything like that before.

"The Smithsonian is just so large and has such vast collections," says Mahoney, "we find ourselves working in a number of different styles at the same time. We do very traditional, conventional work for the Freer and very experimental work in some of the other buildings. The important thing is the quality of the design and the work. Sure we try to keep in the forefront of communications technology, even down to the smallest details. We're always interested in better saw blades, new color combinations and type faces. But we've gone so far that way, into all manner of sophisticated techniques, I can just picture what's going to happen. One day soon a designer is going to come in here and say 'Hey, I've got this great new idea for a wall — just covered with arrowheads, rows and rows of them in straight lines, every size, every kind, as many as the Smithsonian can provide.' He'll think he's found a wildly inventive way to catch the eye of the public. And we just might go along with him."

X 1,000,000

GLOSSARY

abrade	to scrape away
accession	the acquiring of an object or number of objects (one beetle or 5,000 buttons) at one time from one source, for the museum's permanent collection
archaeology	study of historic and prehistoric peoples, through the examination of recovered artifacts and other remains — usually by excavation
bongo	striped antelope with twisted horns
brontosaur, brontosaurus	dinosaur of the Jurassic Age
bronzes	works of art in bronze, an alloy (combination of metals) consisting mostly of copper and tin
buckboard	light, four-wheel carriage, with a long elastic board used in place of body and spring
canid	member of Canidae, animal group that includes dogs, wolves, foxes
catarrhina	one of Anthropoid group, made up of the Old World monkeys, anthropoid apes, and man
check	crack or split, usually on a painted surface, or on wood
collections manager	the "caretaker" of a collection such as fossils, who keeps order, and is responsible for correct storage of specimens and information about them
condemnation procedure	official elimination of objects from museum collections

Conestoga wagon	large and heavy, broad-wheeled covered wagon used during the days of early migration westward to carry freight
conservator	protects and maintains museum objects, sometimes restoring them as closely as possible to their original state, without concealing repairs and always maintaining integrity of objects
crab shank laster	used in shoe making to grip leather and pull it around last
croker sack	or crocus sack, (southern U.S.) a burlap bag
corrosion	the eating away of metal by chemical action — e.g. rust
curator	is in charge of a museum collection such as postal history or land vehicles; he collects, studies, records, cares for and exhibits
dikdik	small antelope
docent	teacher and lecturer who guides visitors on museum tours
dogtags	identification tags, such as those used by the military with name, blood type, and serial number
ethnology	science dealing with different divisions of mankind, their race, location, characteristics
femur	thigh bone
fibula	smaller, outer bone between knee and ankle
fitch	European pole cat, from whose hair a certain flat kind of brush was made. The word now refers to the shape of the brush used in applying varnish. Other varieties of hair are used also, such as hog bristle
foraminifera	group of micro-marine animals with long geologic record, recognized by the shape of the shell
forensic osteology	detective work on skeletons
geology	science dealing with physical characteristics of the earth
graphic arts	drawing, painting, printmaking, using specific techniques
herpetology	science to do with reptiles and amphibia

hogshead	large cask
horticulture	science of growing fruits, vegetables, shrubs, trees
leech jars	containers found in old-time pharmacies to hold live blood-sucking worms and leeches, used in medicine
loess (pronounced *lohce*)	wind-formed deposit of soil, sand, clay
metamorphosis	change in structure and appearance, that takes place, for example, from caterpillar to butterfly
paleobiology	study of fossil plants or animals
palynology	branch of science dealing with pollens
petrology	study of rocks
physical anthropology	study of skeletons, for evidence of evolution of man
preparator	prepares for exhibit such specimens as skins, skulls, fossils or freeze dries whole animals in lifelike positions
registrar	keeps official records on everything collected
restorer	brings objects, such as machinery, airplanes, musical instruments, as close' as possible to their original condition
rigger	assembles large objects such as an airplane, which are hung from the ceiling, using hoisting tackle and crane
Secretary	director of the whole Smithsonian Institution, used with capital S
suffragists	advocates of further rights for women
taxidermy	preparation of animal skins, stuffing them and mounting in lifelike form
topiary	the ornamental trimming into defined shapes of bushes and shrubs
toponymy	place names of a region and their study
triceratops	dinosaur with horns and bony crest on neck

INDEX to People and the Places Where They Work

Martin, Eleni	MHT	Rowell, Chuck	MHT
Marzio, Peter	MHT		
Mayo, Edith	MHT	St. Hoyme, Lucile	NHM
McMillan, Eleanor	MHT	Sandved, Kjell	NHM
Mead, James	NHM	Sayre, Reginald (Bud)	A&I
Miles, Beth	NHM	Scheele Carl	MHT
Miles, John, Jr.	NHM	Sean, Sylvan	A&I
Monroe, Mike	RG	Simkin, Tom	NHM
Mulcahy, Bob	Zoo	Sivowitch, Elliot	MHT
Myette, Ellen	RG	Sorrel, Walter	A&I
Odell, Scott	MHT		
Organ, Robert	MHT	Thomas, E. J.	NASM
Otano, Hernan	NASM	Thorington, Richard	NHM
Parmley, Charlie	NASM	Vogel, Robert	MHT
Potter, Charlie	NHM		
		Wallace, Susan	A&I
Reed, Theodore	Zoo	Wetmore, Alexander	NHM
Rickman, Vernon	A&I	Wink, John	MHT
Rinzler, Ralph	Performing Arts		
Ripley, S. Dillon	Castle	Zisfein, Melvin	NASM
Roderick, Walter	NASM	Zycherman, Lynda	FGA

INDEX

BIBLIOGRAPHY

About Foucault Pendulums as Shown in the Smithsonian Institution. Greenfield, Massachusetts: Channing L. Bete Co., Inc., Revised Ed. 1976.

Burcaw, G. Ellis. *Introduction to Museum Work.* Nashville, Tenn.: American Association for State and Local History, 1975.

Burns, William. *Your Future in Museums.* New York: Rosen, Richards Press, Inc., 1967.

Celebrating a Century, Smithsonian-produced film on highlights of 1975 Festival.

Celebrating the National Air and Space Museum. New York: CBS Publications, 1976.

Craft Mutliples. Washington, D.C.: Smithsonian Institution Press, 1975.

Dexter, Kerry. *The Display Book.* New York: Morehouse-Barlow, 1977

Festival of American Folk Life, Smithsonian-produced film on highlights of 1975 Festival.

The First Ladies Hall. Washington, D.C.: Smithsonian Institution Press, 1976.

Gettens, Rutherford J., Clarke, Roy S., Jr., and Chase, W.T. *Two Early Chinese Bronze Weapons with Meteoritic Iron Blades.* Washington, D.C.: Freer Gallery of Art, 1971.

Goode, James M. "A View of the Castle," *Museum News* (July/August, 1976), 38–45.

Guide to the Nation's Capital and the Smithsonian Institution. Washington, D.C.: Smithsonian Institution.

Hall of Stamps and The Mails. Omaha, Nebraska: Scott Publishing Co., 1972.

Harpsichords and Clavichords. Washington, D.C.: Smithsonian Institution Press, 1969.

Hellman, Geoffrey T., *The Smithsonian Octopus on the Mall*, Lippincott, N.Y. 1967. *Bankers, Bones and Beetles: The First Century of the American Museum of Natural History*, Natural History Press, N.Y., 1969.

Hudson, Kenneth. *A Social History of Museums.* Atlantic Highlands, N.J.: Humanities Press, 1975.

Marzio, Peter C. (ed.). *A Nation of Nations.* New York: Harper & Row, Publishers, Inc., 1976.

Neal, Arminta. *Exhibits for the Small Museum:* A Handbook. Nashville, Tenn.: American Association for State and Local History, 1976.

Oehser, Paul Henry, *The Smithsonian Institution*, Praeger, N.Y., 1970.

Official Guide to the Smithsonian. New York: CBS Publications, Revised ed. 1976.

Oliver, Smith Hempstone, and Berkebile, Donald H. *Wheels and Wheeling.* Washington, D.C.: Smithsonian Institution Press, 1974.

Post, Robert (ed.). *1876 A Centennial Exhibition.* Washington, D.C.: The National Museum of History and Technology, Smithsonian Institution, 1976.

Setzer, Henry W. *Directions for Preserving Mammals for Museum Study.* Washington, D.C.: Smithsonian, 1968.

The Smithsonian Experience, Smithsonian Institution, 1977.

Smithsonian Institution Research Reports, beginning #1, published quarterly by the Office of Public Affairs, Smithsonian Institution, Washington, D.C., 1972.

Smithsonian magazine. Vol. I-VII. Washington, D.C.

Steinberg at the Smithsonian. Washington, D.C.: Smithsonian Institution Press, 1973.

We The People: The American People and Their Government. Washington, D.C.: Smithsonian Institution Press, 1975.

White, Anne. *Visiting Museums.* New York: International Publications Service, 1968.

Whitehill, Walter M. *Cabinet of Curiosities: Five Episodes in the Evolution of American Museums.* Charlottesville, Va.: University Press of Virginia, 1967.

Williams, Patricia M. *Museums of Natural History and the People Who Work in Them.* New York: St. Martin's Press, 1973.

Zoo Book. Washington, D.C.: Smithsonian Institution Press, 1976.